PRAISE FOR *LGBTQ+ EDUCATORS IN CATHOLIC SCHOOLS*

"Ruiz's book is evidence once again of St. Irenaeus's dictum: the glory of God is the human being fully alive. LGBTQ+ Catholics are made in the image and likeness of God. Their work and vocations enliven and bring hope to a world in desperate need. Ruiz identifies the great harm that strident compulsory heterosexist patriarchy does to the work of evangelization and deepening of Catholic vocations in the world. Ruiz's book also suggests that at the heart of the cooked-up 'culture war' between Catholics and secular culture is the issue of authority, especially the authority of the magisterium. Nevertheless, instead of the scapegoating and dehumanization served up to LGBTQ+ Catholics, Ruiz advocates the theological principle of synodality and communal discernment as respectful paths forward for the Church."

—**Susan Abraham**, VPAA and dean, Pacific School of Religion

"Through the process of integrating his own sexual identity, Dr. Ruiz gives testimony to 'educating through witness' to investigate the challenges of exercising one's vocation as an LGBTQ+ person in Catholic educational institutions. His experiential witness and critical analysis are essential reading for Catholic educators, employees, laypeople, and Church leaders to integrate into Church sexual teaching, ecclesiology, and pastoral sensitivity."

—**Todd Salzman**, Amelia and Emil Graff Professor of Catholic Theology, Creighton University

"Ruiz calls the Catholic Church to deeper realizations of courage and justice in the context of our primary and secondary schools. These commitments mandate that Church leaders must not hide behind religious liberty defenses when there are greater moral goods at stake, the most important of which are honoring the human dignity of LGBTQ+ people as workers, celebrating the contributions LGBTQ+ educators make as excellent teachers and mentors to our students, and remaining open to how their lives witness to the wisdom of a God who uses diversity to propel us to become the Church the future needs us to be."

—**Craig A. Ford Jr.**, assistant professor of theology and religious studies, Saint Norbert College

LGBTQ+ Educators in Catholic Schools

Embracing Synodality, Inclusivity, and Justice

Ish Ruiz

A SHEED & WARD BOOK
ROWMAN & LITTLEFIELD
Lanham • Boulder • New York • London

Published by Rowman & Littlefield
An imprint of The Rowman & Littlefield Publishing Group, Inc.
4501 Forbes Boulevard, Suite 200, Lanham, Maryland 20706
www.rowman.com

86-90 Paul Street, London EC2A 4NE

Copyright © 2024 by Ismael Ruiz Abaunza

All rights reserved. No part of this book may be reproduced in any form or by any electronic or mechanical means, including information storage and retrieval systems, without written permission from the publisher, except by a reviewer who may quote passages in a review.

British Library Cataloguing in Publication Information Available

Library of Congress Cataloging-in-Publication Data Available

ISBN: 978-1-5381-8962-7 (cloth: alk. paper)
ISBN: 978-1-5381-8963-4 (pbk.: alk. paper)
ISBN: 978-1-5381-8964-1 (ebook)

♾️™ The paper used in this publication meets the minimum requirements of American National Standard for Information Sciences—Permanence of Paper for Printed Library Materials, ANSI/NISO Z39.48-1992.

To LGBTQ+ educators in Catholic schools:
You make the Church and the world a better place!

Contents

Acknowledgments — ix

Foreword: From a Challenge to a Blessing — xi
James Martin, SJ

Introduction: Teaching Who We Are: The Experience of LGBTQ+ Educators in Catholic Schools — xv

Chapter 1 The Challenges of Firing LGBTQ+ Educators from Catholic Schools — 1

Chapter 2 The Gifts of LGBTQ+ Catholic School Educators — 31

Chapter 3 The Crux of the Matter: Catholic Doctrine on Homosexuality and Gender — 65

Chapter 4 Synodality in Catholic Schools: A Theological Model for LGBTQ+ Inclusion — 95

Chapter 5 Catholic Social Teaching and Human Rights: Giving Catholic School LGBTQ+ Educators Their Due — 123

Conclusion — 159

Bibliography — 161

Index — 181

About the Author — 191

Acknowledgments

This work would not have been possible without the grace of God and the support of various communities that have offered me boundless encouragement throughout this journey. I thank God for the gifts, perseverance, and hope that have served as sustenance throughout this process. Thanks to Richard Brown and the folks at Rowman & Littlefield for believing in this project and allowing me to share my work far and wide. I also thank my academic advisor at the Graduate Theological Union (GTU), Lisa Fullam, for her encouragement and guidance. Furthermore, her theology on probabilism helped me answer a key question in this project. I am grateful to George Griener and Bryan Massingale for helping me shape my arguments, research, and writing. George was particularly instrumental in developing my understanding of synodality and Bryan's insights helped me craft my work on human rights and LGBTQ+ inclusion in the Church. I am indebted to the theological work of Richard Gaillardetz, James Keenan, Margaret Farley, Todd Salzman, Michael Lawler, Craig A. Ford Jr., Miguel Diaz, Ormond Rush, Brad Hinze, Amanda Osheim, Grzegorz Strzelczyk, Julia Fleming, Leslie Griffin, Bill O'Neill, and many others. I thank my professors and mentors at GTU and beyond who have helped and encouraged me to produce this important work. I also acknowledge the work of my co-researchers—Jane Bleasdale, Kevin Stockbridge, James Everitt, and Mark Guevara—who have helped me capture the experiences of LGBTQ+ educators in Catholic schools.

I am eternally grateful to Pat Maloney for enthusiastically volunteering to proofread and edit this volume front to back. Thank you for your generosity and for your time pouring over every word to ensure that it is intelligible to a wider audience.

I am grateful to my professional communities. Candler School of Theology at Emory University has offered invaluable support as I complete this project. Special thanks to Deanna Womack, Letitia Campbell, and Joel Kemp for pouring over various chapters of the book and helping me clarify my arguments. Other colleagues at Candler and beyond who have offered professional and personal support include Tony Alonso, Susan Reynolds, Joanne Solis-Walker, Jonathan Calvillo, Roger Nam, Keith Menhinick, Kwok Pui Lan, Ted Smith, Teresa Fry-Brown, and Jan Love. I wish to also thank the Sacred Heart Cathedral Preparatory Community in San Francisco for supporting my research and for teaching me to take risks as I advocate for LGBTQ+ inclusion. I am especially thankful to Sal Curcio for his incessant support of this project and for helping me fall in love with queer theory and queer theology.

I am grateful to my family, including my biological family and my chosen family, for grounding me as I write. *A mis padres, Ismael Ruiz Meléndez y Marie Angie Abaunza Pérez, les agradezco las de lecciones de vida que me han enseñado a persistir en momentos de duda y dificultad. Gracias por el apoyo y el amor incondicional que me han brindado. A mi hermano Gabriel Ruiz Abaunza, mi cuñada Melisa Rebecca Calderón Ceramé y mis sobrines Pía Isabel Ruiz Calderón y Gabriel Enrique Ruiz Calderón les agradezco las lecciones de perseverancia y unión familiar. A mi hermanito Daniel Ruiz Abaunza y a mi cuñada Karen Barrera les agradezco por enseñarme a no rendirme aun cuando el mundo está en mi contra. Gracias por ser mi fuerza y mi inspiración.* I am grateful for my friends and loved ones, who forced me to take days off to rest and recharge before diving back into the work. Thank you for listening to me, laughing with me, and being with me. Special acknowledgments go to Jayson, Quiria, Ivan, Joe, Franco, Abdiel, Antonio, Vanessa, Erwin, PJ, Blake, Ken, Danny, Max, Gina, and all of my beloved friends.

Most importantly, I thank my beloved Daniel Jose Gutierrez (and Lester) for being my rock and my home. Thank you for your support as I write this and for believing in me throughout this amazing journey. Also, thank you for contributing your idea for the cover art and for coordinating, shooting, and editing such a beautiful and compelling image. I love you.

Finally, I am thankful to LGBTQ+ Catholic school teachers everywhere for showing me the true meaning of what it means to be a good educator. Thank you for being witnesses of Christ's unconditional love for the students entrusted to our care. Thank you for showing me how to faithfully and actively belong to an imperfect Church that is still learning how to love us. And thank you for showing me the meaning of hope.

Foreword

From a Challenge to a Blessing

James Martin, SJ

Since I began working more intently with the LGBTQ+ community, I've noticed that one of the most intractable problems facing the church and LGBTQ+ Catholics is the question of employment.

To begin with, it's important to note that there are hundreds, perhaps thousands, of holy and hardworking LGBTQ+ people working in Catholic schools, including elementary schools, middle schools, high schools, and colleges and universities across this country—and the world.

While I wasn't fortunate enough to attend Catholic schools before I entered religious life, after I entered the Jesuits, I more than made up for that, studying philosophy at Loyola University Chicago and theology at what is now Boston College's Clough School of Theology and Ministry. During those years I studied with, and came to know, many LGBTQ+ educators, all of whom enriched my academic and personal life. And after my studies were completed, and I began my work at America Media in New York, I continued to meet educators from this community as I covered and wrote about the church. LGBTQ+ people have "educated" me in other ways as well: as spiritual directors, mentors, friends, and even religious superiors, enriching me with their wisdom, encouraging me with their bravery, and enlightening me with their faith.

So, then, what's the issue? Simply put, many Catholic schools see LGBTQ+ educators as a problem. In the last few years, Catholic schools have fired them for either simply being gay or, more commonly, entering into same-sex marriages, which are against church teaching. (For those who aren't familiar with current church teaching, after a Vatican declaration in 2023, while priests can, under certain circumstances, bless same-sex couples, these couples are not permitted to marry in the church.) Others have been fired for undergoing a gender transition, which is also prohibited (in 2023, the US bishops published some guidelines prohibiting medical interventions such as gender-affirming surgery).

To some in the Church and in the outside world, it seems an easy question. People say: Aren't they violating Catholic teaching? So why, the thinking goes, should they be allowed to teach or work in a Catholic school?

The problem is that there are educators from many other groups whose lives also don't fully embody church teaching. To begin with, you could include in that group married straight Catholics who use birth control, something that is also against church teaching. Moving beyond questions of sexual morality, you could include Catholics who don't attend Mass every Sunday. Then, moving past Catholic matters into more broadly Christian ethics, you could include educators who don't help the poor, visit the sick, or forgive their enemies, all important teachings of Jesus. Finally, you could include all non-Catholics: Protestants, Jews, Muslims, Buddhists, and Hindus, as well as agnostics or atheists, none of whom fully embrace all church teachings. The problem, as quickly becomes obvious, is the selectivity with which these rules are applied: for the most part, they seem only to apply to the married LGBTQ+ person.

More positively, the problem is that these incredibly gifted educators are not able to offer their gifts to Catholic schools: to students, to faculty, to staff, to parents, and to the community at large. By excluding them, by firing them, schools and school districts are excluding excellence.

These cases have become even more problematic in the wake of the Vatican document called Fiducia Supplicans, which, as mentioned above, allows priests, under certain conditions, to bless same-sex couples. As a friend of mine put it when I mentioned this new book, "We're supposed to bless them, not fire them."

Often these firings are initiated by someone in the school or parish community (or even outside the school community) poring through the social media accounts of an educator or parish employee or using some other "gotcha" strategy. In one case, a person came to the doorway of the organist at a Catholic parish and filmed the interchange, asking questions about whether it was a gay-friendly neighborhood. The video was then forwarded to the church officials.

In many cases, these educators are fired outright (under the guise of "causing scandal"), and their firings cause great anguish not only in their own lives but also in the life of the school community, especially to LGBTQ+ students, families, and fellow colleagues. As community members have said, the greater scandal for them is the firing. Again, LGBTQ+ educators seem to be the only ones whose moral lives are looked at under a microscope.

Just as often these educators are described by fellow faculty and students and parents with terms like "the best teacher in the school," "beloved," "truly gifted," and other such laudatory adjectives. For a long time, I wondered about this kind of praise and was suspicious that, since many of these cases find their way into the media, this was just "hype."

But in time I realized that the reason that these educators were so valued, so appreciated, and so beloved is because, unlike their straight counterparts, teaching in a Catholic school as an LGBTQ+ person often comes at a cost, or at least carries with it some risk. So these teachers must *really* want to be there. They must make a conscious, often costly, choice to stay. What students and parents are responding to, then, is not simply their talent, but their fidelity to their vocation.

Thus, the church and the LGBTQ+ community face this problem: How can they reverence the gifts of these educators in an environment where, in some places, they are reviled?

This is why Ish Ruiz's new book is so important. He offers a way through these controversies by inviting us to consider three thing: First, we need a theological and moral understanding of what is at play when these dismissals happen. Second, we need to understand how our Catholic tradition, and especially Pope Francis's vision of a synodal Church (as well as Catholic social teaching), supports the retention of LGBTQ+ educators in Catholic schools. Third, we need practical advice on how to articulate the mission of Catholic schools in a way that supports the retention of LGBTQ+ educators—thereby upholding their dignity, cherishing their gifts, and promoting an inclusive environment for LGBTQ+ students/families as well.

Ish is the perfect person to write this book. He is an experienced Catholic educator and gifted scholar, is a member of the LGBTQ+ community, and best of all, has a lively and inviting writing style. Also, I must add that I've been to several of my friend's presentations and have found Ish to be one of the most organized and compelling public speakers I've ever seen. A natural teacher, he has a genius for communicating ideas effectively to a wide variety of people.

So may his book help to shed light on what I've so far described as confronting a challenge but is really a matter of accepting a blessing, that is, the presence of so many gifted LGBTQ+ educators in our church.

***

James Martin, SJ, is a Jesuit priest, editor at large of America Media, and founder of Outreach, an LGBTQ+ Catholic ministry. He is also author of the book Building a Bridge, *about LGBTQ+ Catholic ministry.*

Introduction

Teaching Who We Are: The Experience of LGBTQ+ Educators in Catholic Schools

I come to this conversation as a gay theologian who taught religious studies at Catholic high schools for over a decade. As I prepared to exercise this vocation and even into my first years as a teacher, I was constantly compartmentalizing by separating my identity as a gay man from my call to teach in Catholic schools out of fear of dismissal. Eventually, I was blessed with a teaching position in a school community that allowed me to gradually integrate my sexual identity with my mission as a Catholic school educator. This internal integration unlocked within me the ability to bring my full self to the classroom and convey to my students the message of the Gospel in a unique way, with a particular focus on the importance of loving oneself as a person made in the image of God. Although I never felt the need to make a public announcement about my sexual identity, my internal sense of integration sufficed because I could model self-love for my students as an educator who was comfortable with who he was.

In the words of Parker Palmer, "We teach who we are."[1] When educators embrace a spiritual journey of self-discovery and learn to fully integrate our identity with our vocation, we can present an authentic witness of the richness and diversity of our Catholic faith to the students. While I never officially publicly *came out* to students in my classroom, my ability to fully accept myself as a gay man increased my confidence and dedication as an educator committed to aiding all students on a journey of self-acceptance and a communal quest toward a relationship with God. Furthermore, many students probably sensed (perhaps due to stereotypes or unconfirmed rumors) that I identify as gay, and they sought me out as a safe space and as a mentor. In my classroom, I was blessed to help many students, including a significant number of LGBTQ+ ones, grow and genuinely wrestle with questions of spirituality and identity. I believe I offered significant contributions to their lives through my pastoral care, inclusive pedagogical practices, and critical theological approaches to the study of religion. This process of educating through witness, offering inclusive safe spaces through my practice, and mentoring students toward growth is deeply connected to Catholic doctrine on human dignity and flourishing. For these reasons, I rejoice in my vocation as an educator and hope to continue to carry it out with zeal.

My experience is not unique. In 2016, I cofounded a network of LGBTQ+ educators in Catholic schools throughout the San Francisco Bay Area which was named "Queer Educators in Religious Schools" (or *Qu.E.I.R.S.*, pronounced "Queers"). By 2017, Qu.E.I.R.S. had grown to include over sixty members in various roles in Catholic primary and secondary education. A significant percentage of them taught religion, served as campus ministers, helped lead retreats, or otherwise expressed commitment to the Catholic faith and mission of their schools. More importantly, I noticed that these colleagues, even the ones who taught secular subjects, took great joy in their vocations, which they expressed through their passionate commitment to the Catholic mission of their schools despite experiences of discrimination and risks of dismissal. Because of my experience in this network, I began to question how often LGBTQ+ educators in Catholic schools throughout the United States exercise roles directly tied to the Catholic identity of their communities. To further investigate, in 2018, I collaborated with the two colleagues who helped cofound Qu.E.I.R.S, Dr. Jane Bleasdale of the University of San Francisco and Dr. Kevin Stockbridge of Chapman University, on a national survey of LGBTQ+ educators in Catholic schools to better understand their experiences. The results were similar to my experience with the network in San Francisco: a significant portion of the participants throughout the nation indicated that they either taught religious studies or worked as campus ministers in their schools. Similar to my personal experience as a teacher, the survey indicated that, among many blessings, these educators perceive that they are uniquely positioned to connect with vulnerable students in their schools and serve as role models for commitment to the Catholic tradition despite significant risks. This equips them to meet the spiritual needs of our contemporary teenagers who continue to wrestle with their relationship with God and the Church.

Unfortunately, the participants also expressed significant stress and fear over the possibility of being dismissed from schools due to their identity as LGBTQ+. Their fear is valid: since 2007, there have been over one hundred documented cases of employees fired from Catholic institutions due to their LGBTQ+ identity or for supporting LGBTQ+ rights. At least sixty of these cases involve an LGBTQ+ educator dismissed from Catholic schools in the United States.[2] These dismissals often occur when there is a public awareness that an educator entered a same-sex marriage or began a gender-related transition.[3] In many of these cases, members of the local community (families, parishioners, or other concerned Catholics) investigated the private lives of these educators, found a same-sex marriage license or other evidence of nonconformity with magisterial doctrine on human sexuality, and reported the educators to the ecclesial authorities, who then initiated the process of termination.[4] In other cases, the firings were prompted by voluntary disclosures on behalf of the educators, who announced their decisions to marry or transition.[5] In all cases, the dismissals have sparked significant public outcry from students and families who value the gifts the LGBTQ+ educator brought to the community. It is important to note that, except for one documented case,[6] all reports of fired LGBTQ+ educators were dismissed due to their dissent from magisterial doctrine on sexual morality and not simply for identifying as LGBTQ+. That said, I am personally aware of several cases where LGBTQ+ educators are dismissed and then offered severance pay in exchange for their silence, thus indicating that there are potentially many more dismissals of LGBTQ+ persons (for reasons of identity or behavior) that are undocumented by the media. For these reasons, I consider this issue to be pervasive and in need of a comprehensive theological exploration, which I conduct in this book.

This book is divided into five chapters, each beginning with a personal story connecting my experience as a gay Catholic educator to the theme of the chapter. I begin this project by analyzing the circumstances surrounding the dismissal of LGBTQ+ educators from Catholic schools. Chapter 1 will explore the firings of LGBTQ+ educators and the US Catholic leaders' justifications for dismissing them, and chapter 2 will explore the gifts these educators offer Catholic schools. In the subsequent chapters, I propose a new three-part theological framework to help Catholic school leaders—including bishops, diocesan officials, and Catholic school administrators as well as anyone who has a stake in the employment status of Catholic school educators—navigate instances where an LGBTQ+ educator enters a same-sex marriage or embarks on a gender transition. The framework will address questions of sexual morality, ecclesiology, and Catholic social teaching. Chapter 3 will address the crux of the matter, which is the Catholic moral theology on human sexuality that often operates as a litmus test to determine whether an educator should remain at a Catholic school. In this chapter, I will retrieve the doctrine of *probabilism* (developed during the sixteenth century) to make some room for a reasonable degree of theological pluralism on matters of homosexuality and gender identity. Chapter 4 will construct a theology of synodality to advocate for the inclusion of LGTBQ+ educators as the Church (including its institutions) journey together through uncertain territory. As an emerging ecclesiological modality, synodality makes room for LGBTQ+ persons in Catholic schools and incorporates their unique perspectives as "queer" persons into the life and doctrines of the Church. Based on probabilism and synodality, chapter 5 will invoke key principles of Catholic social teaching, especially its doctrines on human rights and labor, to defend the inherent dignity of LGBTQ+ persons in Catholic schools and the free exercise of religion through the enterprise of Catholic education. Considering Church teaching on human dignity, promoted through a doctrine of human rights, I will argue that Catholic leaders must model to society how institutions might uphold the human rights of the most vulnerable, including LGBTQ+ persons.

This framework is needed for both pragmatic and moral reasons. From a pragmatic perspective, I observe that these firings contribute to the continuous exodus of young Catholics from the Church and cause significant spiritual harm to the local communities, which the Church cannot afford to do if it wishes to retain its members and continue to operate Catholic schools. From a moral perspective, I believe integrity calls upon Catholic leaders to: (1) live into the fullness of Catholic doctrines with particular emphasis on its central teachings, (2) consider the contemporary context of the Catholic Church along with the scientific and cultural insights our society has developed, and (3) emphasize the importance of upholding the dignity of the most vulnerable from systematic oppression (especially within the Church). In other words, the Catholic Church must be better toward LGBTQ+ persons if it is to fulfill its mission of building the Kingdom of God on Earth. Catholic institutions, including Catholic schools, are a significant location where the Church is responsible for living up to this call. The way Catholic schools treat LGBTQ+ educators (and students) will affect the journey and mission of the Church.

In this book, I argue that the Catholic theological tradition not only supports the retention of LGBTQ+ educators as potentially suitable ministers in Catholic schools but also calls for the celebration of the unique and indispensable gifts they bring to the school community. To support this thesis, I will draw from the theological teachings of the Second Vatican Council, the teachings of the magisterium on Catholic education, and Pope Francis's call to synodality. I will also be engaging various contemporary theological perspectives in the United States and abroad. Finally, as illustrated above, the reported experience of LGBTQ+ educators (including the aforementioned study) and the reported needs of Catholic school students also help inform this project. In the coming chapters, I will begin a comprehensive study of this issue. My goal for this book is that it would help Catholic school leaders look at LGBTQ+ educators with compassion and appreciation for the unique indispensable gifts they offer to Catholic schools. I hope this framework helps shape the conversation about LGBTQ+ inclusion in the Church and helps resolve the controversy that often contributes to polarization in the Church, isolation of vulnerable persons, conflict between laity and the magisterium, and spiritual harm to our Catholic school communities.

NOTES

1. Parker J. Palmer, *The Courage to Teach: Exploring the Inner Landscape of a Teacher's Life*, 20th ed. (Jossey-Bass, 2017), 1.

2. New Ways Ministry, "Employees of Catholic Institutions Who Have Been Fired, Forced to Resign, Had Offers Rescinded, or Had Their Jobs Threatened Because of LGBT Issues," New Ways Ministry, accessed December 6, 2022, https://www.newwaysministry.org/issues/employment/employment-disputes/.

3. For an example, see "Woman Fired over Her Same-Sex Marriage Speaks Out," 6abc Philadelphia, July 10, 2015, https://6abc.com/waldron-mercy-academy-lower-merion-news-montgomery-county/839191/.

4. As an example, Shelly Fitzgerald was fired after a parishioner discovered her marriage license and sent it to the pastor that oversaw the school. See Jennie Runevitch, "Roncalli Counselor Speaks Out after She Claims School Threatened to Fire Her over Same-Sex Marriage," August 13, 2018, https://web.archive.org/web/20191104040228/https://www.wthr.com/article/exclusive-roncalli-counselor-speaks-out-after-she-claims-school-threatened-fire-her-over.

5. For an example, see Jim Walsh, "Fired after She Came Out to Colleagues, Totino-Grace Teacher Leaves Dissonance and Silence Behind," *MinnPost*, September 11, 2013, https://www.minnpost.com/education/2013/09/fired-after-she-came-out-colleagues-totino-grace-teacher-leaves-dissonance-and-sil/.

6. See Melinda Selmys, "Thou Shalt Not Be Gay," May 26, 2017, https://www.patheos.com/blogs/catholicauthenticity/2017/05/thou-shalt-not-gay/.

Chapter 1

The Challenges of Firing LGBTQ+ Educators from Catholic Schools

In 2011, I landed my first job teaching at a Catholic school in Honolulu, Hawaii. Less than a month into my tenure, I was mysteriously summoned to the principal's office one day after school (a call that terrifies teachers as much as students). I nervously sat in the office as my principal explained that a picture was circulating among students depicting me exiting a local gay bar in Waikiki. I could feel the blood draining from my face. Up until that moment, my biggest worry in my budding teaching career was lesson planning, the grading workload, and the daily struggles of classroom management as a first-year teacher. While the principal expressed support with phrases like "you are who you are," it was also made clear to me that my (perceived) sexual identity mattered. Thankfully, the students did not appear to be sharing the picture with ill intent, but rather acting out of curiosity typical of a teenager. Nevertheless, I felt anxiety about being scrutinized both at school and in my personal life for signs of my homosexual orientation. I began to modify my attire to make sure it wasn't too perfectly tailored. I was afraid my haircut, my mannerisms, and even my Puerto Rican accent would give me away.

Sadly, this modification did not allow me to bring my full self into my classroom—much to the detriment of my students. I believed they could sense when I was being disingenuous. For example, I once served as a leader for a Kairos retreat (a traditional and popular retreat program for juniors or seniors in a Catholic school) and offered a personal testimony that, instead of modeling authenticity and vulnerability for the students, relied on vague statements about "personal struggles" or "feeling ashamed." Taking my cue, the students responded with similar vagueness in the small-group discussion that followed. This hindered their ability to form deep connections with each other, which other students had typically formed in previous retreats. In my classroom, due to my modified behavior, I became strict—almost militant— as a way to shield myself from deep relationships with the students. I feared that, if the students got too close to me, they would discover my secret. I was also scared because, if I was discovered and fired, I would not be able to exercise my vocation for which I had spent years preparing through my college education. But most of all, I was afraid because, if I did not exercise my vocation, I would be unhappy and I would fail God.

My fears were not unfounded. The dismissal of LGBTQ+ educators from Catholic schools remains prominent in many dioceses across the United States. Considering the legal and theological implications of these dismissals, several bishops and other Catholic leaders across many dioceses have begun to follow a specific "playbook" seen throughout the country that enables them to efficiently fire LGBTQ+ educators. This playbook satisfies two important concerns expressed by bishops who seek to dismiss these educators. The first concern is legal. Given the presence of civil laws protecting LGBTQ+ persons from employment discrimination, the playbook provides an avenue for Catholic schools to dismiss LGBTQ+ educators with legal impunity. The second concern is cultural. Given the emerging acceptance of LGBTQ+ people in the Church, the playbook offers a theological justification for firing these educators grounded in the bishop's responsibility to preserve the Catholic culture of the schools. In my research of the dismissals of LGBTQ+ educators from Catholic schools, I read numerous statements and policies issued by bishops, school leaders, and/or diocesan spokespersons attempting to justify the firings; all of which reflected this common playbook with its twofold strategy. In sum, the statements all amount to the same clear message: LGBTQ+ educators who dissent from magisterial doctrine in word or deed are not suitable employees in a Catholic school and must be dismissed because they threaten the Catholic identity of the school and scandalize the students; furthermore, religious liberty, as enshrined in the First Amendment of the US Constitution, grants Catholic schools the right to dismiss them.

In this chapter, I offer my analysis of the bishops' playbook—or framework—for dismissing LGBTQ+ educators in Catholic schools. More importantly, I argue that their framework is inadequate in promoting the Catholic identity of the school because it represents significant theological inconsistencies with the broader Catholic tradition. As I will demonstrate, the dismissals of LGBTQ+ Catholic school educators betray a deep-seated homophobia, transphobia, heteronormativity, and cisnormativity in the institutional Church grounded in a narrow application of a few peripheral Catholic principles while refusing a consistent application of a more important set of foundational Catholic principles. For this reason, I maintain that it is self-defeating: because it undermines the very Catholic identity it seeks to preserve. Therefore, I propose that the Church needs a new framework to navigate cases of LGBTQ+ educators working in a Catholic setting. This new framework would address the different facets of this question—moral, theological, and social—and would provide Catholic leaders, including bishops and school administrators, with the practical tools to appreciate and celebrate the gifts LGBTQ+ educators bring to the schools. While this book focuses on LGBTQ+ educators in Catholic schools, my proposed framework has significant implications for LGBTQ+ inclusion in the Church more broadly.

I will divide this chapter into four parts. In the first part, I will analyze two cases, one in San Francisco and one in Indianapolis, where the local bishop attempted to implement the playbook. In the second and third parts, I will analyze and challenge the two "acts" in the playbook. Act One contains *legal* strategies and Act Two contains *cultural* strategies. As I will demonstrate, the overall approach generally taken by bishops on this issue is inadequate and morally problematic because it violates key theological principles of our Church and is harmful to the fired LGBTQ+ employee, the students who witness the dismissals, the local Catholic school and parish communities, and the broader Church. The fourth part will highlight the need for a new approach that will respect the dignity of LGBTQ+ educators, cherish their contributions to the schools, support the well-being of the school community, and consistently promote the Catholic identity.

TWO CASE STUDIES: SAN FRANCISCO AND INDIANAPOLIS

From the significant number of cases involving the dismissals of LGBTQ+ employees from Catholic schools, I am choosing to highlight two noteworthy ones: the 2015 San Francisco teachers' contract dispute and the 2018–2019 employment disputes involving four LGTBQ+ educators in Indianapolis. In San Francisco, the archbishop engaged in the legal strategy (Act One of the playbook) to protect archdiocesan schools from discrimination lawsuits through ministerial language and morality clauses in employment contracts and handbooks. However, this case is unique because employees in the archdiocesan schools of San Francisco are organized into a labor union that highly publicized and contested the archbishop's proposals through the union's infrastructure of advocacy and press communication. Since the archbishop needed to convince the majority of dues-paying union members to vote for the contract, he promulgated some letters outlining his rationale for these proposals, which facilitated my analysis of his legal strategy.

The cases in Indianapolis are significant because they involve the dismissals of three LGBTQ+ employees who had signed a "ministry contract" with the archdiocese and the retention of one gay employee in a privately owned Jesuit school despite direction from the archdiocese mandating his dismissal. The three employees who were dismissed were considered "ministerial employees" although they were not campus ministers or religion teachers: two were guidance counselors and one was a social studies teacher. The employee that was retained was a math teacher. These cases highlight the relentless efforts on behalf of the archbishop to exclude LGBTQ+ persons from "ministerial roles" based on their sexual behavior. He considered the presence of these educators to be a threat to the Catholic identity of the school. The fired employees attempted to sue the archdiocese for discrimination but were unsuccessful due to the ministerial classification in their contracts. Furthermore, the archdiocese took retaliatory action against the Jesuit school that refused its directive to fire the LGBTQ+ math teacher. These cases in Indianapolis demonstrate that some factors, such as the ownership and governance model of the school, can determine whether the teacher is retained or dismissed. What follows is an exploration and analysis of these case studies.

San Francisco, California: An Archdiocese's Preemptive Anti-LGBTQ+ Legal Strategies

In 2015, Archbishop Cordileone made two controversial proposals to employees in the four archdiocesan high schools of San Francisco. First, he introduced new language to the employment contract that would reclassify all personnel as "ministers."[1] Second, he introduced new language into the employee handbook that outlined a series of prohibited sexual behavior, among which homosexual activity featured prominently.[2] With these actions, he engaged the Catholic school teacher union, American Federation of Teachers, Local 2240, in a contentious contract dispute. The changes were introduced at the beginning of the collective bargaining agreement negotiation process.

To clarify his motives, Archbishop Cordileone wrote a letter to archdiocesan school employees in which he stated that he appreciated the work teachers do but saw a need to provide more clarity on Catholic teaching through the morality clauses.[3] While he states that the aim is not to seek the dismissal of teachers, he argues that "Catholic schools have to be very clear about what constitutes the true teachings of the Catholic Church. They owe that to the teachers, to the students, and to the parents of the students."[4] He further explains that he perceives a prevalent confusion about the Church's stance in areas of sexual morality, including homosexuality, which is why the statement focuses on those "hot button issues." He states, "because the school fosters holiness, virtue and evangelization, teachers not knowledgeable about the precise contours of Catholic teaching have to be cautious about what they say in the school and what they do in the public sphere outside of the Catholic school."[5] Regarding employees who do not conform to magisterial doctrine, he asserts, "dissenting from Catholic teaching or the natural moral law in a Catholic high school does not promote holiness, virtue and evangelization."[6] He concludes by stating his hope that the proposed documents would help Catholic school employees better fulfill their mission amidst the challenges brought upon the Church's doctrine by secular society.

The two proposals initiated by the archbishop were met with fierce opposition from the teachers' union and local activists. In response, the archbishop began to offer some revisions to the proposed language. The first change was to remove the word "minister" from the contract (although he first tried to substitute it with "ministry" before completely removing the term and its variations). Then, he convened a committee of educators from the different archdiocesan schools to redraft the morality clauses.[7] The morality clause revisions contained more positive and affirming statements on matters of Catholic belief, sacramentality, morality, and justice, and were added as a link in the employee handbook of the archdiocesan high schools.[8]

The dispute in San Francisco was significant because it was the first instance in which the educators were able to successfully deflect the actions of the local bishop. I believe this was made possible due to the infrastructure provided by union organizers, which facilitated effective means of communication and collective action, and the more progressive cultural context of the San Francisco Catholic Church. The relentless organized protests, which involved members of the school communities and the broader San Francisco Catholic community (as well as some Bay Area LGBTQ+ activists), successfully pressured the archbishop to reconsider his use of the ministerial language and morality clauses.[9] However, in other places, bishops have successfully implemented ministerial language and morality clauses despite local opposition.[10]

Indianapolis, Indiana: A Tragic Story of Four LGBTQ+ Employees in Catholic Schools

Shelly Fitzgerald, who had served for fifteen years as a school counselor at Roncalli High School, was suddenly fired in 2018. After a local parishioner found her 2014 marriage license to her same-sex partner and reported her to the archdiocese, Fitzgerald was placed on administrative leave and given four options: resign, dissolve the civil marriage, not renew the contract the following year, or be fired. She refused to dissolve her marriage or leave voluntarily and was terminated.[11] Fitzgerald pursued twofold legal action against the archdiocese and the schools: initially for unjust termination and additionally for retaliation against her father, who was barred from volunteering at some events due to his daughter's initial lawsuit.[12] In 2022, a federal judge ruled in favor of the archdiocese and the school, establishing that Fitzgerald does not have legal standing to sue the school because she is a ministerial employee. The court stated:

> Roncalli entrusted guidance counselors like Fitzgerald to convey the Church's message in addition to their secular duties . . . because Roncalli, through the employment agreement and faculty handbooks, expressly entrusted Fitzgerald with shaping the school's religious policy, Fitzgerald's position as Co-Director of Guidance qualifies for the ministerial exception.[13]

Furthermore, the judge also referred to the contract signed by Fitzgerald, noting that the agreement was titled "Teaching Ministry Contract."[14]

In November 2018, months after Fitzgerald was placed on leave, her fellow school counselor colleague at Roncalli, Lynn Starkey, filed a discrimination charge with the Equal Employment Opportunity Commission due to a "hostile environment" that resulted from the conflict between the school and Fitzgerald.[15] Starkey, who had worked at Roncalli for twenty-one years and had received recognition as "teacher of the year" in 2009, was in a same-sex marriage since 2015. In response to her complaint, the school did not renew Starkey's contract for the following school year (2019–2020). The archdiocese's spokesperson stated, "Ms. Starkey is currently in breach of her contract with Roncalli High School because she is in a civil union that is considered 'contrary to a valid marriage as seen through the eyes of the Catholic Church.'"[16] Starkey also pursued legal action to no avail for similar reasons to Fitzgerald: because she qualified as a ministerial employee and had signed a teaching ministry contract.[17] Therefore, both employees from Roncalli High School were terminated without legal restitution.

In 2017, Joshua Payne-Elliott, who taught social studies at Cathedral High School, and Layton Payne-Elliott, who taught math at Brebeuf Jesuit Preparatory, joined their lives in a same-sex civil marriage. A year later, in 2018, they faced a potential termination from their respective schools. Cathedral High School and Brebeuf Jesuit High School received a directive from the archbishop of Indianapolis: they were each mandated to fire the Payne-Elliotts. For several months, the schools were in negotiations with the archdiocese over the directive. However, in the summer of 2019, Cathedral High School complied with the archdiocesan mandate and fired Joshua Payne-Elliott while Brebeuf Jesuit Preparatory refused the directive and retained Layton Payne-Elliott.[18] In response to Brebeuf's refusal, Archbishop Thompson removed the school's Catholic designation, declaring that the archdiocese no longer recognizes Brebeuf Jesuit as a Catholic institution. Due to this declaration, Brebeuf would have been unable to host some Catholic sacramental rituals, such as the Mass of the Holy Spirit,[19] which prompted them to expedite an appeal process to Rome by asking the Vatican to reverse the archbishop's decision to strip Brebeuf of its Catholic designation.[20] The Congregation for Catholic Education (CCE; now known as the Dicastery for Culture and Education) decided in 2019 to temporarily suspend the archbishop's decree over Brebeuf pending further dialogue. The Vatican then asked Cardinal Tobin of the Archdiocese of Newark to mediate a resolution between the two parties.[21] In the meantime, Brebeuf is allowed to perform the sacraments and function as a Catholic school while the dialogue unfolds.[22]

In response to the public outcry over Cathedral's firing of Joshua, the school responded in defense by explaining that, similar to Brebeuf, they were under threat of losing their Catholic identity. Not having the protections of an independently owned private institution that the other Jesuit schools enjoyed,[23] they insisted that their situations were not the same. Cathedral school officials feared permanently losing their Catholic identity without being able to appeal to the Vatican stating,

> If this were to happen, Cathedral would lose the ability to celebrate the Sacraments as we have in the past 100 years with our students and community. Additionally, we would lose the privilege of reserving the Blessed Sacrament in our chapel's tabernacle, we could no longer refer to Cathedral as a Catholic school, our diocesan priests would no longer be permitted to serve on our Board of Directors, and we would lose our affiliation with The Brothers of Holy Cross. Furthermore, Cathedral would lose its 501(c)(3) status thus rendering Cathedral unable to operate as a nonprofit school.[24]

While the sacramental standing of the school is indeed affected by a potential decree from the archbishop removing their Catholic designation, the claim about losing nonprofit status is questionable as educational institutions can retain nonprofit status regardless of whether they are religious or not. Nonetheless, it is clear that the school perceives that it would not have been able to function in the same way Brebeuf functioned if the archdiocese stripped Cathedral of its Catholic designation.

In defense of his actions, Archbishop Thompson issued a statement of "key facts" that ground his decision on the need to protect the Catholic identity of the school and to ensure employees serve as role models. He also stated that, in cases of dissent, the archdiocese would work to reconcile and bring back the employee into compliance with the Church. The archdiocesan fact sheet stated:

> When a minister is living a life not in accordance with Catholic teaching, we try to accompany them, hopefully to reconciliation with Church teaching. If an employee chooses to walk this path of accompaniment and no additional scandal is to be created, we do so with them. If they do not seek reconciliation with the Church—which is always available to them—we regrettably must part ways in

regard to employment. But we continue to pray for and welcome that individual to be part of our faith family.[25]

The document concludes with an invocation of the Church's right to religious liberty, which, according to the archdiocese, "acknowledges that religious organizations may define what conduct is not acceptable and contrary to the teachings of its religion, for its school leaders, guidance counselors, teachers and other ministers of the faith."[26] The archbishop further stated that he believes he is in compliance with Pope Francis's vision of a Church that is both inclusive and pastoral but also proclaims Christ's truth.[27]

PLAYBOOK ACT ONE: LEGAL STRATEGIES TO DISMISS LGBTQ+ EMPLOYEES FROM CATHOLIC SCHOOLS

Analyzing Legal Maneuvers: Ministerial Classifications and Morality Clauses

Firing an employee in the United States may have legal consequences. For this reason, the first part of the playbook for firing LGBTQ+ educators from Catholic schools involves a legal defense strategy. Even in states, such as California and Indiana, that have specific legal employment nondiscrimination protections for sexually minoritized individuals, the firing of LGBTQ+ educators from Catholic schools can occur with legal impunity due to a legal doctrine called the *ministerial exception*. This exception featured prominently in the Indianapolis court cases of Starkey and Fitzgerald. A product of the *Hosanna-Tabor Evangelical Lutheran Church and School v. Equal Employment Opportunity Commission et al.* US Supreme Court case decision in 2012, the ministerial exception offers protection to religious institutions by recognizing their autonomy to determine suitability for service in a ministerial capacity. This ruling is based on the right to religious liberty granted by the First Amendment and offers religious institutions immunity against any antidiscrimination lawsuits directed at them by their ministerial employees. In other words, if a religious institution fires a ministerial employee on the basis of race, gender, sexual orientation, age, disability, nationality, or any other classification under state Title VII policies or federally protected categories, the fired ministerial employee is unable to sue the institution for discriminating. Because theological questions about the suitability of ministers fall outside of the competence and jurisdiction of US courts due to the separation of church and state enshrined by the First Amendment, courts will offer what is known as an *affirmative defense* of the religious institution's right to appoint its own ministers without interference.[28] In other words, religious institutions are legally allowed to discriminate on the basis of (sexual or other) identity as they decide who is a suitable minister. If a fired employee tries to sue the religious institution and is deemed by the courts to be a "minister," the lawsuit would be dismissed by the courts, and the ministerial employee would not receive any legal redress or restitution for the faced discrimination. However, if the courts conclude that the fired employee is *not* a "minister," then regular civil state and federal employment protection laws apply and the lawsuit can proceed to litigation.[29] In the event of a lawsuit, the onus first falls on the religious institution that fired the employee to demonstrate that the employee in question is a "ministerial employee" and has no legal standing to sue for discrimination.

Crucially, the Supreme Court has refused to adopt a rigid legal definition for the term "minister," allowing lower courts to determine how this exception is to be applied on a case-by-case basis considering the titles and functions of each employee in their specific work setting. However, in 2019, the Supreme Court issued a decision on *Our Lady of Guadalupe School v. Morrissey-Berru* that significantly broadened the classification of "minister" to potentially apply to all employees of the institution, regardless of their personal religious affiliations. In the legal cases of Starkey and Fitzgerald in Indianapolis, which were both decided after the *Our Lady of Guadalupe School v. Morrissey-Berru* case, the school was able to successfully argue that both school counselors were ministerial employees because they were explicitly entrusted to transmit the faith via their "Teaching Ministry Contracts" irrespective of their day-to-day duties or whether they chose to explicitly evangelize through their work. As seen in the archdioceses of Indianapolis and San Francisco (and many others throughout the country), there is an increase in the ministerial classification of all employees in Catholic schools, which ultimately grants them legal immunity via the ministerial exception to discriminate by firing any LGBTQ+ employee on the basis of their identity or behavior.

In addition to ministerial classification, the morality clauses added to employment handbooks or contracts establish an expectation that all employees in a Catholic school must abide by magisterial doctrine in their professional and personal lives. This provides schools additional protection under contract law and strengthens their claim that all employees are ministers: they can argue in front of a judge that the expectations of assent toward Church doctrine through word and deed were made clear at the time of ministerial employment. Crucially, while these morality clauses often include statements to the effects of "all ministers must abide by Catholic doctrine in their professional and private lives," some dioceses explicitly mention appropriate sexual conduct in the clauses (e.g., San Francisco's first draft mentioned homosexual behavior several times).

As seen in all cases discussed here, bishops often justify these legal maneuvers through a theology of ministry which argues that all employees in the Catholic schools are tasked with transmitting the content of the Catholic faith to the students and exemplifying Christ through their life witness. Although each employee carries out this task to a different degree, all employees play a part in the overall Catholic mission of the school. Thus, the legal right to religious freedom simply protects religious institutions so that they can hold their ministerial employees (which, according to these bishops, means all employees) accountable for carrying out this mission of evangelization. Bishops who seek to fire dissenting LGBTQ+ educators do so on the assumption that these educators give a public witness contrary to Catholic doctrine on homosexuality or gender and therefore undermine the mission of Catholic schools. For that reason, many US bishops support the legal exercise of the ministerial exception to ensure all Catholic schools are equipped with suitable ministers to carry out this task of preserving and promoting the Catholic identity of the school through word and deed.

It is also important to note that the successful implementation of these legal strategies varies depending on the governance model between the schools and the archdiocese. As seen in the case of Layton Payne-Elliott from Brebeuf, schools owned and operated privately by boards or religious orders can offer additional protections for LGBTQ+ protections targeted by bishops for dismissals. While bishops can exercise direct canonical authority over schools owned and operated by the dioceses,[30] it is unknown how that authority translates to schools privately owned by religious orders. In the case of Brebeuf, the bishop decreed that the school lost its Catholic designation but the decree was suspended by the Vatican pending more dialogue. This raises an important theological question about Catholic schools: Where does the school's Catholicity flow from? Does it come from diocesan recognition? Does it come from their charism—that is, the traditional expression of faith particular to each religious order (e.g., Jesuits, Vincentians, Marianists)? Or from their general commitment to the Catholic tradition?

My Challenges to the Current Use of the Ministerial Exception and Morality Clauses

The United States Conference of Catholic Bishops (USCCB) published a document in 2005, titled *Co-Workers in the Vineyard of the Lord: A Resource for Guiding the Development of Lay Ecclesial Ministry*, in which they offer insights about the theological foundations, adequate preparation, and suitability of lay ministers in the Church. The bishops state, "By their baptismal incorporation into the Body of Christ, lay persons are also equipped with gifts and graces to build up the Church from within . . . lay ecclesial ministers carry out responsibilities rooted in their baptismal call and gifts."[31] They further explain, "Baptism initiates all into the one priesthood of Christ, giving each of the baptized, in different ways, a share in his priestly, prophetic, and kingly work."[32] The document also calls for the proper formation of those who pursue the call to lay ministry. Reflecting on this document, Richard R. Gaillardetz underscores that his call is grounded in the baptismal reality of the ministers, stating, "All Christians by baptism are called in discipleship to follow the way of Jesus of Nazareth, to grow in holiness, and to help further the reign of God."[33] He further remarks that this commitment creates in the layperson a new reality: a life of vocation.[34] In sum, through baptism, the lay ministers are called to a life of vocation that is an extension of Christ's offices of priest, prophet, and king to transform the world in the light of the Gospel. Applied to Catholic schools, these ministers give witness to Jesus and lead students to communion with God and the Church.

Considering the teachings of *Co-Workers in the Vineyard*, herein lies a significant set of challenges to the legal strategies employed by the magisterium. First, Catholic schools often hire non-Catholic educators to serve in their institutions. Since the theology of *Co-Workers* grounds the ministerial call in the baptismal reality of the minister, the attempt to classify all employees as ministers represents a legal strategy that is inconsistent with the teachings of the USCCB, considering that baptism is a prerequisite for a ministerial vocation. From a moral standpoint, I argue that bishops' legal use of the term "minister" should reflect the USCCB's theological understanding of the concept. Integrity demands that Catholic leaders engage the public square following their own Catholic theological principles. Therefore, when the bishops participate in American jurisprudence by declaring that non-Catholic educators can serve as ministers for Catholic schools, their actions contradict their own theology and reflect a lack of integrity for the sake of legal expediency. Crucially, I am not arguing that the ministerial exception should not exist nor that bishops should seek to use it in certain cases, but rather that it must be used responsibly and in consistency with Catholic theology of ministry.[35] In other words, not all employees of Catholic schools should be labeled as ministers by the Church, and their employment should enjoy the protection of civil state and federal employment laws.[36]

Second, Catholic schools often admit non-Catholic students without strictly aiming to convert them to Catholicism due to the Church's doctrine on religious liberty.[37] Although all students are certainly invited to participate in the Catholic life of the school, the institutions make room for diversity of faith (or lack thereof) within their student population. Therefore, the attempt to employ ministers who are witnessing the Catholic doctrine to the letter to inspire students to form a relationship with Jesus and the Church may seem at odds with their intent to welcome non-Catholic students without aiming to convert them. Considering that schools have many goals, some of which involve education in secular subjects, it is reasonable to have non-Catholic role models for the diverse student population they admit. Furthermore, non-Catholic ministers can model for non-Catholic students how to form a relationship with a religious community regardless of one's personal affiliation.[38]

Third, the execution of these legal maneuvers to dismiss dissenting educators seems to target LGBTQ+ employees almost exclusively while disregarding other employees who engage in other violations of Catholic faith and morals such as atheism or religious plurality, failure to attend mass, disregard of the poor, support for the death penalty, lack of charity toward immigrants, disregard for the environment, and so on. The dismissals of LGBTQ+ educators from Catholic schools feature prominently in our national news but one would be hard-pressed to find other "ministerial employees" being dismissed for these other violations of Catholic doctrine. Some heterosexual employees have been fired for cohabitating, procuring or supporting abortions, and getting pregnant out of wedlock, but reports of these cases are few in comparison with the number of dismissals of LGBTQ+ employees, and all of these involve "pelvic" matters of human sexuality and anti-abortion efforts. This is problematic because these teachings are arguably less central to the Church's overall doctrine when compared to faithfulness to the creed and commitment to Catholic social teaching (with the exception perhaps of the pro-life efforts, which I will not discuss). The schools seem to have a significant degree of tolerance toward educators who violate central Catholic doctrines unrelated to human sexuality, but such tolerance disappears toward disagreements about sexual morality—particularly LGBTQ+ issues. For these reasons, I argue that the exclusive targeting of LGBTQ+ employees in Catholic schools constitutes a form of unjust discrimination.[39]

Overall, the bishops' use of their right to religious liberty *vis-à-vis* the ministerial exception and morality clauses to dismiss any dissenting LGBTQ+ employee from Catholic schools reflects a theologically and morally inconsistent exercise of this right in a way that ultimately violates other important precepts of the Catholic faith. This is problematic because it represents a single-minded narrow effort to exclude LGBTQ+ persons from participation in a Catholic community under the guise of protection of the Catholic culture of the school but ultimately undermines certain elements of the very culture it seeks to promote. Such use of legal tools is self-defeating because it inevitably hinders the true mission of the Church by causing significant harm to otherwise qualified LGBTQ+ employees and the school communities that cherish their presence. In sum, this legal quest to promote religious freedom and the Catholic culture of the school is ultimately harmful to a genuine cultural vision of Catholic education.

PLAYBOOK ACT TWO: CULTURAL STRATEGIES TO PRESERVE THE CATHOLIC IDENTITY OF THE SCHOOLS

Analyzing the Bishops' Efforts to Protect the Catholic Culture of the School

The right to religious freedom in the case of Catholic institutions that fire LGBTQ+ employees serves a particular purpose: bishops claiming this right are seeking to protect their ability to freely preserve and promote the Catholic tradition in their institutions. Applied to schools, religious freedom helps protect and promote the Catholic identity and mission of the Church through the day-to-day life of the school. According to the Second Vatican Council, Catholic schools exist, in part, to help students grow into the fullness of Christ.[40] The CCE further explains:

> [The mission of Catholic schools is] fundamentally a synthesis of culture and faith, and a synthesis of faith and life: the first is reached by integrating all the different aspects of human knowledge through the subjects taught, in the light of the Gospel; the second in the growth of the virtues characteristic of the Christian.[41]

Catholic schools must therefore seek to live out their Catholic identity in the rapidly evolving pluralistic social context they are in. While many philosophies of Catholic education attempt to guide schools in this task of interacting with a pluralistic society, the bishops' attempts to protect the Catholic culture of a school through ministerial language, morality clauses, and dismissals of LGTBQ+ employees reflect what I refer to as the *distinguishability approach*.

The distinguishability approach to Catholic education in the United States has been advanced by John Piderit, SJ, and Melanie Morey. In their book, *Catholic Higher Education: A Culture in Crisis*, they argue that, to protect the Catholic identity of a school, employees of the institution promote the *inheritability* and the *distinguishability* of the Catholic tradition. Inheritability refers to the school's ability to transmit the faith to future generations. However, distinguishability demands that the Catholic worldview be presented as a countercultural and distinctive element of the school in an attempt to generate deeper commitment.[42] According to Morey and Piderit, "The more distinct the community or culture, the greater the commitment it can command and sustain."[43] Thus, they create a dichotomy between the Catholic culture of the school and the secular culture of the broader society. This separation then yields an urgency to promote what is in accordance with the Catholic culture of the school and to protect this Catholic identity from secular corruption. In other words, the protection of the school's Catholic identity is achieved by presenting Catholicism as being different from and even threatened by the broader secular culture. Crucially, in response to this perceived threat, the book recommends hiring employees who will promote this mission of distinguishability as well as an exaltation of Catholic symbols that will promote a distinctive Catholic culture in the school.[44]

Both proponents of this approach, Piderit and Morey, were hired in 2014 by Archbishop Cordileone of San Francisco as the vicar for the archdiocese and the director of the newly created Office of Catholic Identity, respectively. Within a year of hire, in 2015, they led the aforementioned efforts in the Archdiocese of San Francisco to include ministerial language and morality clauses in employment contracts. In other words, they "wrote the script/playbook" and were then hired to "direct the play." In an interview during a public protest, vicar Piderit explained that educators in Catholic schools are expected to promote the Catholic "product" and should not contradict Catholicism "just as someone who works for Coca-Cola can't expect to go into work each day with a can of Pepsi in their hand and sing the virtues of Pepsi."[45] Thus, he reinforced the dichotomy between Catholic faith and secular culture and the need to protect the former from the influence of the latter.

In a statement explaining his rationale for the proposed ministerial language and morality clauses, Archbishop Cordileone employed this distinguishability approach as he called for an active defense against the secular culture, stating,

> Promoting the faith in our contemporary society is difficult primarily because the ambient culture either explicitly or implicitly promotes secular values that often run counter to Catholic values, or at times do not align well with them. For this reason, in order to live a faithful Catholic life nowadays one needs to be very intentional, even to the point of developing a very deliberate strategy, so as to counteract the impact of secular society on our students.[46]

More poignantly, in 2014 (a year before the teachers' union dispute), Cordileone offered an address to local seminarians where he explicitly declared that the Church was at war with secular society. He endorsed a Catholic culture war mentality, stating,

> Make no mistake about it. Priests and all Catholics are in combat. It has now become unfashionable to speak of the "culture war," or at least, there are some who would like to make it so. They want us to believe that this is a passé concept, or that this war has been fought and won by the . . . well, however you

want to label them—the secularists, the postmodernists, the social anarchists, the deconstructionists. Of course, they try to force us into believing that, because they want us to back off from our position. Some say the language of "culture war" is not helpful to us, and they have a point. After all, the church is all about peace and reconciliation. But in another sense, we Catholic priests are, and always have been, at war. The church has always understood the reality of spiritual warfare. The worst soldier is the one who does not realize he is in a war. . . . In the church, both priests and laypeople are soldiers.[47]

It is not hard to see how this culture war mentality, perhaps disguised through a more benevolent language of *distinguishability*, informed and operated behind the scenes in San Francisco. While other bishops have refrained from publishing these extensive justifications and philosophies of a Catholic culture war, I note that the same script taken from the same playbook is seen throughout different dioceses in the nation as an attempt to protect the Catholic culture of a school by retaining ministers who exhibit Catholic teaching through a life witness that is consistent with magisterial doctrine, with emphasis on sexual morality as if it were a central component of the Catholic faith.[48] The ultimate goal of the distinguishability approach is to promote a distinct Catholic culture that will prevent scandalizing students into following secular values, especially on sexual morality, that run afoul of Catholic doctrine.

Analyzing the Bishops' Efforts to Avoid Scandal

The process of transmitting the Catholic faith in schools often occurs through the relationship between educator and student, so—according to the distinguishability approach—it is important for educators to give a public witness of congruence with the Catholic tradition. Employees in Catholic schools must resist secular cultural temptations and remain steadfast under the magisterial doctrine even in the face of social pressures. This witnessing should take place on and off school grounds since curious students (especially teenagers) often learn about the personal lives of their educators either intentionally or inadvertently. Therefore, all employees of the school must abide by Catholic doctrine in their professional and personal lives to transmit the Catholic tradition in a distinctive countercultural way. According to some bishops, when students find out that a Catholic school educator is contradicting Catholic doctrine in word or deed, the employee would be personifying a sinful witness to the students, which would be detrimental to the Catholic identity of the school because it constitutes *scandal*.[49]

Scandal functions as the operating principle behind the bishops' cultural maneuvers to protect the Catholic identity of schools. The Catechism defines scandal as "an attitude or behavior which leads another to do evil" and calls it a "great offense" (CCC #2284). A person who commits the act of scandal has essentially tempted another and caused that person to sin. According to the Gospel, this is particularly grievous in cases when an adult scandalizes a child—that is, leads the child to do evil (cf. Matthew 18:6), and it is also made worse if the adult in question is tasked with teaching or educating others (CCC #2285). As seen in the case studies above, Archbishop Thompson of Indianapolis and Archbishop Cordileone of San Francisco, in their efforts to rid schools of dissenting LGBTQ+ educators, argue that they are simply attempting to protect the students from the scandal of believing that same-sex marriage, same-sex sexual activity, and gender-affirming surgeries are morally permissible. According to these bishops, since educators are ministers tasked with transmitting the Catholic faith, they must act under magisterial doctrine through word and deed. Any speech or behavior that falls outside of that can tempt the students into sinning and must be avoided. Therefore, the dismissals of these educators are directly linked with efforts to preserve and promote the Catholic culture of the schools.

Other prelates have also developed the argument for scandal. In 1988, Cardinal William Leveda (the former archbishop of San Francisco) wrote an article reflecting on the importance of having religion teachers who give consistent witness to the teachings of the Church through their actions. He claimed that the religion teachers' role is to impart the faith and to offer assurance to the students that there is a clear path to salvation through Church teaching and modeling. He also argued that modeling dissent would encourage students to disregard further teachings.[50] While he was specifically focusing on religion teachers, many bishops have applied the expectations Laveda places upon these teachers to all employees. When bishops reclassify all employees as ministers, they are strategically extending the scandal-avoidance expectations placed upon religion teachers to all educators.

My Challenge to the Distinguishability Approach

In 2022, the CCE, promulgated a document titled *The Identity of a Catholic School for a Culture of Dialogue*, which struck a more balanced collegial tone between the Catholicity of a school and the local diverse cultural context. The document establishes that the Catholic school is not so much an *institution* as it is a *community* that should be animated by a spirit of freedom and charity.[51] While the document insists on the importance of preserving the Catholic identity of schools through the hiring of educators who are witnesses to Christ, it also rejects a "narrow" Catholic school model that makes no room for those who are not "totally Catholic."[52] Notably, the CCE is interested in protecting students from scandal but would only call for the dismissal of an educator after all other options are exhausted.[53] The CCE document establishes that educators in Catholic schools are entrusted to minister to the students and should model integrity of life and abidance by Catholic doctrine. It further encourages Catholic institutions to make that explicit through a code of conduct akin to morality clauses. However, the CCE also states that schools should "practice the 'grammar of dialogue,' not as a technical expedient, but as a profound way of relating to others. Dialogue combines attention to one's own identity with the understanding of others and respect for diversity."[54] Thus the CCE has attempted to strike a collaborative tone between the Catholic culture of a school and the more pluralistic culture that surrounds and permeates it.

Along these lines, I contend that the distinguishability model is unsuited to properly engage the contemporary pluralistic cultural context of Catholic education. The attempt to separate the students from the rest of society due to fear of corruption runs contrary to the central teachings of the Second Vatican Council, which encourages Catholics to engage the world and interpret the signs of the times.[55] It also fails to prepare the students to address the diversity of theological and cultural opinions present in the pluralistic context in which they live. This is problematic because engagement with pluralism is inevitable and failing to equip students to address the realities of contemporary society represents a failure of another component of the mission of Catholic education.[56] Furthermore, I see the implementation of the distinguishability approach through the hiring of teachers who are "total Catholics" in conformity with all magisterial doctrines to be unattainable because all persons, including ministers and archbishops, fall short of the doctrines of the Church or disagree with some doctrines yet are still considered to be competent ministers or Church leaders. In sum, I argue that the sanitized version of Catholic education reflected in the distinguishability approach is unrealistic, harmful to the students, and detrimental to the mission of the Church. This narrow attempt to create a Catholic bubble is reminiscent of a "smaller, purer" Church that would never—and should never—come to fruition.

In addition to the distinguishability approach, I also find the "culture war" mentality problematic because it ignores God's revelation present in ordinary life. Contemporary Catholic theology, including Jesuit spirituality, Latinx Theology, and other expressions of faith, highlight the importance of finding God in all things—of finding God in *la vida cotidiana* [daily life].[57] Attempting to instill a culture war mentality that separates us from so-called secular culture is founded on two incorrect assumptions. First, I argue that it incorrectly assumes that all secular culture is *bad* when, historically, secular culture has often sparked important human advances that the Church eventually incorporates.[58] Second, I argue that Catholic culture is not always *good* as evidenced in the prevalent systemic abuse of minors, the financial corruption of Vatican officials, and even the institutional hypocrisy on matters of homosexuality.[59] The dualism presented by a culture war mentality is, simply put, a superficial oversimplification of the complicated relationship between faith and culture.[60] In the case of LGBTQ+ employees, as I will discuss in this book, their LGBTQ+ identity and cultural experience are often the source of theological insight and compassion toward others that shouldn't be simplified as an antithesis to Catholic identity.

Faith is a tumultuous journey that is best explored in a community that embraces the lived reality of all people. Therefore, a different approach to Catholic education that fosters dialogue, conscience formation, and commitment to community is needed to guide young students along their faith journey. Catholic principles can and should inform these efforts but should not serve as a strict rubric to evaluate a person's employment or overall belonging in a Catholic institution. Instead, more central tenets of the Gospel—which include mercy, charity, and inclusion—should guide policies in all Catholic institutions. The needs of the students must also be considered and prioritized. Young generations are certainly in need of guidance regarding various moral issues, but, in my experience, they seldom respond well to strict top-down behavioral mandates. On the contrary, they tend to rebel against them. Instead, a new approach should engage them in dialogue and empower them to exercise their own agency informed by the values of the Gospels. Employing competent educators from diverse backgrounds who are well trained in theological discourse and who represent and embrace diverse opinions would aid this mission. They can embody the diversity of our Church and model respectful communal dialogue and discernment for the students, which is another way of giving witness to the Gospels. While there are certainly some parameters and expectations that must be established for all employees of a Catholic institution, I maintain that a narrow focus on sexual morality under threat of dismissal to avoid "confusing students" should not be one of those.

My Response to the "Scandal Argument"

The single-minded quest to protect students from scandal is problematic because it often runs the risk of producing "opposite scandal." Opposite scandal refers to the inadvertent creation of a secondary scandal when someone attempts to protect people from an initial risk of scandal. Applying this concept to the firings of LGBTQ+ educators, Christopher Vogt maintains, "efforts to prevent scandal by firing teachers and lay pastoral ministers provide an excellent illustration of the dangers of 'opposite scandal.'"[61] He further explains that, when a Catholic school fires an LGBTQ+ educator, such an attempt to protect the students from the scandal of homosexual sexual activity or gender transitions can yield an opposite scandal because "firing men and women for seeking state recognition of their gay partnership or for being in an openly gay relationship can easily be interpreted as calling into question the church's affirmation of the intrinsic worth and dignity of gay men and women."[62] This second scandal teaches the students that LGTBQ+ people do not belong in the Catholic community, are unsuitable ministers in the Church, and should not be employed. It further represents a serious disregard for Catholic doctrine on the supremacy of conscience, human rights, the dignity of work, and even religious liberty (as I will discuss in a later chapter). Firing LGTBQ+ educators in an attempt to avoid scandal is, therefore, self-defeating because it may also lead children toward the sin of unjust discrimination against LGTBQ+ persons and the disregard of basic tenets of Catholic moral theology and Catholic social teaching. According to Lisa Fullam,

> Opposite scandal is still scandal—it still leads people to a misunderstanding of moral truth, generally by refusing to grant moral weight to the real complexity of our lives, individually and socially. Ignoring opposite scandal too often leads prophets to imply that Christian faith requires keeping one's own hands completely clean of any involvement in morally messy situations.[63]

It seems, therefore that scandal is inevitable when it comes to LGBTQ+ educators: retaining them might cause one scandal, and firing them might cause another.

In response to this apparent inevitability of scandal, Fullam further argues that *fear* of scandal should not prevent Catholics from exploring morally difficult situations by shielding Catholic institutions from disagreement with magisterial doctrine on matters that are peripheral and heavily contested. It is important to wade into uncertain moral territory as a community journeying together. She asserts,

> An argument that stands or falls on risk of scandal alone is generally a weak argument, hinging as it does on asserting the lack of knowledge or discernment of those who would be scandalized. Better that we all talk together as we walk the pilgrim way, helping each other to grow in wisdom, not afraid to risk scandal, lest we stumble and fail in love.[64]

For that reason, I reaffirm: Catholic schools that wish to engage the pluralistic cultural realities of their students, which already contain disagreements, should teach the students to address moral uncertainty through conscience formation and communal dialogue informed by core principles of the Catholic tradition. Attempting to raise students in a distinguishably Catholic setting by sanitizing the Catholic school environment from so-called sin and scandal fails to equip students with important skills of dialogue, tolerance, and respect for the dignity of all persons.

Considering a Social Justice Lens toward LGBTQ+ Inclusion

Often missing from the bishops' rhetoric regarding the dismissals of LGBTQ+ educators in Catholic schools is a consideration for the Catholic social tradition, which—ironically—finds its genesis in the recognition of the dignity of work and the rights of workers with the first social encyclical, *Rerum Novarum* in 1891. More broadly, this social justice lens is also missing on other matters concerning LGTBQ+ people: bishops have been largely silent in the face of two US mass shootings at LGBTQ+ establishments (Pulse Nightclub in 2012 and Club Q in 2022); many bishops oppose civil protections on matters of housing, employment nondiscrimination, same-sex adoption, and civil marriage—even when these protections would be exercised in a secular context and by LGBTQ+ people who may not be Catholic; only a few US bishops signed the Tyler Foundation's statement about suicide prevention for LGTBQ+ youth, and many were *emeriti*; and many bishops across the globe have been silent (perhaps even supportive) toward laws in their countries that criminalize LGBTQ+ behavior, sometimes under penalty of death. While some US bishops have begun to recognize this missing piece in the life of the magisterial Church, the majority of bishops refuse to advocate for these basic rights that would defend the dignity of those who identify as LGBTQ+. This underscores the existence of an opposite scandal when an LGBTQ+ person is fired from a Catholic school.

Because the dismissals of LGTBQ+ persons affect their economic, social, political, physical, emotional, and cultural well-being, it is crucial to apply a social justice lens to these questions in addition to the seemingly exclusive focus on sexual morality and theological/ecclesiological considerations about the identity of Catholic institutions. The Church has long recognized the intrinsic connection between human dignity and work. For this reason, it is important to contend with this controversy as a matter of social justice and to develop a case for LGBTQ+ retention that considers the dignity of LGBTQ+ persons as tied to their work and vocations. Furthermore, the bishops' invocation of the ministerial exception as an extension of the First Amendment's right to religious liberty requires a deeper conversation about the meaning and scope of religious freedom. Considering the Church's incorporation of human rights language, and the recognition of the right to work and the right to religious liberty as human rights, I argue that a deeper understanding of this methodology can help Catholic leaders better live up to the Catholic social tradition. Finally, the Catholic social tradition has long advocated for a preferential option for the poor and vulnerable which, I argue, applies to members of the LGBTQ+ community that are often subjected to social exclusion, vilification, and erasure. Overall, these social justice considerations are also central to establishing a strong Catholic culture in their institutions and, as I will argue, should ultimately inspire Catholic leaders to retain LGBTQ+ educators who disagree with Catholic doctrine on questions of homosexuality or gender.

WE NEED A NEW APPROACH

In addition to the numerous theological inconsistencies reflected in efforts to dismiss LGBTQ+ educators from Catholic schools, the firings represent an obstacle to the Catholic school mission of evangelization in at least two ways. First, the dismissals cause a significant distraction to the everyday life of the school that, instead of focusing on the message of the Gospels, are suddenly contending with a contentious controversy due to the termination of an often-beloved member of their community (as I will showcase in the next chapter). This causes an incredibly tumultuous school environment that is not conducive to learning—much less learning about faith. Second, I observe that the firings could cause significant spiritual harm to the students and the broader school communities as evidenced in the resulting public outcry. During the many protests in support of dismissed LGBTQ+ educators, several parents and students have issued public statements of apathy or disdain toward the Church due to the actions of Catholic school leaders. Some have also expressed spiritual harm.[65] It is, therefore, hard to imagine how these dismissals are bringing our contemporary youth closer to Christ. Hence, I argue that the dismissal of LGBTQ+ educators from Catholic schools hinders the effective transmission of the Catholic faith to our youth. This is not only a matter of theological integrity whereby I call upon Catholic leaders to live up to the fullness of our Catholic tradition, but also a matter of pragmatism whereby I observe that the harm caused to the Catholic school community by these firings renders the schools ineffective at fulfilling the Catholic component of their mission.

Finally, and most importantly, I argue that these dismissals can cause significant harm to LGBTQ+ students in Catholic schools who receive a clear message that they are not welcome or safe. If I had witnessed one of my LGBTQ+ teachers being fired when I was a gay teenager in a Catholic school, I would be thinking, "If my teacher is not safe, I am not safe." These dismissals undoubtedly contribute to the stress LGBTQ+ youth already feel and the erasure the LGBTQ+ community generally faces in society. Considering statistics of heightened depression, suicide ideation and self-harm, high risk of homelessness, as well as low performance in schools for LGBTQ+ youth, this population is particularly vulnerable and these matters of LGBTQ+ inclusion deserve to be addressed with care and compassion.[66] As an example of such struggles, a gay Catholic school student named Gus O'Sullivan attended a protest during the 2015 San Francisco contract dispute and expressed, "The language is offensive and damaging. As a gay student, I understand the severity of this language." He continued reflecting upon his struggles accepting his sexual identity, observing that the archbishop's proposed language "would have been detrimental to my mental health and self-worth."[67] I observe that the firings of LGBTQ+ employees would only exacerbate these issues facing LGBTQ+ youth. In addition, LGBTQ+ youth often rely on adult role models that they can identify with for their well-rounded development. Therefore, the absence of LGBTQ+ adults in a school community deprives LGBTQ+ youth of the necessary representational role models that would aid their growth.

For these reasons, I assert that there is an urgent need for a new approach to the presence of LGBTQ+ educators in Catholic schools. I argue that the misguided use of religious freedom to promote a *distinguishable* Catholic culture that narrowly defends Catholic doctrine on sexual morality at the expense of other significant teachings of the Church is largely inconsistent with the broader Catholic theological tradition. Furthermore, it betrays a homophobic, transphobic, heteronormative, and cisnormative cultural agenda on behalf of the bishops, which is also problematic. In addition to the theological inconsistencies represented by these efforts, the firings result in an impractical obstruction of the mission of Catholic schools due to the distraction and harm caused to the Catholic school community, especially to LGBTQ+ youth. A new approach needs to consider the entirety of Catholic theology (including sexual morality, social justice, and ecclesiology among other areas), the diversity that surrounds and permeates the Church (including diversity of theological views), the importance of communal dialogue and discernment on controversial matters, and the local needs of Catholic school communities. I will develop this new approach in the coming chapters.

CONCLUSION

In this chapter, I analyzed the playbook implemented by bishops and other Catholic leaders to fire LGBTQ+ employees from Catholic schools and I challenged the theological inconsistencies and impractical results of these dismissals. With this challenge, I highlight the need for a new theological framework that can help Catholic leaders properly and pragmatically respond to the presence of LGBTQ+ educators in Catholic schools. Considering the legal and cultural (i.e., Catholic culture) strategies deployed by Catholic leaders to exclude LGBTQ+ Catholic school educators, this new framework requires a multifaceted theological approach that engages the fields of personal sexual morality, ecclesiology, and Catholic social ethics. Since Catholic sexual morality remains at the crux of the dismissals because Catholic teaching on sex functions as the litmus test for ministry suitability, my new framework will propose new ways to engage with Catholic sexual morality in the context of a theologically diverse community. In light of the institutional questions pertaining to Catholic identity and culture, I enter the field of Catholic ecclesiology, or the study of the nature of the Church, to reflect on how Pope Francis's synodal vision for the global Church should affect the local Catholic school communities in the United States. Finally, considering Catholic leaders' use of religious liberty to adjudicate matters of employment, I retrieve some key principles of the Catholic social tradition on human rights to help Catholic institutions better uphold the dignity of all people and contribute to the common good. In sum, the coming chapters will develop this framework that will help Catholic schools remain true to the Catholic theological tradition, fulfill their mission of evangelization more effectively, and respect the dignity of all members of their community with particular attention to LGBTQ+ educators and students. But first, before developing this framework, in the next chapter, I will highlight the importance of retaining and celebrating LGBTQ+ educators in Catholic schools by delving into some of their beautiful and inspiring stories of vocation and grace.

NOTES

1. "Archdiocese Releases Q&A; on Union Contract Proposals," *Catholic San Francisco*, February 4, 2015, https://web.archive.org/web/20150206080928/http://www.catholic-sf.org/ns.php?newsid=25&id=63174.

2. Salvatore Cordileone, "Archdiocese Releases Statement on Church Teachings, Practice in High Schools," *Catholic San Francisco*, February 4, 2015, https://web.archive.org/web/20150211095801/http://www.catholic-sf.org/ns.php?newsid=25&id=63175; Dan Morris-Young, "New Faculty Handbooks in San Francisco to Include Statement Developed by Archbishop," *National Catholic Reporter*, February 4, 2025, https://www.ncronline.org/news/parish/new-faculty-handbooks-san-francisco-include-statement-developed-archbishop.

3. Salvatore Cordileone, "Archbishop's Letter to Catholic High School Teachers," *Catholic San Francisco*, February 4, 2015, https://web.archive.org/web/20150207014731/http://www.catholic-sf.org/ns.php?newsid=25&id=63177.

4. Cordileone, "Archbishop's Letter to Catholic High School Teachers."
5. Cordileone, "Archbishop's Letter to Catholic High School Teachers."
6. Cordileone, "Archbishop's Letter to Catholic High School Teachers."

7. Dan Morris-Young, "Teachers Union: Revised Faculty Handbook Could Reduce San Francisco Legal Protections," *National Catholic Reporter*, June 3, 2015, https://www.ncronline.org/news/parish/teachers-union-revised-faculty-handbook-could-reduce-san-francisco-legal-protections.

8. Salvatore Cordileone, "Draft of Revised Faculty Handbooks for San Francisco Archdiocese," May 29, 2015, https://www.scribd.com/document/267577184/Draft-of-revised-faculty-handbooks-for-San-Francisco-archdiocese.

9. "Archbishop Cordileone Thankful for San Francisco Teacher Contract Agreement," Catholic News Agency, August 23, 2015, https://www.catholicnewsagency.com/news/32507/archbishop-cordileone-thankful-for-san-francisco-teacher-contract-agreement.

10. For an extensive list of these other diocesan policies, see Dan Guernsey and Denize Donohue, "Faith and Morals Language in Catholic School Teacher Employment Documents: Best Practices Brief," Cardinal Newman Society, June 25, 2015, https://cardinalnewmansociety.org/faith-morals-language-catholic-school-teacher-employment-documents-best-practices-brief/.

11. Holly V. Hays and Vic Ryckaert, "'My Faith Hasn't Been Shaken,' Says Roncalli School Counselor Whose Job Is on the Line," *The Indianapolis Star*, August 14, 2018, https://www.indystar.com/story/news/2018/08/14/roncalli-high-school-counselor-catholic-school-same-sex-marriage-conflict/986631002/.

12. "Roncalli Counselor Suspended for Same-Sex Marriage Files Second Discrimination Charge," *The Indianapolis Star*, March 1, 2019, https://www.indystar.com/story/news/fox59/2019/03/01/shelly-fitzgerald-files-second-charge-against-roncalli-archdiocese-same-sex-marriage-case/3028812002/.

13. Fitzgerald vs. Roncalli High School and Roman Catholic Archdiocese of Indianapolis, No. 1:19-cv-04291-RLY-TAB (Southern District of Indiana 9/30).

14. Fitzgerald vs. Roncalli High School and Roman Catholic Archdiocese of Indianapolis.

15. Crystal Hill, "Another Roncalli Guidance Counselor Alleges Discrimination over Sexual Orientation," *The Indianapolis Star*, November 16, 2018, https://www.indystar.com/story/news/2018/11/16/roncalli-guidance-counselor-files-federal-complaint-against-school-archdiocese/2029962002/.

16. Vic Ryckaert, "A Second Roncalli Counselor Has Been Told She Will Lose Her Job over Same-Sex Marriage," *The Indianapolis Star*, March 25, 2019, https://www.indystar.com/story/news/2019/03/25/roncalli-counselor-losing-job-same-sex-marriage-shelly-fitzgerald-lynn-starkey/3265868002/.

17. Starkey v. Roman Catholic Archdiocese of Indianapolis and Roncalli High School, No. 21–2524 (7 Circuit Court July 28, 2022).

18. Arika Herron, "Cathedral Fired a Gay Teacher. Brebeuf Protected One. They Are Married to Each Other, Lawyer Says," *The Indianapolis Star*, July 10, 2019, https://www.indystar.com/story/news/education/2019/07/10/cathedral-teacher-fired-same-sex-marriage-sues-indianapolis-archdiocese-identifies-himself/1694669001/.

19. This mass refers to the first mass of the year, which most educational institutions refer to as "Mass of the Holy Spirit." It is not an official celebration recognized by the global Church.

20. Arika Herron, "Brebeuf Jesuit Appeals Split with Catholic Church, Barred from Holding All-School Mass," *The Indianapolis Star*, August 5, 2019, https://www.indystar.com/story/news/education/2019/08/05/brebeuf-jesuit-appeals-split-catholic-church-barred-holding-mass/1920187001/.

21. "Cardinal Tobin Asked to Mediate Indy High School Standoff," *The Pillar*, January 27, 2021, https://www.pillarcatholic.com/cardinal-tobin-asked-to-mediate-indy/.

22. Bill Verbryke, "Update from Brebeuf Jesuit President, Fr. Bill Verbryke, S.J., Brebeuf Jesuit Preparatory School," February 25, 2019, https://web.archive.org/web/20210225032948/https://brebeuf.org/update-from-brebeuf-jesuit-president-fr-bill-verbryke-s-j-2/.

23. As an independent school, Brebeuf Catholic does not fall under the direct legal and governance authority of the Archdiocese. Cathedral and Roncalli, however, are owned and operated by the Archdiocese.

24. Matt Cohoat and Rob Bridges, "Dear Cathedral Family," June 23, 2019, https://www.gocathedral.com/about/news-marketing/school-news/news-post/~board/homepagenews/post/dear-cathedral-family.

25. Charles C. Thompson, "Key Facts and Answers to Frequently Asked Questions," Archdiocese of Indianapolis Website, June 27, 2019, https://www.archindy.org/archbishop/press-2019-faq.html.

26. Thompson, "Key Facts."

27. John Shaughnessy, "Archbishop Encourages Christ-Centered Approach to Move Forward in Unity," July 12, 2019, https://www.archindy.org/criterion/local/2019/07-12/archbishop.html.

28. The term "affirmative defense" refers to an instance in which a defendant proves that they are not to be held *liable* for what they did, while at the same time admitting that they did in fact do what the prosecution accused them of doing. See Wex Definitions Team, "Affirmative Defense," Legal Information Institute, June 2022, https://www.law.cornell.edu/wex/affirmative_defense.

29. As an example of an employee deemed by the courts to not be a minister, Matthew Barrett successfully sued Fontbonne Academy in Massachusetts after they fired him as a food service provider. The case was settled in 2016. See Astead W. Herndon, "Catholic School, Gay Man Settle Discrimination Lawsuit," *Boston Globe*, May 9, 2016, https://www.bostonglobe.com/metro/2016/05/09/dorchester-man-settles-with-catholic-school-discrimination-lawsuit/tCU2x8z18VlhcVQXk3H1TP/story.html.

30. According to the Code of Cannon Law, bishops serve as the sole stewards of their diocese and are specifically in charge of the religious education aspects of the schools in their territory. They have direct authority over the hiring of religious studies teachers and campus ministers. Furthermore, the decision of whether a school can receive its "Catholic" designation is relegated to "competent ecclesiastical authority." It is unclear whether that is solely at the discretion of the bishop of whether the Vatican and/or a religious order can bestow that designation. See "Code of Canon Law," Vatican Website, nos. 803–806, accessed December 30, 2022, https://www.vatican.va/archive/cod-iuris-canonici/eng/documents/cic_lib3-cann793-821_en.html#CHAPTER_I.

31. US Conference of Catholic Bishops, "Co-Workers in the Vineyard of the Lord: A Resource for Guiding the Development of Lay Ecclesial Ministry," USCCB. org, 2005, 12, https://www.usccb.org/upload/co-workers-vineyard-lay-ecclesial-ministry-2005.pdf.

32. US Conference of Catholic Bishops, 18.

33. Richard R. Gaillardetz, "The Theological Reception of Coworkers in the Vineyard of the Lord," in *Lay Ecclesial Ministry: Pathways toward the Future*, ed. Zeni Fox (Rowman & Littlefield, 2010), 22.

34. Gaillardetz, "The Theological Reception of Coworkers," 22.

35. I support the existence of a ministerial exception that allows religious institutions the right to determine who is fit to minister for their congregations. To offer an example of why it must exist, I turn to the question of women's ordination in the Church. The Catholic Church does not ordain women priests for theological reasons (regardless of how sound they are) but the United States has federal nondiscrimination protections on the basis of gender. It would be unreasonable for a woman in the United States to be able to levy a lawsuit against the US Catholic Church because they refuse to ordain her. Irrespective of the theological justifications for male-only ordinations, the state has no competence to adjudicate any matter of theology and must, therefore, refuse to entertain such a lawsuit. For this reason, the ministerial exception exists: to offer an affirmative defense for Catholic institutions to be able to discriminate in determining suitability for ministry.

36. As I will discuss in chapter 2, there are many dissenting LGBTQ+ employees in Catholic schools who do teach religious studies and/or serve as campus ministers. In the next chapter, I will argue that these educators can still be suitable ministers despite their dissent with magisterial doctrine.

37. This was acknowledged by the CCE. See Congregation for Catholic Education, "The Religious Dimension of Education in a Catholic School: Guidelines for Reflection and Renewal," Vatican Website, April 7, 1988, no. 6, https://www.vatican.va/roman_curia/congregations/ccatheduc/documents/rc_con_ccatheduc_doc_19880407_catholic-school_en.html.

38. I will discuss the presence of Catholic LGBTQ+ educators serving in direct ministerial Catholic school roles (e.g., campus ministry and teaching religion) in the next chapter.

39. James Martin agrees that the selectivity of the firings reflects a problematic inconsistency that reflects a form of unjust discrimination. See James Martin, *Building a Bridge: How the Catholic Church and the LGBT Community Can Enter into a Relationship of Respect, Compassion, and Sensitivity*, 2nd ed. (HarperOne, 2018), 46.

40. Second Vatican Council, "Gravissimum Educationis," Vatican Website, October 28, 1965, no. 2, https://www.vatican.va/archive/hist_councils/ii_vatican_council/documents/vat-ii_decl_19651028_gravissimum-educationis_en.html.

41. Congregation for Catholic Education, "The Catholic School," Vatican Website, March 19, 1977, no. 37, https://www.vatican.va/roman_curia/congregations/ccatheduc/documents/rc_con_ccatheduc_doc_19770319_catholic-school_en.html. It is also important to recall the CCE's recognition of the welcomed presence of

non-Catholic students who also benefit from the more secular components of Catholic education (see note 37).

42. Melanie M. Morey and John J. Piderit, *Catholic Higher Education: A Culture in Crisis* (Oxford University Press, 2006), 29–32.

43. Morey and Piderit, *Catholic Higher Education*, 254.

44. Morey and Piderit, *Catholic Higher Education*, 110–12, 227–28.

45. Barnard, "Hundreds Protest Morality Clause for Teachers Proposed by SF Archbishop," ABC7 San Francisco, February 8, 2015, https://abc7news.com/morality-clause-teachers-san-francisco-archdioceses/524464/.

46. Salvatore Cordileone, "Knowledge, Virtue, and Holiness," Catholic Culture, February 6, 2015, https://www.catholicculture.org/culture/library/view.cfm?recnum=10849.

47. Salvatore Cordileone, "Valiant in Battle," *Catholic San Francisco*, December 3, 2014, https://web.archive.org/web/20150423193639/http://www.catholic-sf.org/ns.php?newsid=4&id=62989.

48. A summary of Catholic leaders making statements about preserving Catholic school culture by ensuring ministerial employees at the school do not engage in sexual activity that runs afoul of magisterial teaching can be found in the 2015 brief published by the Cardinal Newman Society, which encourages school leaders to protect the Catholic identity of their school through methods like morality clauses, ministerial language, etc. The brief chronicles cases in which schools have implemented such measures. See Guernsey and Donohue, "Faith and Morals Language in Catholic School Teacher Employment Documents: Best Practices Brief."

49. In 2015, Archbishop Cordileone released a Q&A statement outlining the justification and implementation of his proposed language to the San Francisco teacher's contract and handbook. In responding to particular doctrinal conflicts that might arise, Cordileone outlined a course of action based on the public nature of each incident due to the threat of scandal. See "Archdiocese Releases Q&A; on Union Contract Proposals."

50. William Levada, "Dissent and the Catholic Religion Teacher," in *Readings in Moral Theology No. 6: Dissent in the Church*, ed. Charles E. Curran and Richard A. McCormick (Paulist Press, 1987), 133–51.

51. Congregation for Catholic Education, "The Identity of the Catholic School for a Culture of Dialogue," Vatican Website, no. 16, accessed December 5, 2022, https://www.vatican.va/roman_curia/congregations/ccatheduc/documents/rc_con_ccatheduc_doc_20220125_istruzione-identita-scuola-cattolica_en.html.

52. Congregation for Catholic Education, no. 72.

53. Congregation for Catholic Education, no. 80.

54. Congregation for Catholic Education, no. 30.

55. Second Vatican Council, "Gaudium et Spes," Vatican Website, October 7, 1965, no. 4, https://www.vatican.va/archive/hist_councils/ii_vatican_council/documents/vat-ii_const_19651207_gaudium-et-spes_en.html; Second Vatican Council, "Gravissimum Educationis," nos. 4–5.

56. According to the CCE, the Church "encourages the co-existence and, if possible, the cooperation of diverse educational institutions which will allow young

people to be formed by value judgments based on a specific view of the world and to be trained to take an active part in the construction of a community through which the building of society itself is promoted." See Congregation for Catholic Education, "The Catholic School," no. 13.

57. For an example of such theological perspectives, see Miguel H. Diaz, "The Word That Crosses: Life-Giving Encounters with the Markan Jesus and Guadalupe," in *The Word Became Culture*, ed. Miguel H. Diaz (Orbis Books, 2021), 1–24.

58. A classical historical example of this involved Galileo Galilei who, after being condemned by the Catholic hierarchy for his findings in the natural sciences, was later vindicated by another pope centuries later. For an analysis of this affair applied to contemporary issues, see Craig A. Ford, "Our New Galileo Affair," *Horizons* 50, no. 2 (December 2023): 255–92, https://doi.org/10.1017/hor.2023.41.

59. "Number of Priests Accused of Sexually Abusing Children as Reported by the USCCB," bishopsaccountability.org, February 16, 2020, https://www.bishop-accountability.org/AtAGlance/USCCB_Yearly_Data_on_Accused_Priests.htm; Elisabetta Povoledo, "Vatican Indicts Cardinal and 9 Others on Money Laundering and Fraud Charges," *New York Times*, July 3, 2021, sec. World, https://www.nytimes.com/2021/07/03/world/europe/vatican-cardinal-becciu.html; Frederic Martel, *In the Closet of the Vatican: Power, Homosexuality, Hypocrisy*, trans. Shaun Whiteside (Bloomsbury Continuum, 2019).

60. An important analysis of the relationship between faith and culture is seen in the classical work of H. Richard Niebuhr. See H. Richard Niebuhr, *Christ and Culture* (Harper & Row, 1975).

61. Christopher P. Vogt, "The Inevitability of Scandal: A Moral and Biblical Analysis of Firing Gay Teachers and Ministers to Avoid Scandal," in *The Bible and Catholic Theological Ethics*, ed. Yiu Sing Lucas Chan, James Keenan, and Ronaldo Zacharias (Orbis Books, 2017), 265.

62. Vogt, "The Inevitability of Scandal," 266.

63. Lisa Fullam, "'Giving Scandal' in 'The Call of the Catholic Citizen: Theologians and Other Scholars Respond to Cathleen Kaveny,'" *America Magazine*, November 1, 2010, https://www.americamagazine.org/issue/753/100/call-catholic-citizen.

64. Fullam, "Giving Scandal."

65. As an example, bisexual student Brooklyn Thorpe reacted to the dismissal of Joshua Payne-Elliot by stating, "Getting this from the church is kind of like a hit to the face. . . . Does this show that I really am not accepted by the church?" See Arika Herron, "Catholic School Controversy: Rainbow Streamers Welcome Back Cathedral Students," *The Indianapolis Star*, August 8, 2019, https://www.indystar.com/story/news/education/2019/08/08/catholic-school-controversy-rainbow-streamers-welcome-back-cathedral-students/1952923001/.

Another student in San Francisco named Gino Gresh remarked, "Saying that someone's nature is inherently evil, that shocked me . . . I do see this as an injustice." See Lee Romney, "S.F. Archbishop's Imposition of Morality Clause at Schools Outrages Many," *Los Angeles Times*, February 12, 2015, sec. California, https://www.latimes.com/local/california/la-me-san-francisco-archbishop-20150212-story.html.

66. James Martin, "Why Should the Church Reach out to L.G.B.T.Q. People? Some Shocking Statistics Can Answer That," *America Magazine*, August 2, 2021, https://www.americamagazine.org/faith/2021/08/02/james-martin-lgbtq-catholics-statistics-241139.

67. Mandy Erickson, "Hundreds Attend Forum Opposed to San Francisco Handbook Changes," *National Catholic Reporter*, March 17, 2015, https://www.ncronline.org/news/parish/hundreds-attend-forum-opposed-san-francisco-handbook-changes.

Chapter 2

The Gifts of LGBTQ+ Catholic School Educators

I first realized I was gay as a student in an all-boys Catholic high school in Puerto Rico. After being taught through my religion classes that homosexual sexual activity was sinful, and after enduring years of bullying from my classmates who perceived I was gay before I knew I was, I entered a period of emotional and spiritual crisis when I became aware of my sexual attraction to other boys. My only consolation at school was a religion teacher who saw my struggle and accompanied me as I came to terms with my sexual identity. This teacher responded to my need by providing a safe space where I could ask questions and discern what God wanted me to do in light of who I was. Doing so posed a risk for him, as we lived in a Catholic and Latinx culture that was hostile to LGBTQ+ persons.[1] In many ways, I owe my faith to that man for I would probably not consider myself Catholic if it were not for his ministry to me. It saddens me to think about what my life would be like if I did not embark on my current spiritual and faith-filled journey as a gay Catholic.[2]

Interestingly, I never knew about the teacher's sexual identity (which is none of my business). He simply emphasized that his role was to remind me that God loves me and that I am not alone in my struggles. In the same way, after receiving God's call to teach and becoming an educator several years later, I sought to provide a safe space for my LGBTQ+ students to explore both their identity and their faith. I similarly noticed that, in addition to my LGBTQ+ students, my straight cisgender students were also in need of a safe space to discern their faith and relationship to a Church that constantly oppresses their fellow LGBTQ+ friends and family members. Therefore, LGBTQ+ inclusion in my work as an educator was never just an LGBTQ+ issue: it also affected young allies who struggled to be part of an exclusive Catholic institution. More importantly, as a minister, I worried about the spiritual harm LGBTQ+ students and allies would suffer due to their exclusion from the Church, and I sought creative ways to continue to engage them on their faith journey. In this process, I was constantly reminded of queer icon Billy Porter, who reflected on LGBTQ+ oppression by lamenting, "the first thing they take away from us is God" and I vowed to not take away from my LGBTQ+ students their experience of God's grace.

At first, when I began this ministry, I attempted to model my work after my teacher who accompanied me. However, through years of therapy and spiritual direction, I recognized that I deeply yearned for openly gay Catholic role models during my teenage years.[3] For that reason, in my role as a gay educator who advised the school's LGBTQ+ student group, I decided to come out to the members of the group so they knew that I am not only a safe space but also a potential role model to them about how a person can navigate their faith and their LGBTQ+ identity. Through this ministry, I realized that my experience as a gay Catholic equipped me with a unique perspective that students could meaningfully connect with. A proud moment along this journey came from a gender-queer student who came up to me at the end of one of our meetings and said, "I didn't know I could like a Catholic community this much." Another similar moment came from a colleague who told me she felt encouraged to convert to Catholicism via the Rite of Christian Initiation for Adults (RCIA) in my parish after seeing how I proudly lived my Catholic faith as a gay man. More importantly, through my work with other LGBTQ+ educators in Catholic schools, I learned that my experience was not unique. Those of us who were open about our sexual identities (and our struggles in a Catholic community) with our students and colleagues provided them with an important sense of safety and guidance on their spiritual journey and broader questions of identity, human relationships, and social justice. In other words, I have experienced firsthand how LGBTQ+ educators can serve as agents of evangelization and positive transformation in a Catholic community.

These experiences of co-ministering with other LGBTQ+ educators are the main impetus as I write this book: LGBTQ+ educators are a largely untapped resource in our schools that the schools desperately need given how apathetic many contemporary teens are toward Catholicism. Moreover, their dismissals cause significant harm to school communities. When an LGBTQ+ educator is fired, the school sends a clear message to LGBTQ+ students and allies that says, "you are not welcome here." That message can cause significant spiritual harm and it likely contributes to the alarming statistics we see on suicide ideation, depression, and other issues among LGBTQ+ youth. Furthermore, as a sexually marginalized and oppressed community, LGBTQ+ people possess a unique perspective, a queer epistemology,[4] about faith, sexual morality, relationships to community, and social justice. In Catholic schools, LGBTQ+ educators apply this unique perspective as they accompany LGBTQ+ youth and young allies. Furthermore, as I will argue in a later chapter, these queer perspectives are important for the Church as a whole. For this reason, the celebration of LGBTQ+ educators in Catholic schools carries a much broader impact on the global Church.

In this chapter, I will explore the unique gifts that LGBTQ+ educators offer to Catholic school students and the broader Church by virtue of their LGBTQ+ identity and behavior. First, I will analyze the experiences and needs of Catholic school students. To do this, I will examine several studies on youth that have tried to understand their struggles with their faith as well as some statistics and anecdotes relating to LGBTQ+ youth. Second, in light of the needs of our modern Catholic school students, I will examine the purpose of Catholic education and the role of Catholic school educators. Here I retrieve the work of Thomas Groome, who crafts a philosophy for Catholic education that I find best responds to the needs of Catholic school students. Third, I will explore the role of Catholic school educators by synthesizing Groome's philosophy for Catholic education with the USCCB statement on Catholic school educators, *To Teach as Jesus Did*. This part will outline a three-part criterion to evaluate suitability for ministry in a Catholic school. Finally, I will survey the existing research on LGBTQ+ educators in Catholic schools, some of which I helped conduct, to argue that, based on the outlined three-part criteria, LGBTQ+ educators are uniquely equipped to fulfill the mission of Catholic schools. More importantly, they offer essential contributions as ministers in Catholic schools despite (or even because of) their LGBTQ+ identity or lifestyle.

SERVING THE NEEDS OF CATHOLIC SCHOOL STUDENTS

Those of us committed to the Catholic Church's mission of evangelization are observing a distressing trend among students in Catholic schools.[5] Research shows that young people in the United States, both Catholic and non-Catholic, are developing an increasingly apathetic relationship with their religious communities and are exhibiting high levels of disaffiliation from them. In 2005, Christian Smith published a book titled *Soul Searching: The Religious and Spiritual Lives of American Teenagers*, in which he explored the dynamics of disaffiliation among US youth. Specific to Catholic youth, he observed,

> Catholic youth [are] scoring 5–25 percentage points lower than their conservative, mainline, and black Protestant peers on many of variety of religious beliefs, practices, experience, commitments, and evaluations. Perhaps more important for Catholics, our findings regarding teenagers show many of them to be living far outside of official Church norms defining true Catholic faithfulness.[6]

These higher levels of disaffiliation, according to Smith, are attributed to multiple factors such as demographics, parental religiosity, parish and diocesan programs, and Catholic schools. Regarding schools, he notes that they "no longer function as well as they had for decades as means by which the Church evangelized, ministered to, and educated its youth."[7] He further perceives that educators in Catholic schools are generally not receiving robust theological training and that Catholic schools are now more focused on "getting their students admitted to prestigious colleges than to teaching the about the Trinity, sin, the Virgin Mary, the atonement, and faithful Christian living."[8]

Other studies have contributed additional insights into the causes and dynamics of teenage disaffiliation from religion. The Pew Research Center has recently conducted several major studies to understand the religious trends in the United States. In 2009, they discovered that the vast majority of people who leave the Catholic Church do so before the age of eighteen, and over half of them cite the Church's teachings on homosexuality as a reason for their departure (though participants listed many reasons). Other Pew Research Center studies in 2014 and 2018 similarly concluded that questions of human sexuality factored in US teens' decision to leave their religious communities.[9] In 2017, Saint Mary's Press commissioned an in-depth qualitative study to understand disaffiliation among young Catholics. In their publication, *Going, Going, Gone: The Dynamics of Disaffiliation in Young Catholics*, they identified the median age of disaffiliation at thirteen and also concluded that, among the many reasons for disaffiliation, a significant group disaffiliated because they dissent from Church teaching on certain hot-button topics including same-sex marriage.[10]

Such findings may seem alarming considering the Church's mission to spread the joy of the Gospels throughout the generations.[11] It also places educators in a difficult position since many young Catholics are leaving the Church due to a magisterial teaching on sexual morality that is out of their control. However, perhaps more alarming than the declining numbers of members in the Church is the fact that many of these young Catholics are leaving *because* they disagree with the teaching. In other words, disagreement *itself* leads to disaffiliation. As a Church, we have not been able to foster among our youth (or among our adults) an environment where legitimate diversity of theological opinion can coexist and lead to meaningful communal dialogue and discernment. Ironically, Catholic leaders who fire LGBTQ+ educators contribute to this problematic culture by discouraging such a communal mentality through their "submit to magisterial teaching or leave" attitude toward LGBTQ+ ministers. For this reason, I return to the call I made in chapter 1 for a new framework for addressing LGBTQ+ people in Catholic institutions. While, in the previous chapter, I criticized the *distinguishability* framework for Catholic education due to its impractical, cultural, and theological inconsistencies (which are all reflected in the dismissals of LGBTQ+ educators), in this chapter I am exploring a suitable alternative philosophy of Catholic education that would help schools fulfill their responsibility toward Catholic youth who, through their dynamics of disaffiliation, are communicating an important message to Catholic leaders about the need for a more inclusive Church. Catholic education is called to serve these needs as we evangelize and guide young students, whether LGBTQ+ or not, toward a relationship with God and the Church rooted in community.

In addition to the pragmatic questions about disaffiliation and evangelization in Catholic schools, a more pressing moral concern—in my view—relates to the aforementioned alarming statistics among LGBTQ+ youth who experience disproportionate rates of homelessness, consider/attempt suicide, and suffer through other mental health struggles when compared to their heterosexual cisgender peers. These statistics become even more dire for transgender youth.[12] Research suggests that family exclusion and bullying at school are the root causes of these issues.[13] Furthermore, research also shows that religion often serves as a motivating factor in cases involving familial and cultural exclusion of LGBTQ+ youth.[14] While many of these statistics are derived from the public sector (and there is little research on the experience of LGBTQ+ youth in Catholic schools), they nonetheless indicate that LGBTQ+ youth in general are an at-risk population. A devastating story involving the suicide of an LGBTQ+ youth in a Catholic context is captured in the podcast "Dear Alana," where her parents recount how Catholic leaders convinced their daughter that her same-sex attraction was a temptation toward sin to the point where she decided to take her own life.[15] In her diary, she wrote,

> Fr. Peter told me that I should not identify by my temptations, for the cause is much deeper than I could imagine. The cause was the doubt and isolation. From a young age I did not know God. From a young age I was isolated because of my sexual addiction. I felt so much shame and hopelessness. Because of my parents, I could not relate to them or be known by them. They were too strong and I was weak.[16]

Catholic leaders who take seriously their responsibility, as Catholics, to recognize and affirm human dignity are called to exercise proper pastoral care toward vulnerable LGBTQ+ youth. They must go to the margins, exercise a preferential option for the poor and vulnerable, and accompany them on their journey. Considering that this is a matter of life and death for many LGBTQ+ youth, Catholic schools cannot afford to further isolate, marginalize, or oppress this vulnerable population. Unfortunately, Catholic schools have largely fallen short of their call to care for them.

The limited research on LGBTQ+ student inclusion in Catholic schools highlights this failure. In 2001, Michael Maher published a book titled *Being Gay and Lesbian in a Catholic High School: Beyond the Uniform*. In his research, he discovered that there was a serious *disintegration* of LGBTQ+ students in Catholic schools, which means that these students did not feel a sense of internal or external harmony.[17] Internally, disintegration applied to the students' academic, social, spiritual, and emotional components of their development which did not develop in tandem. Externally, disintegration manifested as a disconnect from their home and/or school environments. In some cases, the external experience of disintegration students faced through violence, direct discrimination from teachers, inadequate pastoral care, and lack of adequate curricular references to LGBTQ+ experiences led to a serious internal disintegration in their intellectual, social, emotional, and spiritual development.[18] Furthermore, Maher concluded that this disintegration contributes to the alarming statistics facing LGBTQ+ youth. In 2012, Mick Mominee published a dissertation titled "Lesbian, Gay, Bisexual, and Queer/Questioning Catholic School Alumni: High School Experiences of Support and Challenge," which surveyed the experience of some LGBQ (not transgender students) in Catholic schools. He also noticed issues of discrimination, silence, and negligence toward LGBQ students, particularly in the area of pastoral care. Mominee proposes the following recommendations based on the suggestions offered by the people he interviewed: creating support groups (i.e., Gay Straight Alliances), offering professional development for teachers, establishing nondiscriminatory policies, establishing "safe spaces" in the classroom, and making a conscious effort to educate all students regardless of their orientation.[19] Maher and Mominee's studies were based on a small sample of Catholic school students, but all tell the same story of LGBTQ+ youth struggling in our schools.

The struggles of LGBTQ+ students are underscored by the repeated instances of bullying and outright or subtle discrimination, which are prominent in Catholic schools. In a series of stories published by *Outreach* (a Catholic LGBTQ+ resource website), one teenager named Christian Figueroa recounted the torment he experienced as a gay student in an all-boys Catholic school. This experience caused him significant pain and he chose to stay "in the closet" out of fear of further rejection.[20] Another student named Joseph Larson told a story about serving as a representative of a Catholic school's LGBTQ+ student group during the school's open house for prospective students. His optimism for representing his LGBTQ+ club quickly vanished as he experienced discriminatory stares, invalidating inquiries, and some hollow sympathetic remarks from some of the families in attendance. As he left the event with a friend, he saw a rat walking on the street, told his friend "There's a rat" and proceeded toward the subway. He then stopped and realized "I looked at that rat better than anyone looked at us tonight."[21] A third student, named Henry Herbert Jr., reflected on his experience by stating, "The dissonance between the love of Christ that I knew to be true and the judgement of my church, my school, and my peers was deafening. Eventually I entered into my own Gethsemane. I pleaded to understand. I wept to be freed from my cross."[22] These devastating stories, along with the ones captured in Maher and Mominee's studies and the increasingly alarming statistics on mental health, should compel Catholic schools to prioritize strategies for LGBTQ+ inclusion.

Fortunately, despite the troubling statistics and anecdotes from LGBTQ+ students, there are also signs of hope: research shows that the risk of suicide ideation or attempt on behalf of an LGBTQ+ youth significantly decreases if that youth encounters at least one supportive adult in their school community (and the risk further decreases with more than one adult).[23] For example, despite his struggles, Henry Herbert Jr. also expressed gratitude toward his theology teachers who aided his faith journey. He recounted, "During the 'dark age' of my life as a queer student in my Catholic school, I saw Christ embodied in a select group of people. My theology teachers pushed me to see through the politics and human error and into Christ. They were the church for me."[24] I echo that feeling and again express gratitude to my own theology teacher who, as Herbert articulates, became the Church for me. My hope for Catholic education is that school leaders learn to appreciate educators who serve LGBTQ+ students and especially LGBTQ+ educators who can serve as crucial role models for LGBTQ+ youth by offering a firsthand account of an LGBTQ+ experience.

In summary, it is clear from the contemporary dynamics of youth disaffiliation, the alarming statistics on LGBTQ+ youth, and the anecdotal evidence of LGBTQ+ students that Catholic education faces a unique challenge to its mission of evangelization and its moral responsibility to care for all students (particularly the most vulnerable ones). Furthermore, Catholic schools have failed to respond adequately to these challenges. It is hard to imagine how the dismissals of LGBTQ+ educators, and their subsequent absence from the schools, represent an appropriate response. On the contrary, it further alienates many Catholic youth who yearn for more LGBTQ+ inclusion and it deprives LGBTQ+ youth of the role models they need to navigate matters of faith, identity, and well-being. For the remainder of this chapter, I will continue to argue that LGBTQ+ educators in Catholic schools are uniquely prepared to respond to the current needs of Catholic school students. They can potentially serve as important role models, suitable ministers, and as a safe space for all students. Furthermore, they can offer significant indispensable contributions to the broader mission of Catholic education and the global Church.

Chapter 2

RE-ENVISIONING THE MISSION OF CATHOLIC EDUCATION

The Church is called to proclaim the Gospels throughout the world and throughout the ages as it guides humanity toward salvation.[25] The mission of Catholic schools is derived from this global Catholic mission because schools function as a key point of contact between the magisterial Church, represented by the school's institution (its pastors, ministers, teachers, administrators, etc.) and the lay faithful (the students and families, i.e., the flock). Furthermore, Catholic schools exercise their mission in a multifaceted way, engaging all components of the human person and guiding them toward flourishing and salvation through a relationship with God rooted in community.[26] Key to that mission is a twofold dynamic of personal development and social or communal engagement. Regarding personal development, the Second Vatican Council states, "Among all educational instruments the school has a special importance. It is designed not only to develop with special care the intellectual faculties but also to form the ability to judge rightly, to hand on the cultural legacy of previous generations, to foster a sense of values, to prepare for professional life."[27] Regarding society and community, the Council states that a Catholic school "leads its students to promote efficaciously the good of the earthly city and also prepares them for service in the spread of the Kingdom of God, so that by leading an exemplary apostolic life they become, as it were, a saving leaven in the human community."[28] Both efforts, however, take place harmoniously. Here I return to the Dicastery for Culture and Education's statement explaining that the mission of Catholic schools is "fundamentally a synthesis of culture and faith, and a synthesis of faith and life: the first is reached by integrating all the different aspects of human knowledge through the subjects taught, in the light of the Gospel; the second in the growth of the virtues characteristic of the Christian."[29] Catholic schools must endeavor to help students develop internally a sense of faith and values in connection with an external communal and social relation given their current context.

With that foundation, I note that many bishops implement the mission of Catholic education in different ways. In chapter 1, I critiqued Morey and Piderit's distinguishability approach to Catholic education, which Archbishop Cordileone attempted to implement in San Francisco Catholic schools with disastrous effects because this approach seeks to promote the mission of Catholic schools by separating the school from secular culture. According to the *distinguishability* approach, a Catholic school can only fulfill its mission if it does so in a way that is distinctive from secular influence. Furthermore, it must safeguard the magisterial doctrines of the Church from secular corruption and hire educators who abide by the teaching and can model it to the students. I argue that such a dualistic mindset runs contrary to the fullness of the mission of Catholic schools, which necessarily integrates faith and culture. Instead, I propose that we revisit the work of Thomas H. Groome, who proposes a more effective and appropriate approach to Catholic education.

According to Groome, Catholic education is best illustrated "by the distinctive characteristics of Catholicism itself, and these characteristics should be reflected in the whole curriculum of Catholic schools. By 'curriculum' I intend the *content* taught, the *process* of teaching, and the *environment* of the school."[30] Thus, he measures the Catholicity of the school not in terms of distinguishability, but in terms of character and relationships considering a comprehensive appraisal of the entire school community: content, process, and environment. Groome then lists *eight* key components of Catholic education, which are divided into five theological and three cardinal characteristics. The five theological characteristics are: positive anthropology, sacramentality, community, tradition, and rationality.[31] Groome interrelates these characteristics to rationality by stating,

> Rationality coupled with Catholic anthropology means encouraging people to think for themselves, to trust their own discernment and decision-making. Its sacramentality suggests helping people to think with imagination and perception, to discern the ultimate in the immediate, and to be critically conscious about society. Rationality coupled with community encourages students to think in dialogue and conversation, to test their reasoning in discourse with others and with communities of wisdom and faith. Catholicism's commitment to tradition coupled with rationality means enabling students to critically appropriate the tradition to their lives rather than passively inheriting it, to make it their own rather than accepting it blindly, and to think about tradition in ways likely to encourage personal and social responsibility.[32]

Key in this perspective is the respect for students' conscience and the encouragement to form communities where diversity and disagreement, including theological diversity and disagreement, serve as avenues for dialogue and joint discernment. Under this model, blind indoctrination runs contrary to the heart of the Catholic tradition, which affirms conscience and freedom in the context of diverse communal relationships.

This idea is underscored by Groome when he introduces an additional three *cardinal* characteristics, which are: commitment to "personhood," commitment to "basic justice," and commitment to "catholicity."[33] These three cardinal characteristics are deeply related to the five theological characteristics. With regard to *personhood*, Groome holds that each individual is capable of engaging with the five theological characteristics through the individual person's own autonomy (including one's conscience).[34] With regard to *basic justice*, the person can interact with the five theological characteristics in the context of "right relationships" with others (i.e., community). Finally, with regard to "catholicity," Groome asserts,

> Our claim to be 'Catholic' should confront us with our sins of exclusion and sectarianism, and ever challenge us to become an inclusive community with hospitality and openness to all. Clearly this commitment must permeate Catholic education. Catholicity is reflected in its *anthropology* as the curriculum affirms each person's worth. . . . Its *sacramentality* of life, is catholic as it encourages people to appreciate both the unity and diversity of life, to experience God's Spirit as the love energy of all creation. Its *community* emphasis is catholic when the school is truly a place of welcome and inclusion, and educates its students that "neighbour" has no limits. Teaching the *tradition* is catholic as it convinces students of the universality of God's saving presence and love for all peoples, and grounds them in this particular tradition without prejudice or sectarian bias. And its *rationality* is catholic as it opens people to the truth, wherever it can be found.[35]

The central component of Catholic education, for Groome, is an inherent appreciation of the diversity present within the Catholic tradition and the world we well as God's love and salvation extended to all. This implies that the evangelization that is to take place in Catholic schools should not be too obsessed with uniformity of belief that conforms to a single Catholic worldview (e.g., as presented in magisterial doctrine on sexual morality), but in the communal interaction with a diverse set of ideas about the Catholic tradition and the communal journey toward salvation. I agree with Groome that Catholic education should seek truth wherever it can be found; therefore, Catholic schools should be more concerned with *how* diverse justifiable ideas are taught in the context of a Catholic community rather than *which* particular ideas are taught.[36]

To protect schools from attitudes that foster exclusion, Groome cautions against *sectarianism* and *parochialism*. He defines sectarianism as "a bigoted and intolerant exaltation of one's own group that absolutizes the true and good in its members, encouraging prejudice against anyone who has alternative identity—especially immediate neighbors."[37] He then defines parochialism as "a narrow-minded, self-sufficient, and insular mentality that closes up within itself, is intolerant to or oblivious of other perspectives, and conceited about its own. . . . Parochialism and 'Catholic' education should be an oxymoron—a contradiction in terms."[38]

Attempting to provide students with a narrow, single-minded conception of the Catholic tradition and expecting them to abide by it without question and without influence from secular culture is both impractical and self-defeating. It is impractical because it would fail to evangelize students (who continue to grow discontent with an exclusive Church) and would fail to prepare the students who do stay in the faith to meaningfully interact with the world; thus rendering the overall mission of the Church unfulfilled. It would be self-defeating because it denies the basic tenets of Catholic anthropology that center around autonomy, personhood, sacramentality, conscience, and relationship in an attempt to inculcate students by presenting them with a sanitized model of the Catholic faith taught by educators who strictly seek to abide by magisterial teachings and reflect no theological diversity. In other words, the previously discussed distinguishability model violates the same Catholic identity it seeks to promote. The heart of Catholicism is not contained in a set of magisterial documents to be followed against all costs, but rather in the free conscientious faith-filled relationships we forge with God, each other, and the Church.

Groome's model for Catholic education applies a more comprehensive and profound Catholic individual and communal anthropology to diverse learners, recognizing that the students (whether Catholic or not) are individuals who are inherently good and capable of forming their conscience and entering into community through dialogue.[39] In his words,

> I call [my educational] philosophy "Catholic" because although it is suggested by core convictions of Catholic Christianity, it can have general appeal and be persuasive apart from confessional Christian faith. It reflects catholicity as in the etymology of the term *kata holos*—"welcoming everyone." When such catholicity is the intent the particularity of Christianity can contribute most richly to the universal enterprise of education.[40]

High school students have the rational capacity to critically appropriate the Catholic tradition and apply it to their lives. This is why we allow Catholic teenagers to receive the sacrament of confirmation at the age of fourteen, which is typically a ninth grade student. Groome's anthropological focus on the rational autonomous learner is key to Catholic education. Furthermore, considering the aforementioned rates of disaffiliation and the particular struggles of LGBTQ+ students, respecting student autonomy in the context of a Catholic community is crucial for the school's mission to evangelize and the students' overall well-being. For these reasons, I argue that Groome's philosophy for Catholic education offers a more adequate framework to meet the needs of our contemporary youth.

THE ROLE OF THE CATHOLIC SCHOOL EDUCATOR

Adopting Groome's *universal* approach to Catholic education, Catholic schools should not exclusively seek to hire and retain educators who are in strict conformity with magisterial doctrine but rather should seek to hire role models that can give witness to a relationship with the Church that is grounded in diverse theological and moral perspectives. In other words, it is permissible and even beneficial to have educators who represent a wide range of reasonable theological and moral positions who can still model for students how one can participate in a Catholic community while celebrating such diversity.[41] Catholic school educators, therefore, are called to serve as witnesses of the Catholic faith in all of its diversity. They are also called to teach students how to interact with differing theological and moral views while still respecting the dignity of each person. Under this model, the presence of LGBTQ+ educators who disagree with magisterial doctrine on homosexuality and gender offers the school a unique opportunity to fulfill its mission to evangelize.

Reflecting on the role of Catholic school educators, the USCCB's classic publication *To Teach as Jesus Did* proposed a trifold purpose of Catholic education. According to the US bishops, "[Catholic school] programs must strive *to teach doctrine fully*, *foster community*, and *prepare students for Christian service.*"[42] With regard to the teaching of the doctrine, the bishops state that schools need to have qualified ministers to transmit the content of the Catholic faith tradition.[43] This transmission, however, must be carried out in word and deed. It is not enough for educators to teach content in their classroom, but rather, they should embody the person of Christ and model for students what a life of faith should look like. The USCCB emphasizes that "This integration of religious truth and values with the rest of life is brought about in the Catholic school not only by its unique curriculum but, more important, by the presence of teachers who express an integrated approach to learning and living in their private and professional lives."[44] Pope Francis agrees and states, "Educators . . . pass on knowledge and values with their words; but their words will have an incisive effect on children and young people if they are accompanied by their witness, their consistent way of life. Without consistency it is impossible to educate!"[45]

With regard to community, the USCCB document states, "Community is an especially critical need today largely because natural communities of the past have been weakened by many influences."[46] Students need to be taught to participate and be responsible for each other's well-being despite pressures toward individualism and apathy. Community requires an individual's commitment to relationships and active participation in the group. However, the opposite is also true: community also implies that the group is committed to the well-being of each individual. That said, communities also have boundaries and a person who does not abide by them can certainly jeopardize their place in the community. With regard to service, bishops establish that "service of the public interest is a notable quality of the Catholic and other non-public schools in America."[47] Catholic schools, however, engage in service out of a commitment to building the Kingdom of God on Earth through works of mercy and through social justice.

Groome's universal model for Catholic education adds an important dimension to a Catholic school's trifold purpose of doctrine, community, and service. Regarding doctrine, the universality model reminds Catholic school leaders that the purpose of transmitting a doctrine is not for students to blindly assent to it. Rather, it is to foster an opportunity for critical thinking about the content of Catholic doctrine in a way that helps generate genuine commitment to the Catholic tradition. Teaching doctrine to inculcate students will likely exacerbate the levels of teenage disaffiliation from the Church, especially from members of the LGBTQ+ community and their allies. Teenagers in Catholic schools need to be engaged and invited to use their gifts of discernment to navigate Church doctrine. More importantly, educators should encourage the student's autonomy to decide how they wish to relate to Catholic doctrine. Only then would any potential appreciation for and commitment to the Catholic tradition be free and genuine. Regarding community, Groome's universality approach highlights the diverse nature of our Catholic tradition. Uniformity has never been a part of Catholicism. As Groome explains, the word "catholic," understood as "universal," does not imply *sameness* but rather *togetherness*. And such a call for togetherness would only make sense when considering the real diversity present in the Church. Finally, service to the Kingdom of God requires right relationships of justice toward all. It also involves a commitment to the flourishing of all people inside and outside the Catholic school community, with particular attention to the most vulnerable. Applying Groome's model to Catholic school service would compel schools to place human dignity at the forefront of their social and political efforts. In sum, synthesizing the USCCB's statement, Groome's universality approach to Catholic education, and Pope Francis's call for educators to serve as role models in schools, I argue that Catholic school educators should (1) reflect the collegial theological diversity present in the Church, (2) demonstrate a genuine commitment to the well-being of the Catholic school community, and (3) orient their service toward the overall betterment of society.

In the following section of this chapter, I will demonstrate that, despite their disagreement with Church doctrine, LGBTQ+ educators can still serve as suitable ministers in Catholic schools and can model the trifold purpose of doctrine, community, and service. More importantly, considering the USCCB's reflections in light of Groome's universal model for Catholic education and the contemporary needs of our Catholic school students (including the vulnerable LGBTQ+ ones), I argue that LGBTQ+ educators are uniquely positioned to serve the mission of Catholic schools in ways other educators are unable to. They are capable of embodying, through instruction and life witness, the mission of Catholic schools. Catholic leaders should seek to hire and retain LGBTQ+ educators who can provide perspectives on doctrine, community, and service in a way that will be well received by the students. When LGBTQ+ educators achieve that, which (as I will illustrate) happens often, they significantly transform the lives of their students and guide them to a deeper relationship with God through community.

THE GIFTS OF LGBTQ+ CATHOLIC SCHOOL EDUCATORS

There is limited research exploring the experience of LGBTQ+ educators in Catholic schools so, in this section, I will draw from the three studies conducted so far to reflect on how these ministers have helped fulfill the mission of Catholic education as role models in the areas of doctrine, community, and service. The first study was a dissertation published in 2010 by James Everitt titled "The Experience of Catholic, Gay and Lesbian, Secondary School Teachers within Northern California: A Participatory Action Research Study." In it, he facilitated participatory action research with a group of eight gay and lesbian Catholic high school educators who identify as Catholic themselves.[48] Everitt explored five themes pertaining to the experience of these educators: Catholic identity, prayer/sacramental life, mentoring of gay and lesbian students, silence/invisibility, and fear.[49] All of the participants disagreed with magisterial teaching on homosexuality. Despite this, Everitt recounts that these educators mostly experienced a mixture of positive and challenging times at the school. According to Everitt, "The primary impact of being homosexual in a Catholic school relates to the participants' concern over job security. All eight of the participants expressed concern over job loss if their sexual orientation was revealed to the diocese within which they worked."[50] However, all participants were very committed to their Catholic identity and this commitment created a positive influence in the school.

The second study was also a dissertation published in 2017 by Kevin Stockbridge titled "Queer Teachers in Catholic Schools: The Cosmic Story of an Easter People." This was also participatory action research involving four gay men who taught at Catholic schools and dissented from magisterial teaching on homosexuality.[51] Three identified as Catholic and taught religious studies. One was a non-Catholic science teacher. Stockbridge's research tried to understand how *queerness* was constructed in a Catholic school setting and how that, in turn, impacted the work of queer educators. Like the participants in Everitt's research, Stockbridge's participants recognized similar blessings and challenges in their experience as queer educators. However, while Everitt focused on the Catholic identity questions of gay and lesbian educators, Stockbridge explored how justice and liberation play a role in the life and work of queer educators. He remarks on this by analyzing a quote from one of the participants, "'We live the truth of the Catholic Social Teaching that it is more than just surviving in the midst of oppression, it is about learning to thrive.' Doing queer is a form of liberation in Catholic schools when it seeks to open new pathways in the face of oppression."[52] He refers to queer educators as "an Easter People" because they reflect the transformation and newness of life brought about by this struggle toward liberation.[53]

I helped conduct the third study along with Jane Bleasdale (and in collaboration with Kevin Stockbridge) in 2018. Our research consisted of a survey of thirty-six LGBTQ+ educators in Catholic schools throughout the United States. We published our findings in a 2021 article titled "Mixed Blessings: Understanding the Experiences of LGBTQIA+ Educators in Catholic Schools." I will refer to this work as "our research." Despite the significant range of experiences we captured, which seemed distributed according to the geographical (ergo cultural) location of the participants, we noticed some important trends: (1) there are a significant number of respondents who teach religion or serve as campus ministers, (2) there is a lack of support for LGBTQ+ students in the curriculum and extracurricular activities, (3) LGBTQ+ educators themselves attempt to serve as role models, and (4) they serve students despite significant risk and stress over being fired. Our study, while it reached a small number of LGTBQ+ educators, contributes some more statistical urgency to the previous two studies.[54]

LGBTQ+ Educators as Role Models in Doctrine

Everitt's research specifically focused on gay and lesbian teachers who identified as Catholic. Some of the participants expressed awareness of their students' spiritual needs and were ready to meet them.[55] These educators were well versed in Catholic teaching and understood their role as witnesses for their students.[56] Everitt observed,

> Working within Catholic schools was a choice made freely by the participants in response to their love for the Church and their hope that their own witness to the Christian life would have an impact on their students. They were intentional

about their commitment to Catholic education, and their love for their vocation within the Catholic education community was clear.[57]

Three of the teachers in Stockbridge's research were religious studies teachers who engaged with their students in dialogue about the many teachings of the Catholic Church. They reflected on how they teach students about the Catholic faith through the lens of justice,[58] which provides an avenue for critical dialogue about the role of the Catholic faith in the world. With regard to magisterial teaching on homosexuality, Stockbridge notes that LGBTQ+ educators are best equipped to impart these teachings with compassion, especially to LGBTQ+ students. He states,

> It isn't easy to be [a] queer [student] in a Catholic school, having to question what lessons about the immorality of homosexual activity might mean about you as a queer young person in the eyes of God and the world. Only a queer teacher is able to answer these questions and give solace to a hurting non-heteronormative, non-gender conforming and/or questioning heart.[59]

The trend of LGBTQ+ educators who teach religious studies or work in campus ministry was noted in our national survey, where 77 percent of participants reported serving in those roles in a Catholic school.[60] It is interesting that, despite the risks of dismissal, so many of these educators still choose to live out their vocation at great personal cost. Such a self-sacrificial posture toward vocation makes LGBTQ+ educators Christ-like role models. To be willing to risk their well-being (including financial, emotional, and spiritual) to offer direct contributions to the mission of Catholic education is a level of commitment many straight and cisgender educators do not have to assume. For this reason, I argue that Catholic leaders would be wise to integrate such dedication into the life of the school.

The presence of LGBTQ+ religion teachers and campus ministers can also help challenge some of the pervasive discourses about homosexuality and transgender identity often present in our schools. As an example, a participant in our study observed:

> The religion department at my school takes an ultra-conservative view of homosexuality and the impact that homosexuality is having on society. Members of the religion department have been known to compare homosexuality to choosing a flavor of ice cream (whatever you are feeling today—that's what you choose), comparing homosexuality to ISIS (that the LGBTQ+ community may bring about the destruction of Western society), and suggesting that homosexuality is extremely sinful and that it will most likely lead to eternal damnation. No student should enter a religion classroom and be taught that homosexuality is comparative to any of those things. And yet—these statements are not

discouraged, reprimanded, or countered by the administration or religious team that is assembled.[61]

These schools need LGBTQ+ religion teachers and campus ministers as witnesses for their colleagues and school leaders about the realities of LGBTQ+ lives. Another participant in our study opined, "Having LGBTQ+ religion teachers is very important. I have seen firsthand how the lack of our presence, accompanied with negative words, policies and treatment, often turns off the spiritual and religious dimensions of the students' lives."[62]

In addition to being witnesses of doctrine and tradition in the classroom, LGBTQ+ educators also express a profound engagement with the sacraments and prayer as a means to affirm their own Catholic and LGBTQ+ identities. A participant in Stockbridge's study talked about how he sees his contributions to school liturgy as a way of inserting queer people's gifts into the liturgical life of the Church.[63] With regard to the integration of prayer and sacraments into their personal life, a participant in Everitt's research remarked,

> When they say, "Love it or leave it," I just stand there and say, "Hey, I have my baptismal certificate. I don't need your approval," and with that, that understanding of my identity has always been through the sacraments. It's always been through my relationship with Christ and with the sacraments that make me a Catholic. So for me, Catholic identity in my prayer life has always been secure.[64]

Even the non-Catholic participant of Stockbridge's research found himself deeply tied to the mission of the school. Stockbridge observed about this participant that

> [he], too, expressed this sentiment in words that spoke of a mission to a work greater than himself. This is the first aspect which [sic] opened my eyes to the presence of a spiritual way of existing for queer teachers in Catholic schools. Being present in the schools itself had meaning because it was tied to a transcendent reality. Transcendence, however, need not be understood as a personal god or Church but could take the form of a disembodied mission.[65]

With that, Stockbridge recognized that even non-Catholic LGB educators are still connected with the values and principles embedded in the Catholic mission of the school. His participant, though not Catholic, was able to associate with the "higher calling," which could refer to morality, justice, community, or other aspects of education. However, this higher calling certainly reflects the sacramental nature of the school and, therefore, may equip non-Catholic LGBTQ+ educators to be good role models on matters of Catholic doctrine by witnessing commitment to these principles espoused by the Church while not necessarily using Catholic terminology in reference to them.

Most importantly, the LGBTQ+ educators saw themselves as unique assets in the school's effort to evangelize the students, which is a central component in the mission of Catholic education. One participant in Everitt's study expressed,

> I think if we get credit for anything [it's for] helping young people navigate their own faith. I mean, I think about the missionary effort of the Church to evangelize people. I meant that, to me, is evangelization right there . . . able to share with a young person our own faith struggles in a way that is going to affirm them in their own faith struggles? If toasters were given out for reaffirming young people in the Catholic faith, I think we'd have a lot of toasters.[66]

Another participant added, "We give meat to the Gospel, not in a sort of 'fluffy' way, but again, the 'rubber hitting the road' of it being painful or a struggle to continue to be a witness in the best sense of the word. If our Church were to recognize us for being the healers and the evangelizers that we are, wow."[67]

This is a significant and unique contribution. These dissenting LGBTQ+ educators, who often feel ostracized by the Church hierarchy due to their identity, are still freely choosing to stay as members of the Church. This makes them incredibly effective as ministers because they can draw from their experience as marginalized members of the Church to impart unique insights about Christ to students who are apathetic or unsure about being Catholic. Everitt concurs,

> Another important implication for Catholic schools is the key role that Catholic gay and lesbian educators play in bridging the gap between the Roman Catholic Church and postmodern teenagers who dismiss the validity of Church membership. All of the participants articulated a concern over the relationship between their students and the Roman Catholic Church. The students with whom the participants interact on a daily basis are largely dismissive of the Church and have little faith in its teachings. The participants reported that students believe the Church lacks credibility on moral issues, rendering it unlikely that they will continue their relationship with the Church into adulthood.[68]

As discussed, most contemporary Catholic school students, whether LGBTQ+ or not, are drifting away from the Church and could benefit from the witness of LGBTQ+ Catholics who have good reason to leave the Church yet choose to stay. These *unlikely ministers* can model for the students what it means to disagree but remain part of the Catholic community. As one of Everitt's interviewees explained, "Why do I stay? Because this is my family, you know, and I might disagree with family members. I might disagree with experiences that have taken place in the past, but I'm not going to walk away from my family."[69] Many Catholic school students would benefit from hearing that message from an LGBTQ+ educator. Catholic leaders who are committed to the evangelization mission of the school would be wise to retain these committed LGBTQ+ role models as indispensable and unique assets toward that mission.

LGBTQ+ Educators as Role Models in Community

The LGBTQ+ educators interviewed by both Stockbridge and Everitt remarked on the different ways they engage in community building with their students. A participant in Everitt's research expressed awareness of students who come seeking a place to belong. He explained how he connects with students outside of the classroom through one-on-one mentoring and support groups like *gay straight alliance* (GSA) clubs. He spoke about how, from an LGBTQ+ standpoint, he addresses students asking questions about sexuality by stating,

> Well, to me, that speaks of the student needing to know if he fits in. A young person coming and asking that question says that they're also struggling, that they have faith questions that aren't resolved, that they have viewpoints that are maturing, that a sixth-grade spiritual education isn't addressing them as young adolescents, and to me, that is sort of like an opportunity for me to share. If there's room for me, there's room for you, you know.[70]

With that, the educator demonstrated awareness of student needs and meaningful engagement with the student in the community in a way that allows the student to feel valued for who the student is.

LGBTQ+ educators are also uniquely equipped to look out for students who are particularly vulnerable. Participants in Everitt's study described ways they specifically support LGBTQ+ students through pastoral support, mentoring, and safe spaces like GSAs. Some of these educators have to advocate for the existence of these safe spaces. One participant in Everitt's study stated,

> I think it is just a matter of having the support of the administration, [and having them understand] that [GSAs exist] for the purpose of supporting a healthy understanding of a young adolescent's sexuality, alleviating some of the anxiety that comes with growing up, feeling and knowing that one is different, sort of "nipping" at its source, that sense of dissatisfaction that might lead to harm to a young student, whether it is emotional or physical or even suicide, you know. I think that's important enough to have an administration see that as a

valuable resource to have for young gay and bisexual students in the school environment.[71]

In our research, a similar theme emerged. One participant stated, "Although I am not openly gay, I think some students know, and it is unspoken between us. . . . I think being a LGBTQ+ educator has made me a more empathetic teacher to all minorities and students who don't 'fit in.'"[72] Another noted that a significant blessing of being an LGBTQ+ educator in a Catholic school is "the ability to relate to students that are not the norm." Moreover, a third participant explained, "My identities have helped me to better understand, empathize, and support my students and their needs. I have become an unofficial support for LGBTQ+ students to come to and share their story with."[73]

In addition to the welcome of LGBTQ+ students, I argue that LGBTQ+ educators, as members of the larger LGBTQ+ community, have a cultural sense of what it means to establish communities against difficult odds. The LGBTQ+ community has a long history of establishing safe spaces for its members in the face of hostility and exclusion.[74] LGBTQ+ educators who are aware of this history have a useful tool for applying it in a Catholic school by helping establish these safe spaces for LGBTQ+ students and staff. One participant in Stockbridge's study expressed, "I wish that people could see that we are more than our sexuality, we are a culture!"[75] That sense of community helps LGBTQ+ educators build communities within the Catholic school as a matter of justice.

Community also involves collaboration among fellow faculty. According to Stockbridge's participants, "By being in personal relationships with others in our schools, we transform the sense of justice and solidarity in our community. We can align ourselves with faculty members who are homophobic or have negative attitudes and change them by our friendship."[76] Thus it is clear that these dissenting LGB educators, by virtue of their identity, have become bridge-builders in Catholic schools, offering students and colleagues the opportunity to enter into communities of solidarity and justice with each other. Catholic school leaders committed to the building of Christian communities in their schools should retain and celebrate these educators for the gifts they offer.

LGBTQ+ Educators as Role Models in Service

The presence of LGBTQ+ educators in Catholic schools serves to promote the schools' mission of justice and work toward the common good.[77] This is significantly showcased in Stockbridge's work. His participants were very aware of the diversity of experience in their school environments. Stockbridge observes, "In many ways, these queer teachers see themselves as acting in concert with the deepest heart of the Catholic mission by pushing against oppressive forces. They do this in ways that masterfully negotiate the world they inhabit."[78] These educators were committed to fighting against oppressive forces that expect members of their community to conform to a singular conception of goodness.[79] They state, "We are a safe space for those who don't fit into the norm because of the pressures of school, expected life timelines, due to sexual phobias, or any number of non-normative experiences. We can help others who are caught in a binary tension to live in the grey of this world."[80] This awareness allows them to fight for the liberation of their students (and colleagues) and empower them to fight for justice in the world.

LGBTQ+ educators are very aware of the oppression they and their LGBTQ+ students experience in Catholic schools. Stockbridge states, "Because the queer experience questions, the boundaries of cisgendered [sic] and heteronormative assumptions of human ontology, queer teachers enter the Catholic classroom with very particular vantage points."[81] This vantage point brings about awareness of the oppression LGBTQ+ people face in Catholic environments. As stated, Stockbridge sees "doing queer" as a form of liberation in Catholic schools because queer educators who learn to survive in this setting are posing a radical challenge to forces of oppression in the school, which creates ripples that affect other members of the community.[82] Thus, by virtue of their LGBTQ+ identity, these educators serve to liberate those who are oppressed.

LGBTQ+ educators' engagement with justice is notable because their efforts involve self-liberation as well as external liberation since they are often under threat due to their dissent. One participant in Stockbridge's research stated, "Queer teachers are often the recipients of the very injustices in Catholic schools that they teach are wrong according to the Church's teaching." For this reason, sometimes, LGBTQ+ educators' effort toward justice and liberation is often done covertly. According to Stockbridge,

> Queer teachers acknowledged that they were actively working towards improving their schools but they were doing this quietly. When they are their authentic selves in the classroom, especially if they are not trying to hide non-gender conforming interests or ways of behaving, the teachers say that they "show that there are different paths for moving through life."[83]

The educators seem confident that some students who suspect that they are LGBTQ+ can also perceive this quiet effort to promote justice and liberation. Stockbridge observed,

[The educators] are making a safer and better place for students and faculty by remaining. "Our very presence in schools in the midst of the oppression is a light of hope and a work of activism." Teaching in Catholic schools is a way of changing it from the inside. Some have done this by coming out to select colleagues and students and sharing their own journeys.[84]

This work will bring about a new generation of Catholic laity committed to justice. Everitt noted,

The level of hurt the Church has caused varies among the participants; however, the ability to transcend the pain is consistent among these individuals. They remain hopeful about the future and long for a Church that is more inclusive, loving, and supportive of all members. The participants acknowledged that they remain in the Church with the hope that they can contribute to reshaping the mind-set of a new generation of Catholic laity.[85]

LGBTQ+ educators' awareness of their justice-based role is evident when they reflect on how their "queerness" contributes to the mission of Catholic schools. LBGTQ+ educators, like most LGBTQ+ people, have to first wrestle in their personal journey to come to terms with their LGBTQ+ identity. Part of this process involves forming their own conscience about how to live their lives. Finally, they must take the courageous step to live out their call as LGBTQ+ educators in the face of serious threats to their spiritual, economic, and emotional well-being. Their experience of discovering their identity and living lives that are as authentic as possible in the face of oppression serves as a microcosm of the larger struggle for justice and liberation they attempt to impart to their students. For this reason, given their personal journey and experience of oppression as well as their efforts to build a just world, I argue that their vocation is not only beneficial for the students and the school but also a prophetic witness to the broader Church. Furthermore, it is a unique experience that other non-LGBTQ+ educators do not have access to in the same way. For this reason, it is indispensable. Stockbridge explained,

[Participants stated,] "When we move beyond fear (or tell the story of our lives moving into self-power[ment] when coming out to ourselves) we then give the gift of truth [and] power to our students." . . . This spiritual call to immerse themselves into the oppressive structure of the Catholic school while holding tightly to a solidarity which identifies them as the school itself, makes the queer teacher the living example and promise of what can be when injustice is conquered. That is why they said: "We show that the locus of solidarity is in the work of justice." Only in the pursuit of justice could solidarity make any sense, particularly the Easter solidarity of the queer, Catholic school teachers.[86]

The Gifts of LGBTQ+ Catholic School Educators 53

LGBTQ+ educators who struggle to live authentically have a unique indispensable perspective of the work of justice. This perspective is often shared in the context of the larger experience of the LGBTQ+ community and infused with a Catholic worldview. Stockbridge stated,

> The teachers have been "building resiliency [that] comes through learning how to deal with the obstacles in our life in schools." This is in the community's DNA and their long tradition as an oppressed people. They said they are a people that don't give up. The teachers said that when there is the temptation to leave and wash their hands of working within a Catholic system, they think back to when times were worse. There was a time in the history of the Christian world that we were killed for simply existing. Now we are so much closer to a life of justice. "We value the long battle," they explained. As teachers working in schools which [sic.] don't honor them, they learn powerful ways to endure and become better. [One participant] put it plainly: "We grow in the virtues." The queer virtue par excellence is something they called "stick-to-it-tiveness."[87]

For this reason, when LGBTQ+ educators whose lives run afoul of magisterial doctrine choose to remain committed to the mission of the school, they are uniquely positioned to promote this mission and model to the students what it means to struggle for justice and liberation. Catholic leaders should appreciate this work and seek to incorporate these valuable experiences in their schools.

AN EASTER PEOPLE: THE PASCHAL MYSTERY AND LGBTQ+ EDUCATORS

The journey of LGBTQ+ educators in Catholic schools, in many ways, reflects a Christological image of the Paschal Mystery.[88] Instances of suffering and death—as seen in the challenges these educators navigate—are also mixed with the hope of the resurrection. Nonetheless, an analysis of the data on LGBTQ+ educators reveals that the suffering they experience is significant in at least four different ways. First, there is a culture of silence fueled by fear that keeps educators from being fully authentic. Educators in Everitt's study noted how there was a "don't ask don't tell" policy that permeated throughout their work.[89] This fear is founded upon the valid belief that they may lose their job. The continual dismissal of LGBTQ+ educators from Catholic schools fuels that fear and makes teachers live double lives. Stockbridge noted, "Describing their lives in relation to these two worlds of public and private life, the teachers said: 'We must dance between how public and private we need to be in our lives and schools.'"[90] This presents an oppressive challenge for these teachers. Everitt observed the following of one of his participants, "[she] explained that it was difficult to balance the real possibility that she could lose her job with the impossibility of denying the existence of her partner with her students."[91] Living a double life is stressful for LGBTQ+ educators, which may inadvertently affect any students who could potentially sense distress in their teacher or any attempts to mask an LGBTQ+ sexual identity. Furthermore, it is a contradiction to the Catholic tradition which holds integrity and honesty as important values. Catholic schools that pressure LGBTQ+ educators to live double lives to preserve the Catholic identity of their schools are undermining this identity by engaging in these oppressive practices.

Second, despite their bridge-building efforts, LGBTQ+ educators sometimes experience some isolation from their school community. Stockbridge observed,

> Queer teachers feel like they are kept at a safe distance from the rest of the school community because of the danger associated with them. [A participant noted,] "Queer existence is always seen as a problem. Administration always sees us from a problematic viewpoint and speaks of queerness in that way."[92]

The participant also noted, "In many ways, queer teachers find themselves in the 'back of the bus' of the school, he said. We are separated from the rest of the faculty by silence and we know where our proper place is in the grand scheme of things. Our marginal place in the school is part of our oppression."[93] These educators are aware of the separation. Again, I argue that such efforts to isolate and hide LGBTQ+ educators undermine the very mission of Catholic education, which—according to the USCCB's document on Catholic school educators—holds *community* as a significant component.

Third, the awareness of the separation brings about a sense of paranoia. LGBTQ+ educators are afraid to do something to be found out. A participant in Stockbridge's research highlighted this through a humorous, yet powerful, story that he shared with the other participants,

> [The participant, who was new at the school,] was committed to be himself, but not in a way that would draw any attention to himself. In some sense, [he] was making sure to play down the queer so that he could connect with everyone else. He says that things were going well with his ["downplaying queerness"] project when he went out for a social event with a group of male teachers at the school. As they sat at the table, everyone ordered a drink and they began to talk and laugh. Things were going great, [the participant] said, "until I looked down at the table and my heart stopped." He said all of a sudden a sense of dread overcame him and his breathing became tense at what was before his eyes. . . . [The participant] recalled looking at the drinks around the table and, in his head, taking note: "Corona, Corona, Corona, Strawberry Margarita!" He had let his guard

down and his non-masculine drink was threatening to break his cover . . . The group quickly analyzed the story saying: "We live in paranoia."[94]

The emotional distress experienced by LGBTQ+ educators is, simply put, harmful. Another central theme of Catholic doctrine is the respect for the intrinsic dignity of each person. I argue that the emotional duress reflected in these testimonies constitutes a significant violation of LGBTQ+ person's dignity and, therefore, also undermines the mission of Catholic education.

Fourth, because they are aware of their isolation and difference, and because they are in a paranoid state of being found out, LGBTQ+ educators often try to work harder and overachieve to overcompensate for the "handicap" of being queer. A participant in Stockbridge's work said, "Queer teachers have to work harder just to prove that they are as good as any other worker."[95] One participant in Everitt's study expressed, "I do find it exhausting, I mean, and I feel like sometimes it's exhausting just to do a lot of stuff, but being gay is another part; it's a piece of that."[96] Another participant in Everitt's study explained,

> Well I always figure, see to me, I mean—and this is maybe where I get more paranoid or whatever—I always feel like, if someone just, like I always get more anxious about other stuff in my job. I make sure that I do everything. . . . I get like this sometimes, when I'm really feeling paranoid, like, do everything perfectly because they can fire me and say it was because I did it, this other thing, but really, they don't want a gay person in the school anymore, so they get rid of me because I did this other thing. So it is, like, don't do any of those things wrong because they always have this other information [about sexual orientation].[97]

Such an excessive and emotionally distressing pressure to overachieve, when it is not expected from other employees who may or may not conform to various other Catholic doctrines, constitutes unjust discrimination and is, therefore, another violation of Catholic doctrine, which asserts that, toward LGBTQ+ persons, "all signs of unjust discrimination must be avoided."[98] Again, I highlight the logical inconsistencies reflected by the exclusion of LGBTQ+ educators to protect the Catholic identity of the school (preserved through adherence to Catholic doctrine) all the while undermining the same identity by violating other parts of Catholic doctrine.

Fortunately for Catholic schools, despite these challenges, the educators choose to stay because they are committed to the mission of the school. Summing up the fears and the commitments, Stockbridge states,

> They acknowledged that if all queer teachers were to leave the Catholic school system, there would be no one to fight from within. As much as these teachers

wished that they could have honest discussions about their struggles in schools and the parts of their lives that they currently keep hidden, they were all keenly aware that doing so would likely cost them their jobs.[99]

LGBTQ+ educators are aware of their unique indispensable role in Catholic education and choose to remain at the schools despite the risks to fulfill their mission. They know their perspective is unique and offers particular contributions to the school. They are role models of doctrine, community, and service as well as a deep commitment to the Catholic mission of the school. They have significant valid reasons for leaving but still choose to stay for the benefit of the school and students. They acknowledge the risk and choose to be courageous in their work. Stockbridge establishes, "There is no doubt that the presence of these teachers advances the mission of a school seeking to love, honor, and develop all students authentically. Doing queer in a Catholic school means being a light of hope."[100] As stated, some participants in Stockbridge's study called themselves an "Easter people," which is a term bearing beautiful significance. Being an Easter people is different from being a "Resurrection people." One of the participants elaborated,

> To be identified only with the newness of life that comes in the resurrection is to miss the journey of the queer teacher in schools. Jesus' story did not begin with rising from the dead, he first had to suffer and die on the cross. Easter embraces the mystery of death and rising. The teachers all had stories in which they felt the pain of being seen as "less than human" but pushed beyond this to thrive in their teaching.[101]

Therefore, despite the suffering, fear, and exclusion they experience, these educators carry out their ministry with a spirit of hope. Their work reflects a Christological image of the Paschal Mystery: their suffering (daily struggles) and death (potential termination) often lead to resurrection (hope-filled commitment to the mission of Catholic education) and ascension (deeper communion with God and God's mission). With their reflection on queer educators as an Easter people, the participants in Stockbridge's research expressed that their experience as LGBTQ+ educators bear a profound resemblance to Jesus' life and reflect the teachings of the Church best captured in the title of the USCCB document discussed earlier, *To Teach as Jesus Did*. Their vocational work very much belongs in Catholic schools and should be celebrated by school leaders and the entire Catholic school community. Catholic school students could not ask for better role models than LGBTQ+ educators.

CONCLUSION

As a gay man, the most difficult times in my life have been moments of isolation, especially during my teenage years. Life in the closet was marked with depression, anxiety, and deep shame. My lack of connection to role models and other LGBTQ+ community members made me feel alone and unworthy of love. This was particularly true as a teacher because I was often afraid to bring my full self into the classroom. My spiritual life was in crisis as I believed God condemned me for my queer love yet also called me to be a teacher. My time as a Catholic school educator was also marked by a feeling of isolation despite being constantly surrounded by and interacting with others. The trauma inflicted on me and many of my fellow LGBTQ+ Catholic friends and colleagues during these times of isolation is something we carry for the rest of our lives. Fortunately, the best moments of my life, which have been numerous, have been times of integrity and connection to community, particularly communities of faith. These times have been filled with authentic expression, shared mission, and a common quest toward justice—especially by exercising my vocation as an educator. Reading these stories of LGBTQ+ educators in Catholic schools fills me with joy in knowing that our Catholic schools are stewarded by such prophetic ministers who, as I discussed in this chapter, are often excellent role models in doctrine, community, and service. As an educator, I also find comfort in the support that other LGBTQ+ educators have offered me, which helps promote our sense of shared mission and community. However, a part of me grieves for my younger self who would have significantly benefited from having these educators, who are an Easter people, as explicit guides along the journey. As a younger teacher, I also could have benefited from such role models in the form of colleagues. While I was fortunate to find those communities of LGBTQ+ educators in San Francisco, I needed them earlier; and I am keenly aware of many LGBTQ+ teachers in other parts of the country who still carry out their vocation in isolation. I hope that this book brings some healing by helping Catholic school leaders and bishops value the gifts of LGBTQ+ educators. I pray these leaders stop depriving their Catholic school communities, and especially their LGBTQ+ students, of these amazing, unique, and indispensable role models.

NOTES

1. Hostility toward LGBTQ+ persons are prevalent in Latinx communities as evidenced by higher rates of violence, disregard for sexual healthcare, and overall religious attitudes that condemn their experiences. See Emanuel Jiménez Del Toro, Andrés Cruz Santos, and Adam Rosario Rodríguez, "Escala de masculinidad

hegemónica en una muestra de adultos gais de Puerto Rico: Desarrollo y validación," *Revista Puertorriqueña de Psicología* 34, no. 1 (May 17, 2023): 14–27, https://doi.org/10.55611/reps.3401.02; Sheilla L. Rodríguez-Madera et al., "Experiences of Violence among Transgender Women in Puerto Rico: An Underestimated Problem," *Journal of Homosexuality* 64, no. 2 (January 28, 2017): 209–17, https://doi.org/10.1080/00918369.2016.1174026; Lindsay Mahowald, "Hispanic LGBTQ Individuals Encounter Heightened Discrimination," Center for American Progress, July 29, 2021, https://www.americanprogress.org/article/hispanic-lgbtq-individuals-encounter-heightened-discrimination/; Anastasia Moloney, "LGBT+ Murders at 'Alarming' Levels in Latin America—Study," *Reuters*, August 8, 2019, sec. EverythingNews, https://www.reuters.com/article/us-latam-lgbt-killings-idUSKCN1UY2GM.

2. To qualify this more, I believe LGBTQ+ people who do not affiliate to the Catholic Church, belong to any organized religion, or even engage in a spiritual practice can still thrive and flourish. However, I believe spirituality is a part of our human nature and I rejoice in my particular spiritual journey as a Catholic. I also notice similar joy present in the lives of my fellow LGBTQ+ Catholic friends. For that reason, I see it as part of my vocation to help build a Church where LGBTQ+ people can experience the joyful grace of God.

3. Sadly, one of the first adult gay men I met passed away from AIDS-related causes a few years after I met him. This impressed in me a terrifying misconception of the fate of gay men.

4. Epistemology refers to the study of knowledge or, more specifically, how we learn and come "to know" things. An epistemological perspective is a particular way of knowing grounded in a particular experience. Furthermore, epistemological vantage points are intersectional. For example, a Black queer person cannot separate a "queer" way of knowing from a "Black" way of knowing. In this book, however, I focus on the queer component of educators' comprehensive epistemologies. For reflections on intersectional queer epistemologies, see José Esteban Muñoz et al., *Cruising Utopia: The Then and There of Queer Futurity*, 2nd ed. (New York University Press, 2019); José Esteban Muñoz, *Disidentifications: Queers of Color and the Performance of Politics* (University of Minnesota Press, 1999); Gloria Anzaldúa, *Borderlands / La Frontera: The New Mestiza*, 5th ed. (Aunt Lute Books, 2022); Kaustav Bakshi, "Writing the LGBTIHQ+ Movement in Bangla: Emergence of Queer Epistemologies in Kolkata in the Early Days of Queer Political Mobilizations," *South Asian History and Culture* 13, no. 2 (April 3, 2022): 231–45, https://doi.org/10.1080/19472498.2022.2067636; Jon Binnie, "Coming out of Geography: Towards a Queer Epistemology?," *Environment and Planning D: Society and Space* 15, no. 2 (April 1, 1997): 223–37, https://doi.org/10.1068/d150223.

5. I am cautious about my use of the word "evangelization." In this book, I refer to evangelization as an overall attempt to guide students toward flourishing and toward a relationship with God through the Catholic community. However, I acknowledge that this word can invoke harmful practices that colonize and erase cultural and religious differences. For this reason, I assert that the call to evangelization can be exercised in diverse ways not limited to the confines of the Catholic Church. For example, I can "evangelize" atheistic students by guiding them on matters of discernment,

relationships, happiness, and even exploration of theological questions without specifically attempting to convert them to Catholicism; though that invitation to belong to the Church is always gently extended. For these students, concepts like "God" and "Catholic Church" can be translated to secular language (e.g., "universal principles" and "community," respectively) as a way to aid those students' path toward flourishing. In this sense, evangelization becomes a mission that goes beyond conversion. In other words, I argue that—even in a Catholic context—evangelization can be applied to whatever practice can lead a person to flourish, given the many ways God's grace is present in our diverse world. That said, in this chapter, I focus on evangelization in the context on the Catholic tradition considering my overall desire for the Church to be welcoming to LGBTQ+ people and for LGBTQ+ people to appreciate the beauty of the Catholic Church.

6. Smith offers a footnote at the end of this statement that references the entire Catechism as a guide to determine what "true Catholic faithfulness" means, which I find vague and insufficient because, as I will discuss in chapter 3, the Catechism is not a seamless garment. See Christian Smith and Melinda Lundquist Denton, *Soul Searching: The Religious and Spiritual Lives of American Teenagers* (Oxford University Press, 2005), 194.

7. Smith and Denton, *Soul Searching*, 211.

8. Smith and Denton, *Soul Searching*, 212.

9. Michael Lipka, "Why America's 'Nones' Left Religion Behind," Pew Research Center, last modified August 24, 2016, accessed May 5, 2020, https://www.pewresearch.org/fact-tank/2016/08/24/why-americas-nones-left-religion-behind/; "Why America's 'Nones' Don't Identify with a Religion," Pew Research Center, last modified August 8, 2018, accessed May 5, 2020, https://www.pewresearch.org/fact-tank/2018/08/08/why-americas-nones-dont-identify-with-a-religion/.

10. Robert J. McCarty and John M. Vitek, *Going, Going, Gone: The Dynamics of Disaffiliation in Young Catholics* (Saint Mary's Press, 2017), 14–21, and Nicholas Wolfram Smith, "Study Shows Young Adults Leaving Church Start Down That Path at Age 13," National Catholic Reporter, December 11, 2018, https://www.ncronline.org/news/study-shows-young-adults-leaving-church-start-down-path-age-13.

11. Second Vatican Council, "Lumen Gentium," November 21, 1964, no. 1, https://www.vatican.va/archive/hist_councils/ii_vatican_council/documents/vat-ii_const_19641121_lumen-gentium_en.html.

12. The Trevor Project, "National Survey on LGBTQ Youth Mental Health 2021," 2021, https://www.TheTrevorProject.org/survey-2021/; James Martin, "Why Should the Church Reach out to L.G.B.T.Q. People? Some Shocking Statistics Can Answer That," *America Magazine*, August 2, 2021, https://www.americamagazine.org/faith/2021/08/02/james-martin-lgbtq-catholics-statistics-241139.

13. "Facts About LGBTQ Youth Suicide," The Trevor Project, December 15, 2021, https://www.thetrevorproject.org/resources/article/facts-about-lgbtq-youth-suicide/.

14. Families are often motivated by religious reasons when they exclude or oppress their LGBTQ+ youth. These familial dynamics become more complex at the intersection of race as some racial/ethnic cultures tend to unquestioningly follow LGBTQ+ exclusive religious teaching. See The Trevor Project, "Religiosity and

Suicidality among LGBTQ Youth," The Trevor Project, April 14, 2020, https://www.thetrevorproject.org/research-briefs/religiosity-and-suicidality-among-lgbtq-youth/.

15. Simon K. Fung, "Dear Alana," accessed September 14, 2023, https://dearalana.com/.

16. Quoted in Chris Damian, "'Dear Alana,' Hit No. 1 on Apple Podcasts. Are Church Leaders Listening?," *National Catholic Reporter*, September 14, 2023, https://www.ncronline.org/culture/dear-alana-hit-no-1-apple-podcasts-are-church-leaders-listening.

17. Michael Maher Jr., *Being Gay and Lesbian in a Catholic High School: Beyond the Uniform* (Harrington Park Press, 2001), 4.

18. Maher, *Being Gay and Lesbian*, 49, 68, 71, 89.

19. Mick Mominee, "Lesbian, Gay, Bisexual, and Queer/Questioning Catholic School Alumni: High School Experiences of Support and Challenge" (PhD Diss., University of Cincinnati, 2012), 180–212, accessed May 11, 2020, https://0-search-proquest-com.grace.gtu.edu/docview/1316620177?accountid=11175.

20. See Christian Figueroa, "Coming out as a Gay Catholic Teenager," Outreach, April 15, 2023, https://outreach.faith/2023/04/coming-out-as-a-gay-catholic-teenager/.

21. See Joseph Larson, "I Am a Queer Graduate of an Elite Catholic High School. And I Am Tired of the Homophobia," Outreach, July 7, 2023, https://outreach.faith/2023/07/i-am-a-queer-graduate-of-an-elite-catholic-high-school-and-i-am-tired-of-the-homophobia/.

22. Henry Herbert Jr., "I'm a Catholic High School Student Who Came out. It's Time for Catholic Schools to Come out, Too," Outreach, May 13, 2022, https://outreach.faith/2022/05/im-a-catholic-high-school-student-who-came-out-its-time-for-catholic-schools-to-come-out-too/.

23. The Trevor Project, "The Trevor Project Research Brief: Accepting Adults Reduce Suicide Attempts among LGBTQ Youth," The Trevor Project, June 2019, https://www.thetrevorproject.org/wp-content/uploads/2019/06/Trevor-Project-Accepting-Adult-Research-Brief_June-2019.pdf.

24. Herbert Jr., "I'm a Catholic High School Student Who Came."

25. Second Vatican Council, "Lumen Gentium," November 21, 1964, nos. 1–8, https://www.vatican.va/archive/hist_councils/ii_vatican_council/documents/vat-ii_const_19641121_lumen-gentium_en.html.

26. *Gravissimum Educationis* states, "A Christian education does not merely strive for the maturing of a human person as just now described, but has as its principal purpose this goal: that the baptized, while they are gradually introduced the knowledge of the mystery of salvation, become ever more aware of the gift of Faith they have received, and that they learn in addition how to worship God the Father in spirit and truth (cf. John 4:23) especially in liturgical action, and be conformed in their personal lives according to the new man created in justice and holiness of truth (Eph. 4:22–24); also that they develop into perfect manhood, to the mature measure of the fullness of Christ (cf. Eph. 4:13) and strive for the growth of the Mystical Body; moreover, that aware of their calling, they learn not only how to bear witness to the hope that is in them (cf. 1 Peter 3:15) but also how to help in the Christian formation

of the world that takes place when natural powers viewed in the full consideration of man redeemed by Christ contribute to the good of the whole society." See Second Vatican Council, "Gravissimum Educationis," Vatican Website, October 28, 1965, no. 2, https://www.vatican.va/archive/hist_councils/ii_vatican_council/documents/vat-ii_decl_19651028_gravissimum-educationis_en.html.

27. Second Vatican Council, no. 5.

28. Second Vatican Council, no. 8.

29. Congregation for Catholic Education, "The Catholic School," Vatican Website, March 19, 1977, no. 37, https://www.vatican.va/roman_curia/congregations/ccatheduc/documents/rc_con_ccatheduc_doc_19770319_catholic-school_en.html.

30. Thomas H. Groome, "What Makes a School Catholic?," in *The Contemporary Catholic School: Context, Identity and Diversity*, ed. Terence McLaughlin and Joseph O'Keefe (Routledge, 1996), 107.

31. Groome, "What Makes a School Catholic?," 108.

32. Groome, "What Makes a School Catholic?," 120.

33. Groome, "What Makes a School Catholic?," 109.

34. Groome, "What Makes a School Catholic?," 121–22.

35. Groome, "What Makes a School Catholic?," 123.

36. What is "within reasonable Catholic tradition" will be discussed further in chapter 3 when I explore the concept of probabilism. In sum, the doctrine of probabilism helps people sort out matters of doubt within Catholic tradition and offers tools for determining whether dissenting opinions have a high probability of containing truth. In chapter 3, I will argue that the doctrine of probabilism, when applied to the issue of homosexuality, should bestow upon the individual's conscience the freedom to make decisions that have been discerned as true, even If the decisions dissent from magisterial teaching.

37. Thomas Groome, *Educating for Life: A Spiritual Vision for Every Teacher and Parent* (Herder & Herder, 2001), 42.

38. Groome, *Educating for Life*, 44.

39. Groome speaks of the students' capability to generate wisdom in the context of community. See Groome, *Educating for Life*, 289–90.

40. Groome, *Educating for Life*, 12.

41. I will expound on what makes a position "reasonable" in the next chapter.

42. US Catholic Conference, *To Teach as Jesus Did: A Pastoral Message on Catholic Education* (United States Catholic Conference, 1972), 24. Italics added.

43. US Catholic Conference, *To Teach as Jesus Did*, 30.

44. US Catholic Conference, *To Teach as Jesus Did*, 27.

45. Francis, "Address of Pope Francis to Students of Jesuit Schools of Italy and Albania," Vatican Website, June 7, 2013, https://www.vatican.va/content/francesco/en/speeches/2013/june/documents/papa-francesco_20130607_scuole-gesuiti.html#:~:text=Dear%20Young%20People%2C,home%E2%80%9D%20with%20all%20of%20you.

46. US Catholic Conference, *To Teach as Jesus Did*, 30.

47. US Catholic Conference, *To Teach as Jesus Did*, 31.

48. Participatory action research is a methodology of research that takes place through dialogue. According to Park, "Participatory research is action-oriented research activity in which ordinary people address common needs arising in their daily lives and, in the process, generate knowledge." See Peter Park, "Knowledge and Participatory Research," in *Handbook of Action Research: Participative Inquiry and Practice*, ed. Peter Reason and Hilary Bradbury (Sage, 2005), 83.

49. James Everitt, "The Experience of Catholic Gay and Lesbian Catholic Secondary School Teachers within Northern California: A Participatory Action Research Study" (PhD Diss., San Francisco, CA, University of San Francisco, 2010), 78, https://repository.usfca.edu/diss/376.

50. Everitt, "The Experience of Catholic Gay and Lesbian Catholic Secondary School Teachers," 89.

51. Kevin Stockbridge, "Queer Teachers in Catholic Schools: Cosmic Perceptions of an Easter People" (PhD Diss., Orange County, CA, Chapman University, 2017), 153, https://doi.org/10.36837/chapman.000032.

52. Stockbridge, "Queer Teachers in Catholic Schools," 166.

53. Stockbridge, "Queer Teachers in Catholic Schools," 181.

54. Ish Ruiz and Jane Bleasdale, "Mixed Blessings: Understanding the Experience of LGBTQIA+ Educators in Catholic Schools," *Journal of Homosexuality* 69, no. 12 (October 15, 2022): 2148–66, https://doi.org/10.1080/00918369.2021.1984787.

55. Everitt, "The Experience of Catholic Gay and Lesbian Catholic Secondary School Teachers," 94–96.

56. Everitt, "The Experience of Catholic Gay and Lesbian Catholic Secondary School Teachers," 97–98.

57. Everitt, "The Experience of Catholic Gay and Lesbian Catholic Secondary School Teachers," 83.

58. Stockbridge, "Queer Teachers in Catholic Schools," 155.

59. Stockbridge, "Queer Teachers in Catholic Schools," 163.

60. Ruiz and Bleasdale, "Mixed Blessings," 2155.

61. Ruiz and Bleasdale, "Mixed Blessings," 2156.

62. Ruiz and Bleasdale, "Mixed Blessings," 2156.

63. Stockbridge, "Queer Teachers in Catholic Schools," 166.

64. Everitt, "The Experience of Catholic Gay and Lesbian Catholic Secondary School Teachers," 84.

65. Stockbridge, "Queer Teachers in Catholic Schools," 224.

66. Everitt, "The Experience of Catholic Gay and Lesbian Catholic Secondary School Teachers," 99.

67. Everitt, "The Experience of Catholic Gay and Lesbian Catholic Secondary School Teachers," 100.

68. Everitt, "The Experience of Catholic Gay and Lesbian Catholic Secondary School Teachers," 139.

69. Everitt, "The Experience of Catholic Gay and Lesbian Catholic Secondary School Teachers," 99.

70. Everitt, "The Experience of Catholic Gay and Lesbian Catholic Secondary School Teachers," 99.

71. Everitt, "The Experience of Catholic Gay and Lesbian Catholic Secondary School Teachers," 100.
72. Ruiz and Bleasdale, "Mixed Blessings," 2158.
73. Ruiz and Bleasdale, "Mixed Blessings," 2158.
74. Richard Peddicord outlines the history of the *Gay Liberation Movement* in his work as he argues that the correct treatment of LGBTQ+ people is a question of social justice and not of sexual morality. See Richard Peddicord, *Gay and Lesbian Rights: A Question: Sexual Ethics or Social Justice?* (Sheed & Ward, 1996), 3–26.
75. Stockbridge, "Queer Teachers in Catholic Schools," 177.
76. Stockbridge, "Queer Teachers in Catholic Schools," 243.
77. For a classical work on the relationship between Catholic schools and the common good see, Anthony S. Bryk, Valerie E. Lee, and Peter B. Holland, *Catholic Schools and the Common Good*, Reissue ed. (Harvard University Press, 1993).
78. Stockbridge, "Queer Teachers in Catholic Schools," 164.
79. For these educators, oppression refers to the mechanisms of isolation the school uses to prevent them from authentically expressing their sexual identity. Stockbridge uses a Foucauldian analysis of these methods of oppression in his dissertation. See Stockbridge, "Queer Teachers in Catholic Schools," 18, 45–48.
80. Stockbridge, "Queer Teachers in Catholic Schools," 243.
81. Stockbridge, "Queer Teachers in Catholic Schools," 160.
82. Stockbridge, "Queer Teachers in Catholic Schools," 166.
83. Stockbridge, "Queer Teachers in Catholic Schools," 165.
84. Stockbridge, "Queer Teachers in Catholic Schools," 200.
85. Everitt, "The Experience of Catholic Gay and Lesbian Catholic Secondary School Teachers," 113.
86. Stockbridge, "Queer Teachers in Catholic Schools," 243.
87. Stockbridge, "Queer Teachers in Catholic Schools," 183.
88. In Catholic theology, the Paschal Mystery traditionally refers to the suffering, death, resurrection, and ascension of Jesus.
89. Everitt, "The Experience of Catholic Gay and Lesbian Catholic Secondary School Teachers," 81.
90. Stockbridge, "Queer Teachers in Catholic Schools," 170.
91. Everitt, "The Experience of Catholic Gay and Lesbian Catholic Secondary School Teachers," 79.
92. Stockbridge, "Queer Teachers in Catholic Schools," 174.
93. Stockbridge, "Queer Teachers in Catholic Schools," 162–63.
94. Stockbridge, "Queer Teachers in Catholic Schools," 157.
95. Stockbridge, "Queer Teachers in Catholic Schools," 171.
96. Everitt, "The Experience of Catholic Gay and Lesbian Catholic Secondary School Teachers within Northern California," 80.
97. Everitt, "The Experience of Catholic Gay and Lesbian Catholic Secondary School Teachers, " 109.
98. "Catechism of the Catholic Church," Vatican Website, no. 2358, accessed June 7, 2023, https://www.vatican.va/archive/ENG0015/_INDEX.HTM.

99. Stockbridge, "Queer Teachers in Catholic Schools," 165.
100. Stockbridge, "Queer Teachers in Catholic Schools," 163–64.
101. Stockbridge, "Queer Teachers in Catholic Schools," 182.

Chapter 3

The Crux of the Matter
Catholic Doctrine on Homosexuality and Gender

When I was a sophomore at the University of Dayton, I participated in a Lenten reconciliation service where I expressed to my confessor my sincere belief that I was going to hell for giving in to my homosexual inclinations. The Marianist priest listening to my confession smiled and gently encouraged me to embrace the complexity of human sexuality by assigning me an unusual penance. To atone for my "sins," I was instructed to further educate myself by researching at least three differing Christian theological viewpoints on LGBTQ+ persons. In addition to Catholic magisterial doctrine, which was taught to me as a high school student, I now read some Catholic scholarship affirming LGBTQ+ identities or behaviors and I became aware of the wide range of theological perspectives within the Church. I was also shocked to discover that there were Catholics who carried out their various ministries while openly disagreeing with magisterial doctrine on homosexuality. Encountering these "dissenting" perspectives, which were all well-reasoned, well-sustained, and well-articulated, forced me to rethink how I approach matters of "truth" regarding the mysteries of human sexuality through my vocation as an educator.

Crucially, the experience of encountering such diverse theological perspectives made me feel deeply betrayed by the Church because, until then, the ones responsible for my education had presented magisterial doctrine on sexuality as universal uncontested objective truth. With the exception of the pastorally sensitive religion teacher mentioned in chapter 2 (who nonetheless still taught magisterial doctrine as definitive in his classroom), my religion classes throughout elementary, middle, and high school constantly stressed the infallible nature of magisterial doctrine and did not expose me to other perspectives. Because I trusted my teachers, I blindly subscribed to magisterial doctrine and did not dare to question it. Upon discovering the diversity of theological perspectives on sexual morality after that Lenten reconciliation experience, I began to resent the institutional Church for attempting to inculcate and manipulate me throughout my youth. By not exposing me to the diversity of theological opinions on the matter (all in the name of "guiding me to follow God's will"), I felt that the Church was hindering my ability to discern and conscientiously choose how to live my life. This felt like a violation of my dignity and my God-given freedom.

After graduating college, while teaching in a Catholic school, I was constantly reminded that some Catholic leaders would protect their understanding of truth to the point that they would fire me if I gave witness to any alternative lifestyle that integrated my homosexual identity and my vocation. For that reason, as I pursued doctoral studies in theology while teaching high school, I sought answers to these key questions: Can a person be considered Catholic while conscientiously disagreeing with Church doctrine on sexuality? Can that Catholic still minister in a Catholic institution? Has Catholic doctrine ever changed? And what are conscientious Catholics supposed to do in matters of moral doubt (i.e., when it is unclear what the correct moral choice is)? Considering that magisterial doctrine on homosexuality and gender often becomes the litmus test for firing LGBTQ+ educators from Catholic schools, it was important to further understand how Catholics are called to respond to magisterial doctrine and to matters of conscience and truth, especially when there is ample evidence, contained in theological scholarship and anecdotal/statistical human experience, of competing defensible perspectives.

This chapter attempts to answer these questions by exploring how Catholic school leaders should interact with Catholic doctrine on homosexuality and gender considering the presence of LGBTQ+ educators in their schools. Despite the incredible and evident blessings these educators may provide the community, as established in the previous chapter, their ability to minister in Catholic schools often hinges on their adherence to these doctrines, which prohibit homosexual sexual activity and gender-affirming surgery or social transitions.[1] For Catholic leaders who fire them, Catholic doctrine on sexual morality holds supremacy over any other qualification for ministry. This narrow legalistic approach devalues the positive impact LGBTQ+ educators have had in Catholic schools. In many ways, the educators' sexual behavior has become the crux of the matter and the sole criterion to determine their suitability for ministry.

In this chapter, I will argue that magisterial doctrine on homosexuality and gender-affirming transitions should not serve as a litmus test for ministerial suitability. To give such importance to violations of these particular teachings is to ignore the reasonable disagreements that exist at all levels of the Church hierarchy, from the laity to the pope, regarding human sexuality and the inclusion of LGBTQ+ persons in the Church. The Church is still wrestling with these questions and magisterial teaching is, I contend, dubious at best. Therefore, taking drastic action, such as firing an educator, over a teaching that is considerably credibly contested reflects a significant lack of leadership and judgment. To support my claim, in this chapter I will retrieve the moral tool of probabilism, which was crafted in the sixteenth century to help Catholics navigate matters of moral doubt. I argue that probabilism applies at two levels. First, at the individual level, it frees up persons to act according to their conscience in matters of moral doubt. This has significant implications for how Catholic leaders should interpret the sexual behavior of an LGBTQ+ educator who conscientiously disagrees with magisterial doctrine. Second, at the global ecclesial level, probabilism proposes a paradigmatic shift in how we address doctrine on certain theological and moral matters by making room for continued communal discernment as a Church. As I will argue, probabilism provides an important moral foundation for Pope Francis's ecclesiological vision of synodality.

This chapter will be divided into three parts. Part one will explore the tool of probabilism (including its origin and methodology), part two will apply probabilism to questions of homosexual activity and gender-affirming transitions, and part three will discuss the paradigmatic shifts probabilism brings to the Church.

RETRIEVING PROBABILISM

Probabilism is a methodological tool that validates various reasonable (i.e., probable) moral positions and permits the conscience to act with freedom when there is such moral doubt. Julia Fleming explains the relationship between *truth* and *probability* as follows:

> Truth and falsehood are opposites. What separates the probable claim from the improbable . . . is the presence or absence of reasonable grounds for supporting it, when clear proof is lacking on either side. . . . Probability comes into play when both sides of a debate are reasonably defensible but not demonstrable.[2]

Thus, probabilism enters into play in cases of moral uncertainty where more than one position on a moral question is arguable or justifiable. In other words, probabilism is based on good "grounds" for supporting an argument whenever there is no definitive "proof."

A Brief History of Probabilism

The first explicit mention of the tool of probabilism is found in the 1577 writings of Spanish Dominican theologian Bartolomeo Medina at a time when personal morality was assessed through the ecclesiastical practices of the Church, namely the confessional. Due to the absence of widespread Catholic education through modern schools or parish programs at that time, lay Catholics would receive informal instruction about the moral life through the sacrament of reconciliation. Therefore, since the priest was in charge of teaching penitents about the moral life, he needed to be well informed about contemporary Catholic morality which, at the time, employed *casuistry*. James Keenan explains, "Casuistry emerges as a method of moral reasoning to respond to the extraordinary new issues that materialized in the sixteenth century."[3] Casuists would draw moral conclusions by analyzing new moral situations in light of past moral precedents. If a new issue arose (let us call it scenario C), moral theologians would first examine other similar adjacent moral issues (let us call these scenarios A and B, which—let us suppose—had already been considered at a prior time in history) to determine how those have been previously resolved to decide how to proceed in the new scenario (e.g., scenarios A and B inform how moral scenario C is to be resolved). Therefore, as new moral issues emerged, were debated among theologians, and were then adjudicated by ecclesiastical authorities, a system of interrelated moral principles was formalized and disseminated to the faithful through the confessional (in scenario A, do this; therefore, in scenario B, do this; therefore, in scenario C, do this; therefore, in scenario D, do this; etc.). These moral systems were legalistic, as they were based on a set of precedents that were constructed over time, and were eventually codified into the moral laws of the Church. However, before such codification could happen, each moral issue entered a period of debate as casuists debated back and forth how to resolve the issue and often arrived at different conclusions. During this period of deliberation, the particular moral issue in question (or any new variation of a previously adjudicated moral issue) could be classified as a matter of moral doubt, which is where probabilism comes in.[4]

Probabilism was a key component of sixteenth-century casuistry because it gave confessors the ability to decide how to guide penitents when they came forward with an unresolved moral question—that is, a question of moral doubt. According to Jonsen and Toulmin, during that time, "The moral life was a tissue of laws, from the eternal laws of God to the canon law of the Church. The confessor often had to face the problem whether to place an obligation on a penitent, when one or another of those laws seemed less than absolutely binding."[5] After Medina's initial use of the concept, several Jesuit theologians, such as Gabriel Vazquez, Francisco Suarez, and Juan

Caramuel, continued to develop the concept.[6] A debate eventually emerged about whether, in cases of doubt, a confessor should lean toward freedom for the moral agent (laxism) or strictness toward the moral law (tutiorism). Probabilism affirmed the freedom of the moral agent regardless of the state of the moral arguments up for consideration while its counterpart, probabiliorism, advocated for a safer course of action by attempting to make decisions that are most congruent with preestablished moral law or with the "best" moral argument (if preestablished moral law did not sufficiently answer the question). As such, probabilism has a greater appreciation for moral diversity and probabiliorism has a tendency toward moral rigorism. Both concepts were in tension under the broader umbrella of casuistry.[7]

As casuistry continued to be applied to moral issues, more and more cases were considered to be "established" by ecclesiastical authority and casuistry itself fell into disuse. Furthermore, several historical factors, such as the suppression of the Jesuit order in 1773 and the overall efforts to centralize and establish the Church's global authority through the institutional Church, contributed to the abandonment of casuistry and—along with it—the tool of probabilism. The systems of moral precedent developed during the use of casuistry eventually became codified in moral manuals during the nineteenth century and provided a foundation for our current magisterial moral doctrine. Since the Church's hierarchy continued to establish itself as the centralized Catholic religious authority on moral matters, few Catholics who wished to remain in good standing with the Church could argue that there were moral issues considered dubious. Thus, the Church entered a new era marked by a significant degree of doctrinal legalism that claimed certainty and universality on various matters of faith and morals.[8] This doctrinal rigorism also informed the Church's initial resistance to modernity which was later revisited during the Second Vatican Council.[9]

Along with casuistry, probabilism has been considered by many contemporary moral theologians a relic of the past. However, I argue that probabilism needs to be retrieved, disassociated from the broader umbrella of casuistry, and applied to many complex present-day issues of moral theology, particularly in the area of sexuality. I make this argument for four reasons. First, the Second Vatican Council calls the Church to embrace the pluralism and globalism ushered in by modernity. In its introductory statements, the Constitution for the Church in the Modern World, *Gaudium et Spes*, tasks the Church with paying special attention to "the signs of the times and reinterpreting them in light of the Gospels."[10] This task is to be carried out globally, thus inviting in diversity of culture and theological perspectives into the Church.[11] This would eventually result in an inevitable decentralization of the Eurocentric epistemology that has so far interpreted many moral questions, including those on sexuality.

Second, new fields in the social sciences such as sociology, anthropology, and psychology (which emerged and developed over the past two hundred years) can shed new insights on matters of embodiment, sexual desire, and identity. We should reconsider our understanding of "human nature" in light of these new findings. Unlike the physical sciences, which are arguably more conclusive, the social sciences contain more room for reasonable, well-founded disagreement on questions of human nature as they address matters that are less tangible in comparison to biology, physics, or chemistry. Along these lines, in her classical work, *Nature as Reason*, Jean Porter argues that it is difficult to derive a long list of ahistorical universal indisputable moral laws by studying human nature since our study of nature always happens through the lens of culture. Rather, we can articulate a short list of very general principles to guide our actions.[12] As Craig A. Ford Jr. explains, "the natural law studies nature *theologically*"[13]; therefore, new insights from the social sciences about various components of human nature (e.g., embodiment and desire) inevitably yield a wide variety of theological perspectives on human sexuality. Most importantly, while the Second Vatican Council acknowledged and validated the benefits of the sciences in generating knowledge crucial to the work of theologizing,[14] such welcome has not been extended to the social sciences which, at least on matters of sexuality, have yet to be taken seriously by the magisterium (though they have been taken seriously by various contemporary Catholic theologians).[15]

Third, the contemporary theological and moral perspectives yielded by the diverse cultural, epistemological, and theological frameworks of our global Church and the theological use of modern social sciences are available to the majority of Catholics who now have access to education and/or can interact with these perspectives through the use of technology and the media. Unlike the sixteenth century when access to Catholic education took place through the confessional, contemporary Catholics can enroll in Catholic schools, have access to public schools (which often incorporate secularized knowledge of the Church's history and of progressive perspectives on sexuality), and can access social media, YouTube, and the news to learn about various theological and moral perspectives. Furthermore, regarding sexual orientation and gender identity, LGBTQ+ people now have technological means to find each other and, through solidarity, craft a common story grounded in community which bestows them with a loose sense of what an "LGBTQ+ collective experience" might be like. This (albeit incomplete) sense of an "LGBTQ+ collective experience" may also be accessible to heterosexual and cisgender Catholics who interact with LGBTQ+ people in their daily lives, have access to their stories on the web, and are exposed to a plethora of LGBTQ+ representation through the media. Perspectives that are inclusive of LGBTQ+ people, including Catholic moral or theological ones, are accessible to most

Catholics throughout the world. Furthermore, these LGBTQ+ Catholic perspectives and life witnesses have become more visible since the publication of *Fiducia Supplicans*, the Vatican document permitting blessings for persons in same-sex unions (which I will discuss).

Fourth, in light of Pope Francis's invitation to build a synodal Church, Catholic leaders are called to listen to new perspectives on different matters of human life, consider them seriously in light of the gospel and the guidance of the Holy Spirit, and walk together as a community that jointly discerns its path forward. I will propose a synodal vision for Catholic education in the next chapter so, for now, I simply argue that the Church is currently undergoing a process of reform in how it interacts with the diverse lay faithful and is learning how to be more in touch with the *sensus fidelium* revealed through their lives.

For all of these reasons, I argue that the doctrine of probabilism should be retrieved and reappropriated as a tool that would help the Church navigate matters of moral doubt as it embarks on a synodal journey that interacts with the diverse and easily accessible theological and moral perspectives found throughout the global Church. I believe that, if Catholic leaders continue to interact with our pluralistic society by expecting people (especially Catholic school communities) to unquestionably fall in line with current magisterial doctrine on sexual morality, they will continue to experience significant resistance, disaffiliation, and resentment toward the Church. This would represent a failure to fulfill the mission of Catholic education and the overall mission entrusted to the Church.

Reappropriating Probabilism for Contemporary Moral Theology

Our contemporary culture is filled with many unanswered moral questions. I argue that probabilism is a suitable tool for navigating this doubt. The originator of the concept, Bartolomeo Medina, argued that an opinion can be considered probable "because wise men propose it and confirm it by excellent arguments."[16] Therefore, there are two types of probabilism: the probability of a particular position is determined *intrinsically* by the substance of the arguments defending it and *extrinsically* by the credibility of the experts. When one applies intrinsic probabilism to a moral dilemma, one is basically evaluating the methodological soundness, rationality, and consistency of the argument. Extrinsic probabilism evaluates the authority of the experts proposing the arguments. However, according to Lisa Fullam, "extrinsic probabilism [isn't] merely a matter of counting the experts, but is connected to intrinsic probabilism, the strength of their arguments. . . . Nonsense remains nonsense, regardless of the number of those credulous enough to fall for it."[17] Both criteria are constitutive of and interdependent in the overall process of probabilism, but intrinsic probabilism should be prioritized over the extrinsic one.

Regarding the spectrum of laxism versus rigorism, Medina also wrote, "It seems to me that, if an opinion is probable, it is licit to follow it, even though the opposite opinion is more probable."[18] The reason for supporting the less probable position may gain or lose probability over time as new information is revealed on a particular topic. This is a matter of intellectual humility. Lisa Fullam explains "As knowledge develops, the balance of probabilism shifts in keeping with the greater understanding of the matter at hand, and what may once have been a probable opinion . . . may drift into moral disrepute as improbable."[19] Stefania Tutino agrees,

> A truly probable opinion, either intrinsically or extrinsically, might not remain equally probable forever, and indeed over time it might actually become improbable. The degree of probability of any given opinion is subject to change, either because other people can find new and more stringent intrinsic arguments in support of the opposite opinion, or because new external evidence piles up against the traditional way of looking at something.[20]

Moral rigorism or exclusive adherence to what is perceived at the time as the best moral argument in a moral dispute, as exemplified by probabiliorism, may result in an obstinate refusal to adapt to new information in a constantly changing moral landscape. Probabilism, due to its tendency toward moral freedom, is cognizant of the possibility of change and can adapt. However, this is not merely a relativistic moral "free for all" as probable opinions still have to be intrinsically and extrinsically validated. In other words, probabilism depends on sound rational justification for moral arguments. That said, probabilism and probabiliorism need not necessarily be seen as either/or choices,

> They can be plausibly understood as alternatives for different situations. When faced with complex issues that you have no chance to reflect on yourself, accepting an opinion that appears reasonable from any sound doctor ("probabilism") may be prudent practical policy; but if you have time to undertake a fresh analysis of the issues, the other ("probabiliorist") course, which demands that you look for the sounder doctor and the more reasonable opinion, is surely preferable.[21]

This has strong implications for how we exercise autonomy of conscience. According to Jonsen and Toulmin, "The thesis of probabilism simply asserts that a person who is deliberating about whether or not he [sic] is obliged by some moral, civil, or ecclesiastical norm or law may take advantage of any reasonable doubt about whether the law obliges him [sic]."[22] In other words, probabilism simply frees up the conscience to act in accordance with the probable opinion it considers to be moral, regardless of whether that opinion is considered "more" or "less" probable than others. Fullam further explores the relationship between probabilism and conscience, explaining,

> Because conscience seeks truth, it is always wrong to reject what one knows (or believes after appropriate investigation) to be true. It is also wrong to assert as true what is not known to be true; dealing with the latter is the work of probabilism. . . . Probabilism affirms that in areas of uncertain knowledge, one's conscience weights the degree to which varying stances are supported by good arguments (intrinsic probability) and/or held by experts (extrinsic probability), and is free to choose among probable opinions.[23]

Probabilism prevents ecclesiastical authorities from assuming they know too much. It allows the conscience to operate as the muscle with which we navigate various probable opinions and guide our decision-making.

According to the Catholic Church, conscience does not equate to mere opinion, but rather is the place where we hear the inner voice of God that speaks to us in the depths of our hearts. Furthermore, the conscience needs to be well formed and informed through the process of moral discernment in the context of community where diversity of opinion and moral doubt abounds.[24] Crucially, as our conscience sorts through moral doubt, it is important to note that probabilism does not actually *solve* the doubt in our hearts or in our communal discourse; but rather it emphasizes and validates the freedom of conscience in instances of doubt. The result of such a valid exercise of freedom of conscience is an inevitable theological pluralism within the Church as people will conscientiously choose to act according to diverse perspectives on the question of moral doubt.

Finally, in our contemporary society, an effective retrieval of probabilism requires disassociating it from the casuistry umbrella. My reappropriation of probabilism, therefore, does not necessarily seek to establish legalistic precedent by settling any doubt through ecclesiological adjudication but rather encourages the Church to reconfigure how it addresses matters of moral uncertainty without needing to establish as "definitive" what is still being reasonably debated. Since I am discussing this tool in a Catholic context, I use the word "reasonable" to defend the application of probabilism only to peripheral matters of faith and morals; and I believe that questions of LGBTQ+ inclusion in the Church fall on the periphery when considering the entirety of the Catholic tradition (e.g., LGBTQ+ issues are more peripheral than the content of the Nicaean Creed which outlines the central tenets of the

Catholic faith).²⁵ With that, I now turn to a brief application of probabilism to the question of LGBTQ+ inclusion in the Church.

APPLYING PROBABILISM TO HOMOSEXUAL ACTIVITY AND GENDER-AFFIRMING HEALTHCARE

To apply probabilism, the first order of business is determining whether or not the hierarchy's teachings on sexual orientation and gender are in doubt. While some will deny that the teaching is dubious by stating that it has been well defined and reinforced throughout several magisterial documents (which is technically correct in the case of homosexuality), several key facts, which I will enumerate, reveal that the teaching is indeed doubtful at best or, at worst, in need of significant revision.²⁶ First, as Bryan Massingale points out, during the 2015 Synod on the Family, the paragraphs on homosexuality, which simply restated current doctrine on the matter, did not receive the necessary votes to "pass," thus indicating that the bishops do not have consensus over these teachings.²⁷ Some bishops, like the German conference, have already begun to explicitly issue calls for reform.²⁸ Second, there is a robust body of Catholic theology that affirms LGBTQ+ identities and behaviors by synthesizing new understandings about human sexuality from the social sciences with central themes of the Catholic tradition such as Natural Law, Virtue Ethics, and Catholic social teaching.²⁹ Third, there is a growing number of Catholics in the United States and abroad who support same-sex marriage and gender-affirming surgeries, and a significant number of Catholics worldwide calling for more LGBTQ+ inclusion in the Church.³⁰ Fourth, there is a significant number of testimonies of LGBTQ+ Catholics who report experiencing grace and flourishing through same-sex relationships or gender transitions.³¹ Combined, these factors render the current magisterial doctrine on gender and sexual orientation doubtful at best, or—at worst—indefensible, making room for an evaluation of the intrinsic and extrinsic probability of conflicting arguments.

Evaluating Intrinsic Probabilism on Gender and Homosexuality

When analyzing current doctrine on gender and homosexuality, one can trace historical arguments, mostly grounded in the natural law, declaring the inseparability of the concept of gender from the concept of sex and the prohibition of any sexual activity that does not promote the unitive and procreative purpose of human acts. Regarding the question of gender, the magisterial doctrine is significantly underdeveloped, yet it adopts an essentialist viewpoint, claiming that, while there may be some cultural difference in people's gender expressions, a person's gender itself (1) is innately linked to their biological sex; (2) shares universal characteristics with others of the same gender; and (3) cannot be changed or altered. Conversely, Church doctrine on homosexuality has been more developed over the past several decades and rests on the argument that sexual activity is only permissible in the context of heterosexual marriage and for the inseparable purposes of procreation and the union of the spouses. What follows is an overview of these doctrines.

While people's gender has historically been confined to the binary of *man* and *woman* throughout the Church's early history and had been emphasized in some magisterial documents in the 1970s and 1980s,[32] the first comprehensive theological treatment of gender identity is found in a series of 128 lectures by Pope John Paul II from 1979 to 1984, which have been compiled into what is known today as the *Theology of the Body* (ToB). In his theology, John Paul II observes that God made all creation good and that all creation follows a divine plan reflecting God's will. He also states that our bodies are designed to reflect that will. Part of God's will for humanity involves the idea of sexual difference between males and females as well as sexual complementarity between the two. Due to the complementarity between our genitalia, John Paul II concludes that part of God's divine plan involves the inalterable and essential complementarity of the sexes. Moreover, the union of the two sexes has the capability of producing life, thus creating a family, and further indicating that this is all a part of God's plan. Finally, John Paul II argued in his ToB that the nature of men and women transcended their genitalia and spoke of a complementarity that went beyond a physicalist reading of the body. Since human beings are embodied souls, the body reflects the soul so the complementarity between men and women extends beyond the procreative genital complementary and into a relational, social, and spiritual dimension.[33] Crucially, the document makes no mention of transgender identities, which is understandable given the limited literature on the topic at the time. Furthermore, while this document cannot be considered "official magisterial doctrine" as it did not undergo the canonical processes to be labeled as such, it nonetheless provided a theological backdrop for subsequent magisterial statements on transgender identity (and it also contributed to the doctrine on homosexuality).

In 2015, Pope Francis published an apostolic exhortation on the family, titled *Amoris Laetitia*, where he devoted a paragraph to the question of gender. Without referring directly to transgender persons or identity, he condemned what he termed "gender ideology" by stating that it:

> Denies the difference and reciprocity in nature of a man and a woman and envisages a society without sexual differences, thereby eliminating the

anthropological basis of the family. This ideology leads to educational programs and legislative enactments that promote a personal identity and emotional intimacy radically separated from the biological difference between male and female. Consequently, human identity becomes the choice of the individual, one which can also change over time.[34]

In response to this threat of gender ideology, he links a person's biological sex with their gender identity by stating, "biological sex and the socio-cultural role of sex (gender) can be distinguished but not separated. . . . Let us not fall into the sin of trying to replace the Creator. We are creatures, and not omnipotent."[35] Presumably, the pope is criticizing transgender persons by arguing that their gender transitions reflect an ideology whereby gender becomes a matter of choice that seeks to erase sexual differences and threaten our very nature.

Following a similar line of argument, the CCE published a document in 2019 titled, "Male and Female He Created Them: Toward a Path of Dialogue on the Question of Gender Theory in Education," where they issued warnings to Catholic schools against their perceived dangers of gender theory or gender ideology. In this document, the CCE criticized views of human sexuality as a social construct and condemned "transgenderism," which they defined as a subjective mindset about gender whereby people can choose genders that do or do not correspond with their biological sex. With that, they called upon Catholic schools to ensure that Catholic anthropology of gender as linked to biological sex is taught through curricula and school programs.[36] Several bishops in the United States have responded to this document by issuing policies barring LGBTQ+ people from being enrolled and employed in Catholic schools as well as dictating several policies that encourage conformity with this doctrine.[37]

In 2024, the Dicastery for the Doctrine of the Faith (DDF) published a document titled *Dignitas Infinita* where, after an extensive declaration promoting the intrinsic, inviolable, and infinite dignity of the human person, it rehearsed the previous arguments condemning "gender theory" and "gender ideology" to prohibit gender-affirming surgeries.[38] According to the DDF, "any sex-change intervention, as a rule, risks threatening the unique dignity the person has received from the moment of conception."[39] This document marks the first authoritative magisterial condemnation of gender-affirming surgeries since prior documents came from less authoritative offices in the Vatican or were produce by local dioceses and were not binding to the global Church.

It is important to note that, while these magisterial documents articulate a Catholic anthropology of gender as linked to one's biological sex that applies to all humans, they do not directly or extensively address transgender persons as they understand themselves. The only reference to transgender people (by using the word "transgenderism") in an official magisterial document from the Vatican is found in the CCE's document and it misrepresents the experience of transgender persons and their understanding of gender identity. While most transgender persons interpret their journey as one of discovery, the CCE and DDF documents create a "strawman" argument claiming that trans persons freely choose their gender and seek to erase differences as if they were "radically autonomous" individuals.[40] The vague terms "gender theory" and "gender ideology" are also cast in a negative light as an unsubstantiated threat to the anthropological fabric of society, which is also not how most transgender persons understand gender. This is not surprising considering that these magisterial documents are almost exclusively self-referential. The authors do not demonstrate engagement with a contemporary understanding of gender from the social sciences nor have they consulted the perspectives of transgender persons as they drafted the documents.[41] For this reason, Dan Horan refers to these policies as a theological, scientific, and pastoral disaster, and comments on the 2024 DDF document by stating that "this declaration fails to live up to its claim to affirm and support the 'infinite dignity' of all people."[42]

Unlike Catholic doctrine on gender, which was not significantly developed in official magisterial documents until 2019, Catholic doctrine on homosexuality has been explicitly articulated in various magisterial documents since 1975—though it draws from an earlier theological foundation promulgated by Vatican II and Pope Paul VI's encyclical on contraception, *Humanae Vitae*. Engaging with a Thomistic account of the natural law,[43] the Second Vatican Council established in 1965 that the two purposes of sexual activity are procreation and the unity of the spouses and *Humanae Vitae* (which condemned contraception) declared in 1968 that the two purposes of sex are inseparable.[44] Any sexual activity that violates any component of this inseparable twofold purpose of sex is considered sinful by Catholic doctrine. Subsequent documents from the previously-known-as Congregation for the Doctrine of the Faith (CDF, now known as the DDF) applied this ethical position to homosexual sexual activity and its relationship to the pastoral, sacramental, and political activity in the Church.

In 1975, the declaration on sexual ethics, *"Persona Humana,"* describes homosexual orientations as a pathology, grave depravity, and anomaly, and establishes that "homosexual acts are intrinsically disordered and can in no case be approved."[45] A second document titled "Letter to the Bishops of the Catholic Church on the Pastoral Care of Homosexuals" reaffirmed that "Although the particular inclination of the homosexual person is not a sin, it is a more or less strong tendency ordered toward an intrinsic moral evil; and thus the inclination itself must be seen as an objective disorder."[46] Citing Biblical passages such as the story of creation, the destruction of Sodom and Gomorrah, and various Pauline epistles, the document claims that a condemnation of homosexual activity is consistent with God's revelation. It further determines that "homosexual activity prevents one's own fulfillment and happiness by acting contrary to the creative wisdom of God."[47] Homosexuals are, therefore, called to a chaste life through abstinence from same-sex sexual activity. Crucially, the document laments the violence faced by homosexuals and calls it deplorable. It nevertheless restates that homosexual identity is not to be affirmed and homosexual activity must be condemned by pastors.

Two other documents from the CDF, in 1992 and 2003, respectively condemned legal proposals to extend nondiscrimination rights to homosexuals and legal recognition of same-sex civil unions. The main rationale for these declarations is that extending such political protection to homosexuals would encourage same-sex activity and present a threat to the fabric of society (i.e., the heteronormative family) and the common good. The 1992 document opposing nondiscrimination rights argues that a person's sexual orientation is not analogous to their gender, race, economic status, or nationality because the former represents an inclination toward sin in ways that the other classifications do not. Furthermore, it establishes that, while homosexuals have human rights, no right is absolute, and rights can be reasonably curtailed if homosexuals conduct themselves in ways deemed "objectively disordered."[48] The 2003 document reiterates the concern that recognizing the legal right to same-sex marriage might weaken the anthropological order established by God through the heteronormative family. The document also calls upon Catholics, including Catholic politicians to resist these legal proposals.[49]

In 2021, the CDF published an explanatory note prohibiting Church officials from blessing civil same-sex unions, arguing that God "does not and cannot bless sin."[50] However, in 2023, with the publication of *Fiducia Supplicans*, the newly renamed DDF reversed that decision by developing the understanding of an ecclesial *blessing* and offering a highly nuanced endorsement of blessings for persons in civil same-sex unions who request them from priests spontaneously, in a non-liturgical setting, and without association to a civil same-sex union ceremony. This document preserves Catholic teaching on sacramental marriage and homosexuality but permits pastoral blessings as a means to aid the homosexual persons in their quest toward God's love. In other words, the blessings are imparted on the *persons* and not on the *union*.[51] In response to the significantly polarized reception of *Fiducia Supplicans* throughout the globe, the DDF issued a press release in 2024 further clarifying the document while reaffirming the developments brought forth by the declaration.[52]

Despite the recent developments allowing some pastoral blessings of persons, the substance of magisterial doctrine on homosexuality still considers a homosexual orientation disordered because it leads a person to sin (though it is not sinful in itself), homosexual sexual activity to be intrinsically evil and sinful, and any legal/cultural/political support of homosexual sexual activity to be problematic because it supports evil. Nonetheless, LGBTQ+ persons are to be treated with respect, compassion, and sensitivity and every sign of unjust discrimination must be avoided (keyword: "unjust")—and they may seek blessings from the Church as persons striving to live better lives guided by God's grace and love.

Crucially, the categorization of homosexual sexual acts as intrinsically evil operates as a blanket condemnation of the acts. The word "intrinsic" indicates that the evil of homosexual acts is contained within the act itself and is not attributed to any external circumstance or consequence. This means that homosexual sexual activity can never be justified. Like magisterial teaching on gender, which is labeled as an "anthropology" and therefore applicable to all humans, magisterial doctrine considers all homosexual sexual activity as a categorical violation of human nature.

Regardless of my personal and theological disagreement with these positions, when evaluating these positions through the lens of intrinsic probabilism, I observe that they follow a certain logic and employ a well-established methodology grounded in their historical understanding of the natural law. Like with many ethical arguments, one can raise reasonable criticisms of these magisterial doctrines on gender and sex. As a gay Catholic theologian who is familiar with diverse theological opinions on these matters and who has had personal experiences of grace through same-sex relationships, I am suspicious of the magisterial position and consider it detached from the experiences of LGTBQ+ people and the findings of the biological and social sciences.[53] Nevertheless, my commitment to the Catholic tradition, including my commitment to the institutional Church, compels me to recognize the magisterial position as an intrinsically probable opinion; but, it is not the *only* probable opinion.

For the past three decades, several Catholic theologians have proposed new ways of understanding sexual ethics in the Catholic tradition. Some prime examples, which I will now discuss, include Todd Salzman and Michael Lawler's holistic anthropology of the sexual person, Margaret Farley's virtue ethics approach to just love, and Craig Ford's retrieval and queering of the natural law tradition. These theories also make use of traditional methods of ethical inquiry and, crucially, they take into consideration new findings on human sexuality yielded by contemporary biological and social science. Since the Church has a long tradition of advocating for the use of science to make sense of the moral world around us, these positions possess intrinsic probability within the Catholic tradition grounded in sound reasoning and a deeper connection with people's lived experiences.

Todd A. Salzman and Michael G. Lawler, in their book, *The Sexual Person: Toward a Renewed Catholic Anthropology*, argue that "the attempt to construct a 'one-size-fits all' . . . largely ignores the complexity of history, culture, gender roles and definitions, and socioeconomic variables that have an impact on all human relationships, including sexual relationships."[54] They further observe that modern anthropology, along with other social sciences, has provided new information about human nature that is relevant to sexual ethics. According to Salzman and Lawler, "Sexual activity that is consonant with one's sexual orientation is a premoral value; sexual activity that is not consonant with one's sexual orientation and that does not strive for sexual integrity in light of one's orientation is a premoral disvalue."[55] Therefore, by understanding sexual orientation complementarity as one of many "starting points" upon which sexual moral judgment is constructed, they propose a sexual ethic based on *holistic complementarity*, which they define as an anthropological combination of sexual orientation complementarity (i.e., sexual activity that is integrated with one's sexual orientation), biological complementarity (i.e., embodied interpersonal union that is rational though not necessarily reproductive), and personal complementarity (i.e., affective and communion-based relationships).[56] They assert that "sexual acts are moral when they are natural, reasonable, and expressed in a truly human, just, and loving manner."[57] With that they argue that homosexual acts are moral if they are based on the *nature* (i.e., sexual orientation) of the person if they are reasonable (i.e., when they can reason that these actions will help them flourish),[58] and if they are *truly human* (i.e., when they reflect holistic complementarity).[59]

Using a Foucauldian methodology, Margaret Farley's *Just Love: A Framework for Christian Sexual Ethics* traces the historical construction of sexuality and observes that "our understandings of sexuality in particular remain immersed in the economy of defilement."[60] In response, she proposes a new relational model, grounded in the concept of justice, that should guide all sexual activity. Farley's justice-based ethic considers that "love is true and just, right and good, insofar as it is a true response to the reality of the beloved, a genuine union between the one who loves and the one who loved, and an accurate and adequate affective affirmation of the beloved."[61] She rejects the notion, as proposed by magisterial interpretations of the natural law, that sexual activity can only be moral only if it abides by the magisterium's understanding of the twofold purpose of sex. In her words, "the most difficult question to be asked in developing a sexual ethic is not whether this or that sexual act in the abstract is morally good, but rather, when is sexual expression appropriate, morally good and just, in a relationship of any kind."[62] With that, Farley constructs a justice-based framework for sexual expression that is founded upon the lived experience of the person.

Her framework consists of seven norms for just sex: do no unjust harm, free consent of partners, mutuality, equality, commitment, fruitfulness (not exclusively procreative), and social justice. Crucially, Farley explains fruitfulness as such: "beyond the kind of fruitfulness that brings forth biological children, there is a kind of fruitfulness that is a measure, perhaps, of all interpersonal love. Love between persons violates relationality if it closes in upon itself and refuses to open to a wider community of persons."[63] Finally, she observes that all of these principles, which are grounded in Catholic intellectual tradition, can be met by people in same-sex relationships.[64]

Craig A. Ford Jr.'s article, "Transgender Bodies, Catholic Schools, and a Queer Natural Law Theology of Exploration," which he dedicates to a young transgender girl named Leelah who died by suicide, criticizes Catholic doctrinal anthropology of gender in two ways. First, he critiques the use of vague terms such as "gender theory" and "gender ideology" to create a straw-man argument that misrepresents how transgender people see themselves. Second, and most importantly, he debunks the essentialist claim that natural law somehow establishes a conception of gender as binary, complementary between only men and women, and categorically applicable to all humans. In his words, "Without dismantling this gender essentialism in our theology, which simply moves the rigidity of the category of gender back one step into sexual identity, there can be little hope of depathologizing the existence of all trans persons, since it is precisely the question of the fixity of sexual identity that is at stake, particularly for transgender persons who wish to transition."[65] To do so, he constructs a queer natural law of exploration whereby discernment of one's gender identity, which he claims is socially constructed and taught to us, is a part of human nature.[66] Therefore, this process of constructing an understanding of gender is in and of itself a part of human nature. Ford asserts,

> Sex and gender identity are among the elements of one's self that one must explore not only introspectively in the sacred space of one's conscience, but also in community—perhaps with one's family, with one's close circle of friends, and even with one's Christian community. Indeed, alongside other elements of one's self that must be investigated along similar axes of conscience and community, living into one's sex and gender identity is part of the larger journey towards fulfillment in one's relationship with one's self, with others, with the world, and with God. Or, as Thomas called it, this is part of a larger journey towards *eudaimonia*, or happiness—which Thomas will identify as a life lived by the virtuous person.[67]

This queer account of the natural law does away with normativity about gender identity. Ford explains, "Indeed, if any identity is presumed, it is only that of a seeker. The rest I leave to our personal experiences of conscience, of community, and of the various ways in which we investigate the phenomenon of human life, scientifically, philosophically, or otherwise: What sort of beings are we? What are we like?"[68]

These three theologians join a community of scholars like Lisa Cahill, Lisa Fullam, John Whitehead, Evelyn Whitehead, John McNeill, Richard Peddicord, Jason Steidl, and others[69]; all of whom propose a framework for sexual ethics that supports and validates same-sex relationships and gender transitions. All of these proposed theologies, which are at odds with magisterial doctrine on homosexuality and gender, exhibit sound methodology, engagement with major currents of thought within the Catholic tradition, and—crucially—engage contemporary findings in the social sciences. For this reason, I maintain that they contain intrinsic probability.

Unfortunately, the works of Salzman, Lawler, and Farley have been condemned and censored by the Vatican as erroneous simply because they contradict Church doctrine on sexual morality. In a set of primarily self-referential statements, the Vatican criticized these theologies without engaging in the substance of their arguments but rather by pointing out their error in departing from magisterial teaching.[70] Therefore, while the hierarchy does not recognize the concept of intrinsic probability outside of the magisterial positions, I argue that intrinsic probability is very much present in these arguments.

Evaluating Extrinsic Probabilism on Gender and Homosexuality

The extrinsic probability of the two positions in favor and against LGBTQ+ persons is seen in the expertise and commitment of the authors. Magisterial doctrine is crafted by bishops, with the assistance of some theologians, all of whom possess advanced knowledge of the history of the Catholic tradition. Furthermore, bishops embody a life of service and commitment to the Church and, through their participation in the line of apostolic succession (i.e., the unbroken line of descendants from the twelve apostles to the contemporary bishops), are the recipients of God's grace and revelation. From a Catholic theological standpoint, the bishops' understanding of the Catholic tradition and their commitment to preserve and promote it as fully ordained members of the Church imbues them with the authority to make declarations about human nature and sexual morality.

However, in the case of the other theologians I referenced, they too have advanced degrees in theological ethics and deep commitments to the Catholic tradition. Some are ordained or professed religious, all of them teach theology at a university, and all of them actively participate in various academic societies in the United States.[71] Furthermore, since they are not bishops but rather live as "ordinary Catholics," they may have access to particular ways of understanding the contours of human sexuality. For this reason, they are also experts in the matter and can craft theological positions that are rational and well-sustained. While extrinsic probability depends on the intrinsicality of the documents and not on simply counting the experts, it is important to note that the position of the theologians I explored reflects a growing consensus among theologians in the United States and even abroad.[72] Furthermore, as discussed, an increasing number of bishops and other prelates have joined in this consensus. Therefore, the extrinsic probability of LGBTQ+ affirming theological perspectives is growing and is validated by the ethos of their respective authors.

Probabilism and the Dismissals of LGBTQ+ Educators in Catholic Schools

Considering the intrinsic and extrinsic probability of arguments in favor and against same-sex relationships and gender-affirming transitions, I argue that Catholic leaders should allow and encourage LGBTQ+ people to follow their conscience with regard to their sexual identity and behavior. This would not be the case if the magisterial doctrine on homosexuality and gender was credibly established and uncontested. However, since the doctrine is contested at all levels of the Church, and since opposing viewpoints within the Catholic tradition also possess intrinsic and extrinsic probability, which means they are legitimately defensible, LGBTQ+ people should feel free to follow their conscience and should be allowed to remain in the Church as Catholics in good standing.

Applying probabilism to LGBTQ+ educators in Catholic schools, I argue instead of considering same-sex relationships or gender transitions as a violation of Catholic doctrine and a threat to the Catholic identity of the schools, bishops and Catholic leaders should interpret them as a legitimate exercise of conscience and adherence to the Catholic principles sustaining an opposing probable opinion. To fire an LGBTQ+ educator based on a doctrine that is credibly contested is morally problematic because it denies the legitimate probability of their conscientious choices. I further restate that, considering the global debates in the Church on these topics, dismissing these teachers represents a drastic and hurtful action grounded in a contested doctrine that may develop in the future. The "hill" some of these Catholic leaders are choosing to "die on" is made out of sand and is in flux. Finally, the publication of *Fiducia Supplicans*, while it does not change the magisterial doctrine on same-sex unions, makes room for some LGBTQ+ persons in same-sex marriage to form a part of the Church.[73] Extending a blessing to these persons who approach the Church together is a sign of welcome. This new developlent calls upon Catholic leaders to welcome LGBTQ+ persons who espouse differing theological opinions on the matter, not fire them..

PROBABILISM AND THE CULTIVATION OF A NEW MORAL LANDSCAPE FOR THE CHURCH

Toward a Paradigm Shift on Questions of Sexual Morality

The doctrine of probabilism has significant implications for how the Church addresses questions of homosexuality and gender identity. Because probabilism makes room for defensible conscientious disagreement, the result is a degree of pluralism within the Church on questions of sexual morality. This tolerance and validation of diverse probable opinions reflects a new form of relationship between believers, the institutional Church, and Truth.[74] Prior to this proposal, a grammar of dissent and a grammar of magisterial authority dominated the Church, which has led to the exclusion of any perspective contrary to magisterial doctrine. Because the Catholic hierarchy proclaims that it possesses the correct, inerrant interpretation of God's Law, any tolerance of dissenting opinions is seen as a violation of God's will. Such understanding of ecclesial inerrancy is supported by the First Vatican Council, which teaches, "The doctrine of faith which God revealed . . . has been entrusted as a divine deposit to the Spouse of Christ [i.e., the Church], to be faithfully guarded and infallibly interpreted."[75] The Second Vatican Council further supported this by stating that the "authentic" interpretation of revelation "has been entrusted exclusively to the living teaching office of the Church, whose authority is exercised in the name of Jesus Christ."[76] Given these statements, one may argue that questions of moral theology already outlined by the teaching offices of the Church through conciliar documents, encyclicals, or other magisterial documents (like the ones from the Congregation of the Doctrine of the Faith), enjoy a certain inerrancy and are not open to probabilistic opinion. Anyone who disagrees with these documents is in a state of "dissent" and, therefore, presents a threat to the transmission of these divine truths.

However, as I have discussed, such claims to infallibility are constantly called into legitimate question when theological historians, such as John T. Noonan and Christopher J. Kellerman, chronicle ways in which the Church has "developed" (in the form of reversal) some moral doctrines—namely the one on slavery, which was first endorsed as part of the moral order and later categorized as an intrinsic evil.[77] Therefore, I assert that arguments for the categorical infallibility of all magisterial documents on morality stand on shaky grounds. Furthermore, in addition to the passages on magisterial authority, the Second Vatican Council also broadens the question of inerrancy to include the *sensus fidelium* by stating, "The entire body of the faithful, anointed as they are by the Holy One, cannot err in matters of belief."[78] I argue that this statement and the subsequent extensive theologies on the *sensus fidelium*, which I will discuss in the next chapter, try to gradually democratize the process of theologizing by integrating the lived experiences of the faithful in a way that automatically opens the doors to some pluralism in the Church as it navigates these questions of moral truth together. Furthermore, Pope Francis's statements acknowledging the development of doctrine and highlighting the importance of a Church that journeys together while decrying the Church's obsession with doctrinal orthodoxy further support the need for a paradigm shift in how the Church addresses morality on peripheral matters such as human sexuality.[79] With my retrieval of probabilism, the Church would deemphasize the grammar of dissent grounded in the inerrant teachings of the magisterium and would, instead, adopt a paradigm of joint communal and collegial discernment on mysterious matters of human sexuality.

Probabilism: A Founding Principle for Synodality

Probabilism proposes a new paradigm in which the entire Church walks together as it seeks to better embody an authentic witness to the Catholic tradition, which lies—not in some set of documents—but in the totality of the covenant between God and God's people. This perspective embraces an expansive view of the entire Catholic tradition that also considers society (even secular society) as a potential avenue for revelation through the lived experiences of the faithful, which sometimes contain valuable lessons for the magisterium. In cases where there is disagreement on how to bear this witness, all members of the Church would exercise some theological hospitality, ecclesial humility, and dialogue that could, hopefully, lead to a deeper understanding of our faith. In other words, the Church would walk a synodal path.[80] In *Amoris Laetitia*, Pope Francis states, "We [the magisterium] . . . find it hard to make room for the consciences of the faithful, who very often respond as best they can to the Gospel amid their limitations, and are capable of carrying out their own discernment in complex situations. We have been called to form consciences, not replace them."[81] A synodal Church that adopts a grammar of communal and collegial discernment on matters of sexual morality opens its doors to theological pluralism, fosters fellowship, and reflects an ecclesiology that tells the story of an inclusive Body of Christ.

Regarding questions of magisterial authority in light of the aforementioned ecclesial documents, I would argue that a synodal ecclesiological vision can increase the authority of the magisterium by equipping it with access to the consciences of the lay faithful. This might compel them to revise or reverse some doctrines, but that does not mean the magisterium loses its authority. As John T. Noonan points out: Do parents, teachers, and legal authorities lose their authority when they reverse decisions and/or apologize for their mistakes? He argues that they do not; rather, they increase it by showcasing active continuous discernment and growth.[82] Furthermore, Richard Gaillardetz criticizes those who view power as a zero-sum game. He instead proposes a new way of conceiving power as shared rather than disputed. Gaillardetz explains, "The primary question is no longer who has power and who does not. The main question now becomes: How can the various gifts exercised by all the Christian faithful be best employed in the fulfillment of the Church's mission?"[83] Lay Catholics, including young Catholics, are no longer the helpless, theologically illiterate flock they once were. They are suspicious of "infallible" claims on matters of sexuality that no human fully understands. More importantly, as Pope Francis says, they are capable of their own discernment and have the tools to access multiple perspectives on different matters. The Catholic hierarchy would be perceived as more credible if it recognizes, tolerates, and even celebrates the presence of some of the diverse valid viewpoints on sexual orientation and gender identity that permeate throughout the entire Catholic community.

While *Fiducia Supplicans* represents a step toward greater welcome of LGBTQ+ persons, the document explicitly clings to its "perineal" magisterial doctrine on homosexuality and does not seem to entertain any of the theological perspectives discussed here.[84] Some may consider such welcome and blessings of same-sex unions as superficial without the accompanying relaxation (or development) of the doctrines while others may see it as an important step while the Church continues to wrestle with this complex matter of moral doubt. There are others who defend magisterial doctrine in its present state and fear these blessings are weakening the Church's resolve to pursue, defend, and promulgate its truth. And so the debate rages on throughout the global Church.[85] In the meantime, I argue that Catholic leaders in the United States, especially those who employ LGBTQ+ persons, should employ the doctrine of probabilism and preserve the freedom and inclusion of diverse theological perspectives in Catholic institutions.

Probabilism, LGBTQ+ Catholic School Educators, and a Culture of Communal Discernment

Catholic school educators who enter same-sex marriages or undergo gender-affirming transitions do not do so lightly or in an attempt to frivolously threaten the anthropological basis of humanity. By the time LGBTQ+ people enter into a same-sex civil marriage or begin any physical or social gender transitions, they have likely undergone an extensive process of discernment about who they are and who they love. In the case of Catholic school educators who also identify as Catholics (or Christian, religious, or spiritual), their decisions represent a conscientious response to God's call in their lives, which takes incredible courage against significant odds as showcased in chapter 2. In many cases, I observe that they can articulate (at least to themselves) why they chose to enter into that marriage or process of gender transition. Perhaps, like me, some of them have done research about Catholicism and LGBTQ+ inclusion and have become familiarized with diverse theological perspectives that help them articulate the dictates of their conscience. Their disagreement with Church teaching should be interpreted as a conscientious subscription to an intrinsically and extrinsically probabilistic theological opinion on sexual orientation and/or gender identity. More importantly, their disagreement can serve as a catalyst for further dialogue in the broader Church on matters of sexuality.

Finally, LGBTQ+ Catholic school educators' probabilistic disagreement with Church doctrine offers a unique educational opportunity. Instead of depriving our schools of the indispensable presence of LGBTQ+ educators, school leaders should foster a school culture where probabilistic theological pluralism can serve as a catalyst for joint dialogue and discernment on matters of faith, human nature, moral behavior, and relationships. LGBTQ+ educators can serve as important role models in the process of evaluating probabilistic moral opinions and building community with those who disagree. Rather than sanitizing Catholic schools by attempting to protect students from perceived scandals, Catholic school educators should focus on teaching the skill of conscience formation and communal discernment. The attempt to inculcate students to follow a narrow conception of sexual morality is futile as teenagers have access to diverse opinions, even theological opinions, and can become apathetic toward a Church that presents a narrow and fluctuating conception of truth as if it were universal and unchangeable. Probabilism makes room for such diversity and provides a foundation for a new understanding of how our Church should operate in the face of such inevitable pluralism.

CONCLUSION

This chapter retrieved the moral doctrine of probabilism as a tool to help Catholic leaders make sense of diverse theological opinions in the Church on matters of homosexuality and gender. Probabilism validates such diversity and allows Catholics to act according to the dictates of their conscience while remaining as members of the Church in good standing. Most importantly, probabilism proposes a new paradigmatic shift in the Church whereby conscientious theological disagreement is not seen as a threat to a rigid Church but as an integral part of the Church's pilgrimage as a people of God. As we approach broader questions of Church polity and Catholic moral doctrine through the lens of Pope Francis's vision for a synodal Church, probabilism provides an important foundation for synodality by embodying a popular Catholic phrase, which served as an axiom of the Second Vatican Council: *In necessariis unitas, in non-necessariis libertas, in omnibus caritas*; which translates to, "In essentials, unity. In nonessentials, liberty. And in all things, charity." In the next chapter, I will discuss synodality and its implications for Catholic education.

NOTES

1. Social transitioning refers to a process whereby transgender people change their names, pronouns, and appearance without engaging in any medical or hormonal intervention. Typically, a social transition would precede a medical transition and most times operates as an avenue for exploration or discernment about one's gender identity.

2. Julia Fleming, *Defending Probabilism: The Moral Theology of Juan Caramuel* (Georgetown University Press, 2006), 30.

3. James Keenan, *A History of Catholic Theological Ethics* (Paulist Press, 2022), 170.

4. For a more detailed overview of the history and impact of sixteenth-century casuistry, see Keenan, *A History of Catholic Theological Ethics*, 167–206.

5. Albert R. Jonsen and Stephen Toulmin, *The Abuse of Casuistry: A History of Moral Reasoning* (University of California Press, 1990), 167.

6. Jonsen and Toulmin, *The Abuse of Casuistry*, 167–75; Fleming, *Defending Probabilism*.

7. Keenan, *A History of Catholic Theological Ethics*, 196–99.

8. Keenan, *A History of Catholic Theological Ethics*, 263–64.

9. For an example of resistance to modernism, see Pius IX, "The Syllabus of Errors," Papal Encyclicals, 1864, https://www.papalencyclicals.net/pius09/p9syll.htm. For a discussion on how Vatican II ushered in a new ecclesial culture that embraced modernity, see David Hollenbach, "Commentary on Gaudium Et Spes," in *Modern Catholic Social Teaching: Commentaries and Interpretations*, ed. Kenneth R. Himes et al., 2nd ed. (Georgetown University Press, 2018), 277–82.

10. Second Vatican Council, "Gaudium et Spes," Vatican Website, October 7, 1965, no. 4, https://www.vatican.va/archive/hist_councils/ii_vatican_council/documents/vat-ii_const_19651207_gaudium-et-spes_en.html.

11. In his book, *The Word Became Culture*, Miguel Diaz discusses how revelation is intrinsically linked to culture as it is interpreted through the lens of the exegete's cultural background and viewpoint. See Miguel H. Diaz, "The Word That

Crosses: Life-Giving Encounters with the Markan Jesus and Guadalupe," in *The Word Became Culture*, ed. Miguel H. Diaz (Orbis Books, 2021), 1–4.

12. Jean Porter, *Nature as Reason: A Thomistic Theory of the Natural Law* (Wm. B. Eerdmans-Lightning Source, 2004), 327–42.

13. Craig A. Ford Jr., "Transgender Bodies, Catholic Schools, and a Queer Natural Law Theology of Exploration," *Journal of Moral Theology* 7, no. 1 (January 1, 2018): 91, https://jmt.scholasticahq.com/article/11382-transgender-bodies-catholic-schools-and-a-queer-natural-law-theology-of-exploration.

14. Second Vatican Council, "Gaudium et Spes," nos. 36, 59, 62.

15. For an example, see Daniel P. Horan's criticism of the US Bishops' guidelines for gender-related healthcare, Daniel P. Horan, "US Bishops' Document against Transgender Health Care Is a Disaster," National Catholic Reporter, March 23, 2003, https://www.ncronline.org/opinion/guest-voices/us-bishops-document-against-transgender-health-care-disaster.

16. Bartolomeo Medina, *Exposition in Summa Theologiae Partem I II, q 19, a. 6* cited in Jonsen and Toulmin, *The Abuse of Casuistry*, 168.

17. Lisa Fullam, "Dealing with Doubt: Epikeia, Probabilism, and the Formation of Medical Conscience," in *Conscience and Catholic Health Care: From Clinical Contexts to Government Mandates*, ed. David E. DeCosse and Thomas A. Nairn (Maryknoll, NY: Orbis Books, 2017), 54.

18. Medina, *Exposition in Summa Theologiae* Partem I II, q.19, a.6, Cited in Jonsen and Toulmin, *The Abuse of Casuistry*, 164.

19. Lisa Fullam, "Transgender Students in Catholic Schools, Probabilism, and Reciprocity of Conscience," in *Conscience and Catholic Education: Theology, Administration, and Teaching*, ed. Kevin C. Baxter and David E. DeCosse (Orbis, 2022), 145–46.

20. Stefania Tutino, *Uncertainty in Post-Reformation Catholicism: A History of Probabilism* (Oxford University Press, 2017), 81–82.

21. Jonsen and Toulmin, *The Abuse of Casuistry*, 261.

22. Jonsen and Toulmin, *The Abuse of Casuistry*, 166.

23. Fullam, "Transgender Students in Catholic Schools, Probabilism, and Reciprocity of Conscience," 145.

24. Second Vatican Council, "Gaudium et Spes," no. 16.

25. For a comprehensive treatment on the different levels of authority contained invarious forms of Church teaching, see Richard R. Gaillardetz, *By What Authority?: Foundations for Understanding Authority in the Church*, 2nd rev. ed. (Liturgical Press, 2018).

26. I reaffirm my position that the doctrines of the Church can and have developed in the form of reversal. Things that once were approved by the magisterium have later been condemned and vice versa. See John Henry Newman, *Essay on the Development of Christian Doctrine* (Word on Fire Classics, 2017); John T. Noonan, *Church That Can and Cannot Change: The Development of Catholic Moral Teaching* (University of Notre Dame Press, 2005); Christopher J. Kellerman, *All Oppression Shall Cease: A History of Slavery, Abolitionism, and the Catholic Church* (Orbis, 2022); Jaroslav Pelikan, *The Christian Tradition: A History of the Development of Doctrine,*

Vol. 5: Christian Doctrine and Modern Culture (University of Chicago Press, 1991); Blase J. Cupich, "The Development of Doctrine Is the Tradition," Chicago Catholic, September 13, 2023, https://www.chicagocatholic.com/cardinal-blase-j.-cupich/-/article/2023/09/13/the-development-of-doctrine-is-the-tradition.

27. Bryan N. Massingale, "Beyond 'Who Am I to Judge?' The Sensus Fidelium, LGBT Experience, and Truth-Telling in the Church," in *Learning from All the Faithful: A Contemporary Theology of the Sensus Fidei*, ed. Bradford E. Hinze and Peter C. Phan (Pickwick Publications, 2016).

28. "German 'Synodal Way' Meeting Ends with Call for Same-Sex Blessings, Change to Catechism on Homosexuality," Catholic News Agency, accessed September 9, 2022, https://www.catholicnewsagency.com/news/250313/synodal-way-meeting-ends-with-call-for-same-sex-blessings-change-to-catechism-on-homosexuality.

29. See Todd A. Salzman and Michael G. Lawler, *The Sexual Person: Toward a Renewed Catholic Anthropology* (Georgetown University Press, 2008); Margaret Farley, *Just Love: A Framework for Christian Sexual Ethics* (Continuum, 2008); Ford Jr., "Transgender Bodies, Catholic Schools, and a Queer Natural Law Theology of Exploration."

30. Jeff Diamant, "How Catholics around the World See Same-Sex Marriage, Homosexuality," Pew Research Center, November 2, 2020, https://www.pewresearch.org/fact-tank/2020/11/02/how-catholics-around-the-world-see-same-sex-marriage-homosexuality/; General Secretariat of the Synod, "Enlarge the Space of Your Tent: Working Document for the Continental Stage," synod.va, October 2022, no. 39, https://www.synod.va/content/dam/synod/common/phases/continental-stage/dcs/Documento-Tappa-Continentale-EN.pdf.

31. Jason Steidl Jack, *LGBTQ Catholic Ministry: Past and Present* (Paulist Press, 2022); Michael J. O'Loughlin, *Hidden Mercy: AIDS, Catholics, and the Untold Stories of Compassion in the Face of Fear* (Broadleaf Books, 2021); William D. Glenn, *I Came Here Seeking a Person: A Vital Story of Grace; One Gay Man's Spiritual Journey* (Paulist Press, 2022); Charles Benedict, *Catholic and Gay: My Journey into Roman Catholic Priesthood and Out of the Closet* (CreateSpace, 2017); Donal Godfrey SJ, *Gays and Grays: The Story of the Gay Community at Most Holy Redeemer Catholic Parish* (Lexington Books, 2007); Mark Dowd, *Queer and Catholic: A Life of Contradiction* (Darton Longman & Todd Ltd, 2018).

32. Congregation for the Doctrine of the Faith, "Persona Humana—Declaration on Certain Questions Concerning Sexual Ethics," Vatican Website, December 29, 1975, https://www.vatican.va/roman_curia/congregations/cfaith/documents/rc_con_cfaith_doc_19751229_persona-humana_en.html; Congregation for Catholic Education, "Educational Guidance in Human Love: Outlines for Sex Education," Vatican Website, November 1, 1983, https://www.vatican.va/roman_curia/congregations/ccatheduc/documents/rc_con_ccatheduc_doc_19831101_sexual-education_en.html.

33. John Paul II, *Man and Woman He Created Them: A Theology of the Body*, trans. Michael Waldstein (Pauline Books & Media, 2006).

34. Francis, "Amoris Laetitia," Vatican Website, March 19, 2016, no. 56, https://www.vatican.va/content/dam/francesco/pdf/apost_exhortations/documents/papa-francesco_esortazione-ap_20160319_amoris-laetitia_en.pdf.

35. Francis, "Amoris Laetitia," no. 56.

36. Congregation for Catholic Education, "'Male and Female He Created Them'—Toward a Path of Dialogue on the Question of Gender Theory in Education," Vatican Website, 2019, https://www.vatican.va/roman_curia/congregations/ccatheduc/documents/rc_con_ccatheduc_doc_20190202_maschio-e-femmina_en.pdf.

37. Archdiocese of Denver, "Guidance for Issues Concerning the Human Person and Sexual Identity," n.d., https://www.documentcloud.org/documents/23218852-guidance-for-issues-concerning-the-human-person-and-sexual-identity; Archdiocese of Milwaukee, "Catechesis and Policy on Questions Concerning Gender Theory," January 18, 2022, https://www.archmil.org/ArchMil/attachments/2022GenderTheoryfinal.pdf?utm_source=sendgrid&utm_medium=email&utm_campaign=website.

38. Dicastery for the Doctrine of the Faith, "Dignitatis Infinita," Vatican Website, April 8, 2024, https://press.vatican.va/content/salastampa/en/bollettino/pubblico/2024/04/08/240408c.html.

39. Dicastery for the Doctrine of the Faith, no. 60.

40. "'Male and Female He Created Them'—Toward a Path of Dialogue on the Question of Gender Theory in Education," no. 11.

41. In the "Presentation" section of the 2024 document, the DDF outlines the process of composing the document, which showcases the lack of consultation with transgender persons. See Dicastery for the Doctrine of the Faith, "Dignitatis Infinita."

42. Daniel P. Horan, "US Bishops' Document against Transgender Health Care Is a Disaster," National Catholic Reporter, March 23, 2023, https://www.ncronline.org/opinion/guest-voices/us-bishops-document-against-transgender-health-care-disaster; Daniel P. Horan, "The Strawman of 'Gender Theory' in the Vatican's New Document," *New Ways Ministry* (blog), April 8, 2024, https://www.newwaysministry.org/2024/04/08/the-strawman-of-gender-theory-in-the-vaticans-new-document/.

43. Thomism refers to the theological thoughts of St. Thomas Aquinas, the thirteenth-century Catholic scholastic.

44. Second Vatican Council, "Gaudium et Spes," no. 48; Paul VI, "Humanae Vitae," Vatican Website, July 25, 1968, no. 12, https://www.vatican.va/content/paul-vi/en/encyclicals/documents/hf_p-vi_enc_25071968_humanae-vitae.html.

45. Congregation for the Doctrine of the Faith, "Persona Humana—Declaration on Certain Questions Concerning Sexual Ethics," no. VIII.

46. Congregation for the Doctrine of the Faith, "Letter to the Bishops of the Catholic Church on the Pastoral Care of Homosexual Persons," Vatican Website, October 1, 1986, no. 3, https://www.vatican.va/roman_curia/congregations/cfaith/documents/rc_con_cfaith_doc_19861001_homosexual-persons_en.html.

47. Congregation for the Doctrine of the Faith, no. 7.

48. Congregation for the Doctrine of the Faith, "Some Considerations Concerning the Response to Legislative Proposals on the Non-Discrimination of Homosexual Persons," Vatican Website, July 24, 1992, nos. 10–12, https://www.vatican.va/roman_curia/congregations/cfaith/documents/rc_con_cfaith_doc_19920724_homosexual-persons_en.html.

49. Congregation for the Doctrine of the Faith, "Considerations Regarding Proposals to Give Legal Recognition to Unions between Homosexual Persons," Vatican

Website, June 3, 2003, https://www.vatican.va/roman_curia/congregations/cfaith/documents/rc_con_cfaith_doc_20030731_homosexual-unions_en.html.

50. Congregation for the Doctrine of the Faith, "Responsum of the Congregation for the Doctrine of the Faith to a Dubium Regarding the Blessing of the Unions of Persons of the Same Sex," Vatican Website, March 15, 2021, https://press.vatican.va/content/salastampa/en/bollettino/pubblico/2021/03/15/210315b.html.

51. Dicastery for the Doctrine of the Faith, "Fiducia Supplicans: On the Pastoral Meaning of Blessings," Vatican Website, December 18, 2023, https://www.vatican.va/roman_curia/congregations/cfaith/documents/rc_ddf_doc_20231218_fiducia-supplicans_en.html.

52. Dicastery for the Doctrine of the Faith, "Press Release Concerning the Reception of Fiducia Supplicans," Vatican Website, January 4, 2024, https://www.vatican.va/roman_curia/congregations/cfaith/documents/rc_ddf_doc_20240104_comunicato-fiducia-supplicans_en.html.

53. Horan, "US Bishops' Document against Transgender Health Care Is a Disaster," March 23, 2003.

54. Salzman and Lawler, *The Sexual Person*, 92.

55. Salzman and Lawler, *The Sexual Person*, 109.

56. Salzman and Lawler, *The Sexual Person*, 140–57.

57. Salzman and Lawler, *The Sexual Person*, 233.

58. Salzman and Lawler, *The Sexual Person*, 233–34.

59. Salzman and Lawler, *The Sexual Person*, 234.

60. Farley, *Just Love*, 177.

61. Farley, *Just Love*, 198.

62. Farley, *Just Love*, 207.

63. Farley, *Just Love*, 227.

64. Farley, *Just Love*, 289.

65. Ford Jr., "Transgender Bodies, Catholic Schools, and a Queer Natural Law Theology of Exploration," 80.

66. In his words, "'human nature,' like all concepts—scientific or philosophical—is the product of social construction." See Ford Jr., "Transgender Bodies, Catholic Schools, and a Queer Natural Law Theology of Exploration," 90.

67. Ford Jr., "Transgender Bodies, Catholic Schools, and a Queer Natural Law Theology of Exploration," 94.

68. Ford Jr., "Transgender Bodies, Catholic Schools, and a Queer Natural Law Theology of Exploration," 97–98.

69. Lisa Sowle Cahill, *Sex, Gender, and Christian Ethics* (Cambridge University Press, 1996); Lisa Fullam, "Civil Same-Sex Marriage: A Catholic Affirmation," New Ways Ministry, accessed September 19, 2023, https://www.newwaysministry.org/issues/marriage-equality/civil-sex-marriage-catholic-affirmation/; Evelyn Whitehead and James D. Whitehead, *Fruitful Embraces: Sexuality, Love, and Justice* (True Directions, 2014); John J. McNeill, *The Church and the Homosexual: Fourth Edition*, 4th ed. (Beacon Press, 1993); Richard Peddicord, *Gay and Lesbian Rights: A Question: Sexual Ethics or Social Justice?* (Sheed & Ward, 1996); Steidl Jack, *LGBTQ Catholic Ministry*.

70. Congregation for the Doctrine of the Faith, "Notification on the Book Just Love. A Framework for Christian Sexual Ethics by Sr. Margaret A. Farley, R.S.M.," Vatican Website, March 30, 2012, https://www.vatican.va/roman_curia/congregations/cfaith/documents/rc_con_cfaith_doc_20120330_nota-farley_en.html; US Conference of Catholic Bishops, "Inadequacies in the Theological Methodology and Conclusion of the Sexual Person: Toward a Renewed Catholic Anthropology by Todd A. Salzman and Michael G. Lawler," USCCB.org, September 15, 2010, https://www.usccb.org/resources/inadequacies-theological-methodology-and-conclusion-sexual-person-toward-renewed-catholic.

71. "Michael G. Lawler," Catholic Theological Ethics in the World, accessed June 7, 2023, https://catholicethics.com/ethicists/michael-g-lawler/; "Salzman, Todd A.," Creighton University Website, accessed June 7, 2023, https://www.creighton.edu/campus-directory/salzman-todd; "Margaret A. Farley," Yale Divinity School Website, accessed June 7, 2023, https://divinity.yale.edu/faculty-and-research/yds-faculty/margaret-farley; "Craig A. Ford, Jr.," St. Norbert's College Website, accessed June 7, 2023, https://www.snc.edu/academics/faculty/craig.ford.html.

72. After the publication of *Humanae Vitae*, the Catholic Theological Society of America commissioned a study, which was conducted by several member theologians. The report was published in 1977 and adopted a position contrary to the magisterial position developed through the CDF documents. See Anthony Kosnik et al., *Human Sexuality: New Directions in American Catholic Thought: A Study* (Paulist Press, 1977).

73. Dicastery for the Doctrine of the Faith, "Fiducia Supplicans: On the Pastoral Meaning of Blessings."

74. I am using "capital T" Truth in reference to the overarching mystery of the Catholic faith that our tradition is attempting to grasp.

75. First Vatican Council, "Dei Filius," Vatican Website, April 28, 1870, chap. 4, https://www.vatican.va/content/pius-ix/la/documents/constitutio-dogmatica-dei-filius-24-aprilis-1870.html.

76. Second Vatican Council, "Dei Verbum," Vatican Website, November 18, 1965, no. 10, https://www.vatican.va/archive/hist_councils/ii_vatican_council/documents/vat-ii_const_19651118_dei-verbum_en.html.

77. Noonan, *Church That Can and Cannot Change*; Kellerman, *All Oppression Shall Cease*.

78. Second Vatican Council, "Lumen Gentium," November 21, 1964, 12, https://www.vatican.va/archive/hist_councils/ii_vatican_council/documents/vat-ii_const_19641121_lumen-gentium_en.html.

79. Christopher White, "Pope Francis Blasts Reactionary American Catholics Who Oppose Church Reform," *National Catholic Reporter*, August 28, 2023, https://www.ncronline.org/vatican/vatican-news/pope-francis-blasts-reactionary-american-catholics-who-oppose-church-reform; Ines de la Cuetara and Phoebe Natanson, "Pope Francis Restates Catholic Church Is for Everyone, Including LGBTQ+ People," ABC News, August 7, 2023, https://abcnews.go.com/International/pope-francis-restates-catholic-church-including-lgbtq-people/story?id=102064714.

80. Ish Ruiz, "Synodality in the Catholic Church: Toward a Conciliar Ecclesiology of Inclusion for LGBTQ+ Persons," *Journal of Moral Theology* 12, no. 2 (July 18, 2023): 55–77, https://doi.org/10.55476/001c.84391.

81. Francis, "Amoris Laetitia," no. 37.

82. Noonan, *Church That Can and Cannot Change*.

83. Richard R. Gaillardetz, *The Church in the Making: Lumen Gentium, Christus Dominus, Orientalium Ecclesiarum* (Paulist Press, 2006), 152.

84. Dicastery for the Doctrine of the Faith, "Fiducia Supplicans: On the Pastoral Meaning of Blessings."

85. Aleja Hertzler-McCain, "Vatican Shift on Gay Blessings Has 'Deep Pastoral Implications,' Say Theologians," National Catholic Reporter, December 19, 2023, https://www.ncronline.org/news/vatican-shift-gay-blessings-has-deep-pastoral-implications-say-theologians; Patrick Hudson and Munyaradzi Makoni, "Joy and Alarm in Bishops' Responses to Fiducia Supplicans," The Tablet, December 26, 2023, https://www.thetablet.co.uk/news/18081/joy-and-alarm-in-bishops-responses-to-fiducia-supplicans.

Chapter 4

Synodality in Catholic Schools

A Theological Model for LGBTQ+ Inclusion

In my ministry of LGBTQ+ inclusion in Catholic schools and parishes, the question I am most frequently asked is: "Why do you stay in the Church?" This is a reasonable question to ask considering the prevalent institutional rejection of LGBTQ+ people from the Church, including the threat faced by LGBTQ+ educators such as myself. Answering the question has always been complicated because the joy I feel as a member of the Church is simultaneously marked by repeated instances of pain and exclusion, which often results in an internal dualism in my relationship with the Church. On one hand, "Ish, the gay Catholic" is seeking to connect with God and with community; on the other hand, "Ish, the theologian" is engaged in the theological academy and committed to helping transform the Church beyond its current culture of exclusion. For a long time, these two components of my identity—although related—did not interact much with each other.

As a committed gay Catholic, my faith practice has been rooted in my experience of local Catholic community. Because I have often felt the urge to leave the Church, especially due to the exclusive actions of the Catholic hierarchy, I tried to avoid conversations about the global Church in my personal life and faith journey; and I sought refuge in my local Church community for the sake of my emotional, mental, and spiritual sanity. My parish priest, my LGBTQ+ young adults ministry group, and the weekly liturgy at Most Holy Redeemer parish in San Francisco, along with the amazing school community of Sacred Heart Cathedral Preparatory where I taught, have been the sources of spiritual nourishment in my life.

As a theologian, however, I constantly engage in conversations about inclusion in the global Church through my profession. Because of the spiritual and emotional pain I often felt as a part of these conversations, I first attempted to compartmentalize my personal faith (grounded in a local community) from my theological pursuits in the global academy in order to protect myself from further harm. I figured that if I brought my rational theological mind to the conversation but left behind my "gay self" in a psychological closet, I would not feel so personally hurt by the actions of our Church. Such a dis-integration, however, caused pain in different ways because the separation of these components of my identity made me feel like I was neglecting important parts of myself at different times. This realization compelled me to seek to do theology as an integrated person, bringing my "gay self" more fully into my academic professional theological self. During this process of integration, I realized that a sole focus on our local compartmentalized Catholic contexts without meaningful engagement with the global Church may generate within us a false sense of security. More importantly, it can desensitize those of us who are privileged enough to have an inclusive local Church community to the suffering of those who do not and are more directly affected by the actions of the institutional global Church. This process helped me reconceive my understanding of my theological vocation in a way that integrates "Ish, the theologian" with "Ish, the practicing gay Catholic."

As an integrated gay Catholic theologian, I have sought to promote a new ecclesiology (an understanding of the nature of the Church) that would help the Church become more inclusive of LGBTQ+ people. Key to this ecclesiology is an integration between the local and global experiences of the Church, which I find manifested in Pope Francis's vision of synodality. A synodal Church, at its core, seeks to highlight the lived experiences of local faith communities as the starting point for theological and pastoral reflection. As I have discussed in my previous scholarly work, synodality contains a hopeful promise for LGBTQ+ inclusion in the Church because it represents a new ecclesiological modality where the institutional hierarchy enters into a collegial relationship with all lay Catholics, with particular attention to those who are marginalized.[1] Since the bishops are called to serve the Church, including its laity, synodality proposes a new structure in which Catholic leaders must first consult with God's revelation through the lives of the lay faithful (i.e., the *sensus fidelium*) as they consider ways to guide the Church along its journey. Such an ecclesiological modality contains significant potential for inclusion throughout our Church, especially for LGBTQ+ people. Furthermore, because synodality represents a new ecclesiological modality that affects how the Church operates, I argue that this new way of "being Church" has significant implications for Catholic schools.

In this chapter, I will apply a theology of synodality to Catholic education. With the foundation for a synodal Church provided by my retrieval of probabilism, as discussed in the last chapter, I present synodality as an important ecclesiological model that can help Catholic schools navigate complex questions of human sexuality as a unified community. Furthermore, synodality can provide a theological framework whereby Catholic leaders can learn to cherish the gifts of LGBTQ+ educators in their schools. Crucially, this synodal model for Catholic education represents a circular dynamic whereby synodality affects how the Catholic schools operate and, in turn, the Catholic school communities' lived experiences of synodality affects the broader Church. First, as discussed in the last chapter, synodality can guide Catholic school students and employees along a process of communal discernment on complicated questions of sexual morality while respecting the diversity of probable theological opinions on the matter. Second, since Catholic schools are a significant point of contact between the hierarchical Church and the Catholic laity, I believe applying synodality to Catholic education can significantly improve the relationship between lay Catholics (including LGBTQ+ Catholics) and the Church's hierarchy. In other words, I argue that synodality in the microcosm of the Catholic school offers an opportunity to model, at the local level, what active lay participation can look like in the macrocosm of the global Church; thus gradually shaping the polity of the global Church and creating a deeper sense of integration between local and global experiences of Church.

To construct a synodal model for Catholic education, I will divide this chapter into three parts. The first part will synthesize a theology of synodality as a new ecclesiological modality for the Church. In this part, I will explore the foundation of the Second Vatican Council, Pope Francis's call to synodality, and contemporary theology. Then, I will apply the question of synodality to LGBTQ+ inclusion in the Church. The second part of the chapter will construct a theology of Catholic education grounded in a theology of synodality. The work of Thomas Groome, as discussed in chapter 2, offers an important foundation for this conversation. Finally, the third part will apply a synodal theology of Catholic education to the question of LGBTQ+ educators in Catholic schools. I will conclude with a summary and an introduction to synodality and the question of social ethics.

A THEOLOGY OF SYNODALITY FOR CATHOLIC LGBTQ+ INCLUSION

Lessons from Vatican II

Synodality relies on a robust theological foundation provided by the Second Vatican Council,[2] which ushered in a new ecclesiological direction that redefined the relationship between the hierarchy and the lay faithful. Prior to Vatican II, Catholic ecclesiology emphasized the authority of the hierarchy and described the role of the laity as passive. This pre-Conciliar ecclesiology is perhaps best reflected in Pope Pius X's 1906 encyclical, *Vehementer Nos*, which states:

> The Church is essentially an *unequal* society, that is, a society comprising two categories of persons, the Pastors and the flock, those who occupy a rank in the different degrees of the hierarchy and the multitude of the faithful. So distinct are these categories that with the pastoral body only rests the necessary right and authority for promoting the end of the society and directing all its members towards that end; the one duty of the multitude is to allow themselves to be led, and, like a docile flock, to follow the Pastors.[3]

Conversely, Vatican II's ecclesiology, as reflected in the four dogmatic constitutions authored by the Council Fathers almost six decades after *Vehementer Nos*, empowers the laity to actively partake in and contribute to the life of the Church. For example, this invitation is present in *Sacrosanctum Concillium's* call for active lay participation in the liturgy,[4] in *Lumen Gentium's* description of the Church as the People of God,[5] in *Gaudium et Spes's* emphasis on the supremacy and freedom of the human conscience,[6] and in *Dei Verbum's* developed understanding of God's divine revelation through the lives of the faithful as conduits of the "living tradition."[7] Furthermore, the empowerment of the laity is grounded in a renewed theology of Baptism through which all Catholics share the common vocational call of priest, prophet, and king. In the words of Ormond Rush, "Full and active participation of all the faithful means appropriate participation by the laity in the *teaching, sanctifying*, and *governing* of church life, and in the mission of the church in the world, since the whole People of God . . . share in the prophetic, priestly, and kingly offices of Christ."[8]

Most importantly, in what I consider to be the most significant theological development of Vatican II, the Council introduced the notion of the *sensus fidelium*, or "sense of the faithful," in *Lumen Gentium*, which states,

> The entire body of the faithful, anointed as they are by the Holy One, cannot err in matters of belief. They manifest this special property by means of the whole peoples' supernatural discernment in matters of faith when "from the Bishops down to the last of the lay faithful" they show universal agreement in matters of faith and morals.[9]

The *sensus fidelium* refers to a supernatural and inerrant sense of faith, possessed by baptized Catholics, that allows the laity to intuitively grasp God's will.[10] Gaillardetz observes, "The council asserted that the whole people of God share in that infallibility which Christ gave the church inasmuch as, when they are in agreement on a matter of faith and morals, they cannot err."[11] Crucially, since the *sensus fidelium* operates as a source of God's revelation, I argue that it endows the laity with a special competence on matters of faith and morals that must be consulted by the hierarchy. A detailed synthesis of the role and competence of the laity is offered by Gaillardetz, who summarizes,

> The council taught that the laity has a right and responsibility to be actively involved in the Church's apostolate (*LG*, 30, 33). They are equal sharers in the threefold office of Christ who is priest prophet and king (*LG*, 34–36). They are called to full conscious and active participation in the liturgy, a participation that is demanded by the "very nature of the liturgy" (*SC*, 14). Pastors must acknowledge the expertise, competency and authority of the laity and gratefully accept their counsel (*LG*, 37). The council encouraged laypersons to pursue advanced study in theology and scripture (*GS*, 62). Finally, it is the laity who are to take the initiative in the transformation of the temporal order (*LG*, 31; *GS*, 43).[12]

Unfortunately, the doctrine of the *sensus fidelium* is often perceived to be at odds with the concept of magisterial authority, which—as I discussed in the last chapter—was also affirmed by the Council in *Dei Verbum*: "The task of authentically interpreting the word of God, whether written or handed on, has been entrusted exclusively to the living teaching office of the Church, whose authority is exercised in the name of Jesus Christ."[13] On the one hand, the lay faithful possess God's revelation through their lives as manifested in the *sensus fidelium* and, on the other hand, the Church's hierarchy is in charge of interpreting this revelation and formulating it into doctrine. Conflict arises when the hierarchy and the laity do not agree on particular matters of faith and morals, as is currently the case with questions of sexual morality in the US Church. Even more unfortunate, however, is the result of the conflict, which often involves members of the US hierarchy exercising their canonical power to punish, silence, exclude, or ignore opposing theological positions on behalf of the faithful.[14]

In response to this conflict, I remind Church leaders that, while the hierarchy retains its magisterial authority according to *Dei Verbum*, it is called upon by the Council to exercise it responsibly. The document also states, "This teaching office is not above the word of God, but serves it, teaching only what has been handed on, listening to it devoutly, guarding it scrupulously and explaining it faithfully in accord with a divine commission and with the help of the Holy Spirit."[15] Thus, the hierarchy of the Church is tasked with serving God's revelation by actively consulting the Holy Spirit via the *sensus fidelium*, along with other sources of revelation (e.g., Scripture).

Overall, the ecclesiology of Vatican II envisions a new balance between the Church's hierarchy and the lay faithful, who possess a special competence through the *sensus fidelium* and are called through their Baptism to participate in the priestly, prophetic, and royal/governing mission of the Church. John W. O'Malley asserts that, in light of Vatican II, "the first reality of the Church is horizontal and consists of all the baptized, without distinction of rank. Only then comes the vertical reality, hierarchy."[16] With this new balance between the authority of the hierarchy and the competence of the laity, the Second Vatican Council sets the stage for a new collegial ecclesiological modality which is being retrieved and implemented by Pope Francis's vision of a synodal Church.

Pope Francis's Call to Synodality

Since the beginning of his pontificate, Pope Francis has emphasized the importance of listening to the *sensus fidelium* as a crucial component of the life of the Church. His first apostolic exhortation in 2013, *Evangelii Gaudium*, makes specific calls for an inclusive Church that pays attention to the inerrancy of the *sensus fidelium*.[17] Furthermore, during a general audience in 2013, and in stark contrast with Pope Pius X's *Vehementer Nos*, he explained:

> With the gift of Baptism, each one of us is a living stone. This tells us that no one in the Church is useless, and if from time to time someone says to someone else: "go home, you are no good," this is not true. For no one is no good in the Church, we are all necessary for building this Temple! No one is secondary. No one is the most important person in the Church, we are all equal in God's eyes. Some of you might say "Listen, Mr. Pope, you are not our equal." Yes, I am like each one of you, we are all equal, we are brothers and sisters! No one is anonymous: we all both constitute and build the Church.[18]

With this vision of a Church that emphasizes the experience and participation of the faithful, Pope Francis calls upon the hierarchy to listen to the *sensus fidelium*, stating, "To find what the Lord asks of his Church today, we must lend an ear to the debates of our time and perceive the 'fragrance' of the men of this age, so as to be permeated with their joys and hopes, with their griefs and anxieties. At that moment we will know how to propose the good news on the family with credibility."[19] Considering that ecclesial credibility is in short supply, as evidenced by the high levels of disaffiliation discussed in chapter 2, such efforts to ensure the Church remains relevant are significantly needed.

Building upon this ecclesiological vision of collaboration with the faithful, Pope Francis issued his first explicit call for a synodal Church at the 2015 Synod on the Family, which also marked the fiftieth anniversary of the creation of the Synod of Bishops created by Pope Paul VI after Vatican II.[20] During his address, he offered two significant insights to the bishops.

First, he stated, "A synodal Church is a Church which listens, which realizes that listening 'is more than simply hearing.' It is a mutual listening in which everyone has something to learn. The faithful people, the college of bishops, the Bishop of Rome: all listening to each other, and all listening to the Holy Spirit, the 'Spirit of truth,' in order to know what he 'says to the Churches.'"[21] This ecclesiology retrieves a conciliar notion of the *sensus fidelium* and applies it to the hierarchical composition of the Church. Second, Pope Francis invokes a Christological statement to construct an image of the Church as an inverted pyramid:

> In this Church, as in an inverted pyramid, the top is located beneath the base. Consequently, those who exercise authority are called "ministers," because, in the original meaning of the word, they are the least of all. It is in serving the people of God that each bishop becomes, for that portion of the flock entrusted to him, *vicarius Christi*, the vicar of that Jesus who at the Last Supper bent down to wash the feet of the Apostles.[22]

Furthermore, in a 2016 letter to Cardinal Marc Ouellet, Pope Francis issued an important call: "Let us trust in our People, in their memory and in their 'sense of smell,' let us trust that the Holy Spirit acts in and with our People and that this Spirit is not merely the 'property' of the ecclesial hierarchy."[23] With that, he recognizes the competence of the *sensus fidelium* in discerning God's revelation in their lives.

Toward a Synodal Ecclesiology of Inclusion

Building upon Pope Francis's calls for a synodal Church, various theologians have crafted ecclesiological reflections on a synodality. The International Theological Commission (ITC), which is comprised of the Vatican's "in-house" theologians, published a document in 2018 titled "Synodality in the Life and Mission of the Church," which contained significant insights. From the onset, the ITC describes synodality as a reconfigured view of the Church as the People of God[24] and as a communion of believers.[25] This communion is characterized by the universality of the Church, including the laity and the hierarchy,[26] and a spirit of mutual responsibility.[27] Crucially, the starting point for synodality is the lived experience of the Church. According to the ITC, "In the local Church, Christian witness is embodied in specific human and social situations, which allows for an incisive initiation of synodal structures which serve the mission. As Pope Francis has emphasized, 'only to the extent that these organizations keep connected to the *base* and start from the people and their daily problems, can a synodal Church begin to take shape.'"[28] This process requires an extensive method of active and continual consultation.[29] Synodality, therefore, refers to a collegial ecclesiology whereby the laity and the hierarchy work together, through their respective active participation and magisterial authority, along the Church's journey. This synodal collegiality is not a mere canonical, juridical, or parliamentary process, but is rather a new modality of being Church,[30] specifically a Church that walks together as the People of God.

Since the *sensus fidelium* lies at the heart of a synodal Church, it is important to adopt a pneumatological lens to understand the relationship between the Holy Spirit, the laity, and a synodal Church.[31] Amanda C. Osheim explains, "Francis's metaphor for authority in the church and his vision of synodality are rooted theologically in the presence of the Holy Spirit throughout the church; rather than dividing the church into those empowered to teach and those rendered docile to teaching, through the Spirit all church members are both learners and teachers."[32] Bradford Hinze agrees:

> Consulting the faithful, and I would say, deliberating and engaging in decision-making among the faithful about the life and mission of the church, is based on the central conviction that the Spirit is actively at work in the faithful as they receive the Word of God, understand the self-communication of God, and apply this received revelation. When papal and episcopal teachings are not received by the faithful, this may reveal a breakdown in communication, a failure of understanding on the part of the faithful. However, it may also happen that a teaching is not received due to an accurate, authentic, and possibly truthful discernment by an individual or community. Thus, theologians speak of the dissent of the faithful that emerges through an exercise of an informed conscience.[33]

This process of consultation with the *sensus fidelium* in the hopes of being guided by the Spirit can be interpreted as communal discernment. In the words of Grzegorz Strzelczyk, "through the communal discernment process, individual insights coincide with each other and this reveals direction in which the Holy Spirit desires the community to go."[34] Crucially, Hinze observes that "even with such a capacious vision of synodality there will inevitably be a diversity of pathways"[35] and, as discussed in the last chapter, this diversity must be, at least, respected or, ideally, cherished as a source of theological insight.

Since the faithful are imbued with a particular competence via the *sensus fidelium*, and considering the diversity of pathways they feel called to live as Catholics, the hierarchy's synodal interactions with them contain high probability of surprise. Engaging in synodal discourse with the diverse *sensus fidelium* will present the listener (the hierarchy) with new grace-filled perspectives that should form an integral part of the Church's journey. Strzelczyk explains, "in its very essence, synodality is associated with the possibility of an epiphany of the Holy Spirit. In other words: Every gathering in which the synodality of the Church is realized is (at least potentially) an epiphany of the Holy Spirit. Moreover, expectation of this epiphany should be the reason for such a gathering."[36] Therefore, to genuinely engage in synodal discourse is to open oneself to what Pope Francis refers to as the God of surprises.[37]

This epiphanic process, I argue, unfolds through what Ormond Rush refers to as a circular hermeneutic of understanding.[38] This dynamic draws a four-part connection between listening, formulating doctrine, and imparting teachings in the Church. First, the onus falls on the Church hierarchy's commitment to genuinely listen to the *sensus fidelium* through active consultation. Second, bearing in mind the insights gained from the faithful with a spirit of collaboration and collegiality, the hierarchy articulates a collective understanding of the Catholic faith (i.e., Catholic doctrine). Third, the doctrine is communicated pastorally to the faithful. Fourth, and most significantly, the circle then closes and continues through active consultation that gauges the reception of the teaching. Considering the diversity of theological opinions present among the faithful, I argue that Catholic doctrine—particularly on matters of sexuality—should focus on general principles to guide moral behavior rather than particular mechanical prescriptions of sexual acts. This would make room for the consciences of the faithful to freely navigate diverse probabilistic opinions which, in turn, continue to inform the broader Church through the circular hermeneutic catalyzing various instances of epiphany.

From the Biblical tradition, specifically the story of the Epiphany in which the magi have an encounter with Jesus and return to their lives "by another road" (Matt. 2:1–12), we learn that, when we encounter God in an unexpected way, we cannot go back to being as we were. A synodal Church that listens to the faithful as it engages in communal discernment (and is open to an epiphany of the Spirit) is a Church willing to change and find new ways of being in communion with one another. In the words of Pope Francis, "We must rediscover the word *together*. Walk *together*. Question *together*. Take responsibility *together* for community discernment, which for us is prayer, as the first Apostles did: this is *synodality*, which we would like to make a daily habit in all its expressions."[39] In relation to the LGBTQ+ community, while this may bring about a future development in doctrine on sexuality, at the very least, a spirit of synodality should inspire the Church to recognize and include LGBTQ+ persons in the life of the Church. At best, however, a synodal Church would take seriously the lived experiences and the epistemologies (i.e., the worldviews) of LGBTQ+ people as a source of theological reflection that can inform Catholic doctrine and the overall life of the Church.

Synodality and LGBTQ+ Catholics

Synodality in the Church has two major implications for LGBTQ+ Catholics. The first implication, which I have discussed in previous scholarly work, entails both recognizing the presence of LGBTQ+ persons in the Church and creating safe spaces for LGBTQ+ Catholics to form a part of the daily fabric of the Church.[40] By adopting a synodal ecclesiology, the Church recognizes that LGBTQ+ people have been effectively serving in schools (as evidenced in chapter 2), parishes, hospitals, and other places of ministry. Such recognition includes acknowledgment that LGBTQ+ people exist and that their LGBTQ+ experiences are valid. Preemptively pathologizing the identity of LGBTQ+ persons as intrinsically disordered and their same-sex unions or gender-affirming journeys as intrinsically evil automatically excludes the insights gained from their lived experience from the synodal table.

As an example of such problematic erasure, some bishops, like Archbishop Cordileone of San Francisco and Bishop Barber of Oakland have issued statements invalidating LGBTQ+ identities as such by instead arguing that their "most fundamental identity is that of a beloved child of God."[41] While it is true that we are all God's children, such statements dichotomize an LGBTQ+ identity and an identity as a child of God as if they were opposite or mutually exclusive. LGBTQ+ Catholics are both: LGBTQ+ *and* Children of God. They can fully grow into both identities and a synodal Church should recognize this and welcome them as they are.

Welcoming LGBTQ+ Catholics also entails the creation and nurturing of a spiritual space through which they can participate in all facets of Church life. This includes creating an LGBTQ+ faith-sharing group, celebrating liturgy on important cultural LGBTQ+ events such as Pride and National Coming Out Day, providing opportunities for spiritual direction, inviting LGBTQ+ people to serve as ministers in the community, and explicitly indicating that the Catholic community welcomes LGBTQ+ persons through verbal, digital, and print communications. Furthermore, the staff in the community should receive adequate preparation to serve LGBTQ+ Catholics through cultural competence training, pastoral care training for LGBTQ+ people, direct experiences interacting with the community, and adequate theological training that can help them articulate how the Catholic tradition includes and celebrates LGBTQ+ persons. This has obvious implications for Catholic education, which I will discuss in a later section.

The second implication of synodality for LGBTQ+ inclusion in the Church is perhaps less obvious and more contentious because it involves listening to the experiences of LGBTQ+ persons to decipher what God is communicating to the Church through their lives. This honors the doctrine of the *sensus fidelium* by recognizing that, through baptism, LGBTQ+ Catholics participate in God's ongoing revelation. Therefore, I argue that recognizing the presence of God through LGBTQ+ persons and their lived experiences requires an engagement with the emerging field of queer theology. Up until now, I have used the term "LGBTQ+" to refer to a population of persons who identify as something other than heterosexual and cisgender. However, I now introduce the concept of "queerness" to invoke a sense of social, cultural, and political transgression on behalf of LGBTQ+ persons. While some LGBTQ+ persons would seek to assimilate their sexual identity to hetero and cisnormative lifestyles,[42] many LGBTQ+ persons question and challenge some of the underlying social and religious norms that impose a sense of compulsory heterosexuality and cisnormativity. In that sense, to be an LGBTQ+ Catholic is to transgress against sexual and relational norms that many in our Church and society take for granted and seldom question.

The field of queer theology seeks to understand our religious tradition through the lens of anti-normativity. I argue that, in a Christian context, queer theology reflects on God and Jesus as transgressive forces in our world.[43] Crucially, this field is not so much concerned with the representation of LGBTQ+ people in the Bible or the theological tradition because it does not seek to promote external validation for LGBTQ+ people by using queer religious imagery. Rather, it is an acknowledgment of a queer epistemology (i.e., worldview) present in the Divine and, therefore, in the humans made in the *Imago Dei*. In other words, because God's nature encompasses queerness as transgression (e.g., God blurs the lines between human and divine, between life and death, between natural and supernatural),[44] we who are made in God's image are called to adopt queerness as a worldview and as an ethical project that seeks to deconstruct oppressive norms.[45]

Queer theology was famously pioneered by Marcella Althaus-Reid, who challenges theologians to craft theology "without underwear" so that their theology captures the smell of their sex. With this evocative image, she calls for theological reflections that are not divorced from the embodied experience of human sexuality. More importantly, she questions the concepts of "decency" and "indecency," which are often sustained by religious discourse, to argue that what is often deemed obscene—namely sex or, more specifically, non-heterosexual and non-cisgender sexual expression—is also a location for theological insight. According to her, all theology is sexual theology and should encompass an integrated view of humans as diversely embodied beings, whether queer or not. To drive this point forward, Althaus-Reid provocatively discusses the sexuality of Jesus and Mary in an attempt to invite readers into transgressing against oppressive normativity that seeks to compartmentalize and minimize our sexuality.[46]

Although queer theology is growing in popularity within Christianity, it remains significantly underdeveloped in the Catholic tradition. To explore a contemporary queer Catholic theologian, I briefly return to the work of Craig A. Ford Jr., who retrieves a natural law framework to argue that part of our nature as humans is to explore and construct our identity. Ford rejects the idea that any study of human nature yields a comprehensive set of norms that can be categorically applied to all persons. There is no "one size fits all" discernible through an examination of the natural law. Recall his argument: "if any [human] identity is presumed, it is only that of a seeker. The rest I leave to our personal experiences of conscience, of community, and of the various ways in which we investigate the phenomenon of human life, scientifically, philosophically, or otherwise: what sort of beings are we? What are we like?"[47] Human nature, according to Ford, contains an inherent potential for queerness. Such queerness, especially when intersected with a politically racially oppressed epistemology (i.e., brownness or blackness), can yield a unique important worldview that can aid the Church's journey toward the Kingdom of God on Earth and in heaven. In the words of Craig Ford, "queer persons of color, precisely because of the political and economic disenfranchisement we have endured under white supremacy's many incarnations, possess privileged access to the Reign of God as referenced in the simple yet profound words of Jesus, 'Blessed are you who are poor, for yours is the Kingdom of God' (Luke 6:21)."[48]

A synodal Church that listens to LGBTQ+ people should not simply focus on listening as a superficial act of mere welcome but should rather listen with an openness to being transformed by the queer epistemology of LGBTQ+ persons. Synodality seeks the *sensus fidelium* wherever it can be found and is open to trusting the revelation of the spirit through LGBTQ+ Catholics. Considering that injustice often manifests through oppressive norms that exclude and *otherize*, a queer worldview that challenges oppressive norms, sexual or otherwise, inside and outside of the Church, is crucial for building a genuinely welcoming Church and a just society that reflect the Kingdom of God. Under this vision, LGBTQ+ people—through their transgressive lived experience that yields a queer epistemology—become active participants in the life of the Church and can aid in the formulation of theological insights and doctrine through the process of synodality.

Considering the first implication of welcoming LGBTQ+ persons and the second implication of adopting a queer epistemology, I argue that queerness is an essential component of synodality because it transcends rigid norms that prevent the Church from moving forward. As I have argued in previous work,

> Queerness presents a solution to an ecclesiological problem we encounter too often in our Church. While many in our Church have brought forth significant structural reforms and key developments, these advances are often thwarted or

delayed by Church leaders who cling to outdated ways of thinking. The phrase "old wine in new wineskins" captures this trend.[49]

Because queer theology is a transgressive project, and because synodality seeks to venture into the unknown as the Church journeys together under the guidance of the Holy Spirit, I contend that a Church that is unwilling to transgress against norms is ineffective at being synodal.

Synodality is challenging because it presupposes an openness to the God of surprises and to an epiphany of the Spirit. However, such an epiphany is impossible if one fiercely clings to a particular way of thinking, or a particular set of norms, and is unwilling to question or challenge the supposed "knowledge" that sustains them. This is perhaps why so many bishops in the United States, for example, are resistant to synodality: they are ok with welcoming and listening to the faithful, but they are unwilling to challenge some of the preestablished norms and knowledge that undergird their theology and/or their understanding of the Church. This prevents them from fully embracing the synodal way. As I previously stated,

> Queer theology functions in [the] realm of normative discourse (defined by Foucault as a powerful use of language to produce "knowledge" that generates particular norms). Queer theologizing is not limited to structural reforms, but rather seeks to examine and challenge the operating principles that lie underneath our efforts and the "so called" knowledge that sustains them.[50]

Genuine synodality, therefore, needs a queer theological viewpoint that questions our previously held "knowledge" of what God wants. It entails being willing to walk into uncertainty in search of the Spirit's guidance and revelation. In other words, synodality as a queer project is an epiphanic encounter with the God of surprises.[51]

Such willingness to live in uncertainty applies to both the global and local context of the Church. The Church's hierarchy, at the global level, needs to learn to be uncomfortable with doubt, apply probabilism to peripheral moral decisions as it permits a degree of theological pluralism *ad intra*, and collegially engage with the faithful in a process of communal discernment as it articulates doctrines. But more importantly, this synodal attitude needs to trickle down to local Church contexts whereby communal discernment in the face of uncertainty permeates the culture of Catholic institutions, including Catholic schools. As such, synodal Catholic institutions become microcosms of the global synodal Church.

TOWARD A SYNODAL VISION FOR CATHOLIC EDUCATION

Synodality and the Catholic School Identity

As discussed in chapter 2, Catholic schools exist to promote the spiritual development of their students and to prepare them to meaningfully engage our world. To foster spiritual development, a central component of the school's mission involves transmitting the Catholic tradition to the students so they can grow in holiness and faith as they develop a relationship with God. Regarding engagement with the world, schools strive to teach students about community and justice. I argue that this twofold purpose needs to be carried out in the spirit of synodality. Because Catholic schools function as a significant point of contact between the institutional Church (represented through the school leaders, clergy, and employees) and the lay faithful (i.e., the students and families), they should reflect the global Church's macro-ecclesiological polity at a local micro-ecclesiological polity level. Thus, synodality and probabilism have significant implications on how Catholic schools live out their mission toward the spiritual and sociocultural development of their students.

There are many approaches to how schools may transmit the Catholic faith to the students. Traditional approaches often center around inculcation through memorization and comprehension. These approaches attempt to gauge students' knowledge and understanding of the doctrines of the Catholic magisterium and assess expressions of faith or religiosity through ritual and symbolic practices such as sacraments, prayer services, retreat testimonies, and service projects. An example of this model is seen in Morey and Piderit's distinguishability approach to Catholic education, which I discussed in chapter 1. While well intended, I consider such approaches to be misguided. Simply checking off knowledge of doctrine, rituals, and symbols as we see them performed in the school, students' lives and the lives of the employees is an insufficient indication of its Catholic identity. The transmission of the Catholic tradition cannot be measured with a checklist. Instead, I retrieved the philosophy of Thomas Groome and infused it with a theology of synodality to propose a new model for the transmission of the Catholic tradition to the students.

Thomas Groome's philosophy of Catholic education, which I discussed in chapter 2 and am now reviewing, retrieves central components of the Catholic tradition and reconfigures them,[52] not as checklist items to be crossed off, but as a set of virtues that should be habitually practiced by Catholic schools in their day to day lives.[53] Therefore, the Catholic identity of a school is not about the *content* of the school's polity, but rather their *character* or *process*.

Furthermore, it lives out to its namesake of "catholic" by being universally welcoming to diverse opinions. The main question for a synodal Church is not "Is the school teaching Catholic doctrine effectively, practicing the sacraments periodically, and displaying Catholic symbols prominently?" This represents an attempt to distinguish the Catholic school from secular culture. Instead, the questions we should be asking are: "How is the school guiding diverse students to meaningfully engage with doctrine, sacraments, and Catholic imagery? How is the life of the school reflective of Catholic principles and the diversity (including theological diversity) present within? How is the school's participation in and with the broader society reflective of Catholicism?" These questions incorporate the students' cultural and historical context as they interact with the faith. This philosophy rejects parochialism and sectarianism and places trust in the "wisdom" present through the lives of the students, who Groome considers to be "subject-agents" of knowledge and as participants in the story (past) and vision (future) of the Christian tradition.[54]

Building upon this foundation, I argue that a synodal Catholic school understands its Catholicity as expansive and not as exclusive. A synodal school abandons dualistic perspectives that seek to separate what is "Catholic" from what is "secular" and, instead, understands that God's grace is found all around us and that diversity of thought (including theological thought) represents an opportunity for deeper and more expansive understanding of the Catholic faith.[55] The transmission of the Catholic tradition in a synodal Church involves engaging the student, the entire student,[56] in conversation with the tradition. All should feel welcome to the dialogue. In the words of Bradford Hinze,

> We must be willing to create dialogical processes that promote open, courageous honesty at all levels of church.... Such dialogical processes are essential if we are to name and diagnose the challenges that we are facing in the church, and this requires hospitably inviting and welcoming active participation of the baptized faithful however shaken and unsure they are in their faith. At the same time, I think we must be very clear that even with such a capacious vision of synodality there will inevitably be a diversity of pathways.[57]

The transmission of the Catholic tradition must consider the freedom of the students to pursue these diverse pathways.[58] Students are not "robots," and the Catholic tradition is not "code" to be downloaded onto their brains. Because students have consciences, especially high school students, any engagement with the Catholic tradition should make room for discernment about how it applies to their lives. In my experience as an educator, when teenagers feel manipulated, they are more likely to rebel. But when they are given leadership and when they are encouraged to take active agency (i.e., when they are acknowledged as subject-agents as Groome proposes), they step up to the plate and engage in genuine discernment and what Richard Gaillardetz calls "spiritual wrestling."

For Gaillardetz, the heart of the spiritual journey does not lie in strict obedience to dogma, but rather in the process of wrestling with the dogma. Groome agrees and adds a relational component to this vision, stating, "the defining content of Christian religious education is neither creed nor dogma, Scripture nor Tradition, important as these are, but a person—the person of Jesus."[59] I observe that this relationship with Christ takes place directly with Him, but also through the relationship with each other and with the institutional Church (including its doctrines). Therefore, spiritual relational wrestling is a form of communal discernment that preserves relationships with each other and with the Church as members of the Mystical Body of Christ Jesus. More importantly, spiritual relational wrestling preserves the agency of Catholic school students as subject-agents with the competence to determine how the Spirit is calling them to live their lives.

Because spiritual relational wrestling takes into consideration the sanctity of the Church as a key component of the relationship, I argue that spiritual relational wrestling in a Catholic school should bestow upon Catholic doctrine the initial benefit of the doubt as a product of the wisdom of the bishops preserved through the Apostolic Succession.[60] However, I also argue that spiritual relational wrestling also utilizes any tool (secular or not) that allows students to better understand the truth of our faith. In cases where there is a conscientious disagreement with the doctrine through spiritual relational wrestling, after giving the doctrine as much benefit of the doubt as possible, I maintain that a Catholic student can reasonably follow a probabilistic opinion even if it disagrees with the doctrine. For example, in my experience teaching Catholic theology of human sexuality to high school students, I have noticed that they often employ insights from the social sciences to argue that the Church's position on homosexuality and gender identity needs to develop. Pedagogically, I allow this discussion to take place and then ask the students what their individual role is, and what the role of our school community is, in communicating these unaddressed insights from the social sciences to Catholic leaders. This encourages wrestling with the tradition and a relational model whereby students take active leadership in their faith. Despite their disagreement, I consider their engagement as a victory for the Catholic identity of the school, and I consider the inevitable disagreements on any matter of Church life throughout this process of spiritual relational wrestling to be a crucial part of transmitting the Catholic tradition.

A synodal Catholic school that transmits the Catholic tradition through spiritual relational wrestling must learn to live with uncertainty and with uncomfortableness, which is brought about by the inherent diversity already present in the student body and the broader Church. Synodal schools should not be concerned with sanitizing the schools from the so-called evils of secular culture because that is impossible and problematic. Preventing scandal is impossible because students always have access to diverse theological opinions and can never be fully protected from temptation. It is also problematic because this sanitizing through separation may disregard God's revelation present through the *sensus fidelium* of those who disagree with a particular tenet of Catholic doctrine that needs to develop. Furthermore, synodal schools should abandon the futile quest toward certainty by clinging to narrow applications of Church doctrine. They should lean into the uncomfortableness of doubt and disagreement, guided by the wisdom of the educators, and should model for the students how one can interact with differences in the process of developing a sense of self in our pluralistic society. Most importantly, a synodal school should celebrate diversity and disagreement through spiritual relational wrestling as a potential epiphanic source of revelation along an uncertain spiritual journey.

A free and empowered communal discernment (i.e., relational spiritual wrestling) in synodal Catholic schools, which should be open to reasonable diversity of opinion, will foster long-lasting relationships between students and the tradition, guided by teacher role models, that will ultimately aid the students' incorporation of the Catholic faith into their lives. I believe that it will also improve the relationship between young people and the hierarchical Church as it reflects the active participation envisioned during the Second Vatican Council. Synodality in Catholic schools is the necessary next step in Catholic education and the broader Church which, as we recall, faces increasing disaffiliation from youth.

Finally, synodal Catholic schools exercise an internal and external role. Internally, as discussed, they care for the well-being of all members and serve to foster a relationship with God through each other along the process of spiritual relational wrestling. Externally, they seek to build the Kingdom of God, as revealed by Jesus, on earth by advocating for social justice. Because Catholic schools exercise significant social capital and can influence social policy directly (through active participation in the public square) and indirectly (by forming students who will eventually grow to participate in the public square), I argue that they must ensure their daily operations reflect principles of justice and Catholic social teaching. I will discuss the external, justice-based role of Catholic education in the next chapter.

The Synodal Calling of the Catholic School Educator

Catholic school administrators and educators play a crucial role in implementing a synodal model of Catholic education. Possessing a theological understanding of ecclesial synodality is crucial for its implementation in schools. For this reason, Catholic school administrators must remain informed and continue to reflect on how the historical and contemporary Catholic tradition shapes the Catholic identity of the school. Clear articulation of the synodal nature of Catholic education to employees, students, families, donors, and other stakeholders, will aid its implementation as well. In some cases, school administrators might also need to engage in discussions about synodality with their local bishop, who might be resistant to this model as evidenced in the many firings of LGBTQ+ educators.

In the classroom and ministry space, Catholic school educators, particularly religion teachers and campus ministers but also all teachers, should receive adequate formation on matters of vocation, synodal dialogue amidst diversity, and the appropriate pedagogical tools to implement this dialogue. Catholic teaching, I argue, should always be taught accurately and with genuine respect for the authority of the Church. But, regardless of where educators or ministers stand in their own spiritual and vocational journey in relation to particular doctrines, they should take great care not to inculcate or manipulate students into either blindly following a doctrine or rejecting a doctrine without the process of discernment. Instead, they should create a space and a process in the classroom or ministry space where spiritual relational wrestling can occur. Reflecting on the role of lay ecclesial ministers (which may include Catholic school educators), Regina Bechtle observes,

> In a world where divisiveness grows ever more toxic and civility is in short supply in both political and ecclesial discourse, a "both and" spirituality that integrates love of God and love of neighbor, that seeks to create coalitions and build bridges, will surely better serve today's lay ecclesial minister than a mindset wedded to rigid dichotomies and dualistic thinking.[61]

A synodal mentality that seeks God's revelation wherever it can be found will help heal some of the rifts and polarization present in our society and in our Church.

Pedagogically, I argue that a synodal model of Catholic education complements some of the seminal work of scholars such as Paulo Freire, bell hooks, and Parker Palmer. Freire proposes a liberatory pedagogy whereby students become aware of the oppression they face and acquire the tools to dismantle it.[62] Similarly, hooks proposes an engaged transgressive pedagogy whereby students challenge normative powers that promote oppression.[63] And Palmer's subject-centered pedagogy calls both teachers and students to engage in the process of learning as a community of explorers.[64] Key to these pedagogies is an emphasis on the uncomfortable processes of self-understanding and understanding others. For example, bell hooks discusses classrooms not so much as "safe spaces" but as spaces where people need to be courageous and take risks. In other words, classrooms are places where uncomfortable wrestling takes place. Crucially, these pedagogies emphasize diversity, equity, and inclusion in education. Liberatory, transgressive, and subject-based pedagogy seeks to bring all students to an equitable playing field. For this reason, I observe that Catholic school educators who seek to engage all students in synodal dialogue must first strive to create an equitable school environment where all students have a voice and the agency to wrestle with various aspects of the Catholic tradition spiritually and in the context of community.

On matters of instruction about human sexuality, Catholic school educators should model how to live with the uncomfortableness of the unknown. Despite the significant advances in theological, social science, and biological scholarship as well as the increased prominence of diverse sexual expressions and identities in our culture, our sexual identities remain a mystery. All authoritative sources of knowledge, informed by lived experiences, paint an incomplete picture of human sexuality. Educators must acknowledge this uncertainty, model prayer and discernment, and encourage open dialogue as the learning community grows in its understanding of these human mysteries. Most importantly, teachers must pay special attention to students who are sexually oppressed, including LGBTQ+ students, to ensure their wisdom as subject-agents forms an integral part of the synodal process.

Synodal Catholic Schools and the Local Bishop

Per canon law, bishops serve as stewards and guides of Catholic education in their dioceses.[65] Despite the opposition of some US bishops to Pope Francis's efforts to promote synodality,[66] I remain hopeful that my synodal model for Catholic Education will permeate the US Church and eventually transform its Catholic schools. Since bishops do not operate in a democratic structure and possess absolute institutional authority over many components of their dioceses, such a change might take time because it depends on the goodwill of bishops to reconceive their understanding of power to include the competence of the laity. This may be cause for pessimism. However, I am often accused of being a foolish optimist because I choose to trust in the Holy Spirit's ability to "remove their hearts of stone" (Ezek. 36:26) by inspiring the bishops to seek out the *sensus fidelium* revealed through the lives of the laity, including Catholic school students. I believe this is their responsibility as ordained leaders of the Church, and I agree with Bradford Hinze, who states,

One of the central requirements [for synodality] would be that all Catholics, perhaps especially bishops and clergy, would honour the efforts of each church member who strives to discern the sense of the faith in their own personal life, and that such ordained leaders would likewise respect the collective discernment of the sense of the faithful taking place in communities of faith, ecclesial movements, and base communities.[67]

Furthermore, I argue that, once bishops are onboard with synodality, they should seek to establish consultation structures that allow them to connect with the *sensus fidelium* in Catholic schools. Over time, as teachers and administrators adequately implement synodality in the schools, they will develop a sense of how the school community is responding to the movements of the Spirit on various matters. This *sensus fidelium* of the school community must be conferred to the bishops through the structures of active consultation (which would hopefully include bishops visiting schools and dialoguing with the youth entrusted to their care). Through these structures of active consultation, bishops would be informed by the insights of the *sensus fidelium*, which would aid their discussion on matters of doctrine and development with their colleagues in the USCCB and the Vatican. In other words, through a connection with the *sensus fidelium*, synodality in Catholic education bestows upon bishops a greater competence on matters of faith and morals and, with it, greater credibility to proclaim doctrine and to administer their diocese.

SYNODAL CATHOLIC SCHOOLS AND LGBTQ+ EDUCATORS

The presence of LGBTQ+ educators provides an optimal opportunity to promote synodal dialogue. As discussed in chapter 2, these educators (including religion teachers and campus ministers) often serve as role models of the Catholic tradition, of Catholic community, and of social justice. While their life witness runs contrary to articulated magisterial doctrine, this dissent, which is peripheral when compared to the dissent from more central components of the Catholic tradition that is often tolerated by Catholic school leaders (e.g., when they hire a non-Christian educator), can catalyze some spiritual relational wrestling on matters of sexuality and can bring fellow Catholics into deeper dialogue with the tradition.

In 2024, my colleague Mark Guevarra and I published an anthology of stories of LGBTQ+ employees in Catholic schools and parishes. As we collected stories, we were struck by the power of the queer epistemologies (some of which intersected with racial diversity) these employees brought to their

Synodality in Catholic Schools 115

institutions. The stories were divided into three categories: LGBTQ+ educators who were fired, LGBTQ+ parish ministers who were fired, and LGBTQ+ educators and parish ministers who were retained. Regardless of their fate, all employees witnessed significant moments of grace despite oppression. These stories represent the incredible power of queerness and they contain a lesson for all Catholic institutions and the global Church. To offer some examples of fired LGBTQ+ employees and their stories, I will briefly recount some of the anecdotes.

Sandra, a fired lesbian Church music minister recounted how she continued to return to the Church and the priest that hurt her seeking further dialogue and challenging the oppressive norms that led to her termination. Miguel, a music minister who was fired from a Church in Texas observed how his marriage to his husband remained an example of a powerful grace-filled queer love that grows despite challenges from the institutional Church, much like Jesus's love that conquers death. Margi, a fired religious studies lesbian teacher in Philadelphia remarked that, after her termination, she experienced profound trauma that eventually led her to connect with her own faith more deeply; thus, witnessing the power of vocation despite oppression. Kristen was a lesbian Campus Minister who felt guided by the Holy Spirit to come out to the school's faculty and staff as she facilitated a workshop about bringing one's whole self into the classroom. She was fired for that. Terry, a parish music minister who was fired for marrying a woman, discusses her experience as a messy experience of grace. Overall, it is remarkable how, despite the pain of termination, suffering, and oppression, these LGBTQ+ employees are still able to draw from the power of their queerness to nonetheless connect with God.[68]

Among the stories we collected were stories of educators and ministers who were retained and celebrated by their institutions. For example, Alicia, a queer librarian who was born and raised in Hawaii and remained employed at a school in San Francisco, explained how her coming out to some students challenged the youth to reposition how they interact with those who are LGBTQ+ and articulate that inclusive position. Furthermore, her queerness has allowed her to integrate a traditional Catholic faith with a Hawaiian spirituality that is expansive and allows her to see the divine in the unconventional. Breanna, a Black trans singer hired at Most Holy Redeemer parish in San Francisco celebrated how her singing during mass created an atmosphere of welcome and visibility for other trans Catholics. She also explained how her medical transition moved the local Church to compassion for the plight of trans persons. Gabriel, a Jewish trans English teacher in San Francisco, was also retained and became a visible presence of queerness in the school. He rejoices in his singing voice, which he also uses to offer praise to God's wonders. Michelangelo is a gay teacher who was suspiciously fired from one

Catholic school and then found a new job in another Catholic school where he is an out and proud theology teacher. He continues to provide a perspective of inclusion for his school community and publicly blogs on the New Ways Ministry (Catholic LGBTQ+ organization) website with the support of his administration. All of these retained LGBTQ+ ministerial employees are not only thriving in terms of their personal lives but are also sharing invaluable Spirit-filled insights with their communities.[69]

All of these perspectives, whether explicitly articulated or not, represent a particular transgressive vantage point that aids their local communities in understanding God and the mission of the Catholic community. Specific to Catholic schools, queer educators have a way of detecting underlying operating oppressive norms that adversely affect students and colleagues. They also exhibit a heightened sense of empathy and solidarity for students and colleagues who are sexually oppressed. These educators model for the school community how one can disagree with Catholic teaching yet still commit to the mission of the Church. This is true even after some are fired: some of them continue to approach the Church and call it to greater love. As I stated in chapter 2, these educators are crucial models for students who are apathetic about the Church. Because of their ability to hold the tension between their identity and the Church's doctrines, their queer epistemology transgresses against dualistic binary perspectives that dichotomize Catholicism and LGBTQ+ identity. They show the community how one can commit to a community yet challenge that community to be better. The queer epistemology of LGBTQ+ educators wields discursive power that creates a new reality, a new way of being, in the Catholic school. By their very presence, they gradually transform the hetero and cisnormative spaces they occupy.

Change is uncomfortable. Engaging with the God of surprises, via the epiphany of the Spirit, requires an abandonment of a sense of safety. Catholic school leaders are called to wade into the waters of uncertainty and trust the movement of the Spirit through the lives of LGBTQ+ employees. By doing so, I believe they will be personally transformed for the better. Furthermore, I believe that the school will be transformed into a community that wrestles with their faith together, truly reflects the Mystical Body of Christ, and is better equipped to help build God's Kingdom on Earth.

Finally, authenticity plays a role in how these educators can effect some change. For this reason, Catholic school leaders (including bishops) must seek to provide safety for LGTBQ+ educators to live authentic lives and the structures to translate their creative transgressive queerness into meaningful communal transformation. Active consultation is the first part of this process, but more importantly, taking seriously the *sensus fidelium* of LGBTQ+ educators will aid a synodal school to better walk along God's path with the guidance of the Holy Spirit. Catholic school leaders must allow themselves to be guided by the wisdom of LGBTQ+ educators. Furthermore, they should allow this wisdom to inform the life of the school and eventually help transform the broader global Church. Because of the wisdom of the Spirit-led queer epistemology of LGBTQ+ educators, I believe that students, educators, and families need them in Catholic schools. Catholic leaders, at least, should stop dismissing them based on their queerness. At best, however, they should cherish their presence and celebrate the transformative gifts they offer Catholic education and the broader Church.

CONCLUSION

In this chapter, I constructed a synodal model of Catholic education based on contemporary theology of synodality. I argued that this synodal model would better aid Catholic schools in understanding God's revelation and how they are called to walk together as a community. Synodality in Catholic schools also operates as a bridge connecting the global Church, guided by bishops and the pope, with the local Church, materialized in the Catholic school. Since Catholic schools are a significant point of contact between the faithful and the hierarchy, structures of synodal consultation with the sense of the faithful of the Catholic schools would surely illuminate bishops and help them lead the Church with credibility and relevance.

Synodality in Catholic education goes beyond access or welcome. Rather, it seeks to incorporate (bring into the body—i.e., the Body of Christ) the queer perspectives LGBTQ+ educators bring to the community. Therefore, Catholic schools should strive to go beyond welcoming LGBTQ+ educators (and students and families) and allow themselves to be transformed by the wisdom of queer epistemologies. Theologically, this queer epistemology reflects the guidance of the Holy Spirit through the *sensus fidelium* of LGBTQ+ persons. Catholic leaders should retain and celebrate LGBTQ+ educators as possessors of a unique indispensable perspective that can aid Catholic schools and the broader Church to better reflect the fullness of the Body of Christ.

Finally, to LGBTQ+ Catholic school educators: Be yourselves! While I recognize that it is difficult in some schools and dioceses, the goal is ultimately for us to live an authentic life as integrated educators who embody the fullness of sexual, vocational, and spiritual identity. I believe God calls us to take up as much space as we can (after factoring in our safety and stability) and challenge some of the oppressive norms that undergird many Catholic institutions. While not all LGBTQ+ teachers can be public about their sexual identity, we can still find small ways to be true to ourselves to the extent that we feel appropriate. Ultimately, this quest toward authenticity (however that looks for each individual) will bring about personal fulfillment and will aid the school community as a whole on its journey toward inclusion. While the initial onus falls on Catholic leaders to facilitate a process whereby LGBTQ+ educators can exercise their vocation as their true selves, it also falls upon us to walk out through the closet door and share our gifts with the Catholic school community.

NOTES

1. Ish Ruiz, "Synodality in the Catholic Church: Toward a Conciliar Ecclesiology of Inclusion for LGBTQ+ Persons," *Journal of Moral Theology* 12, no. 2 (July 18, 2023): 55–77, https://doi.org/10.55476/001c.84391.

2. Emile Kouveglo, "La Sinodalidad En La Actualidad, a La Luz Del Concilio Vaticano II," *Revista de Investigación de La Cátedra Internacional Conjunta Inocencio III* 1, no. 7 (October 30, 2018): 280–81, 293, https://vergentis.ucam.edu/index.php/vergentis/article/view/93; Massimo Faggioli, "From Collegiality to Synodality: Promise and Limits of Francis's 'Listening Primacy,'" *Irish Theological Quarterly* 85, no. 4 (November 1, 2020): 6, https://doi.org/10.1177/0021140020916034.

3. Pius X, "Vehementer Nos," Vatican Website, February 11, 1906, no. 8, https://www.vatican.va/content/pius-x/en/encyclicals/documents/hf_p-x_enc_11021906_vehementer-nos.html.

4. Second Vatican Council, "Sacrosanctum Concilium," Vatican Website, December 4, 1963, no. 14, https://www.vatican.va/archive/hist_councils/ii_vatican_council/documents/vat-ii_const_19631204_sacrosanctum-concilium_en.html.

5. Second Vatican Council, "Lumen Gentium," November 21, 1964, nos. 9–18, https://www.vatican.va/archive/hist_councils/ii_vatican_council/documents/vat-ii_const_19641121_lumen-gentium_en.html.

6. Second Vatican Council, "Gaudium et Spes," Vatican Website, October 7, 1965, no. 12, https://www.vatican.va/archive/hist_councils/ii_vatican_council/documents/vat-ii_const_19651207_gaudium-et-spes_en.html.

7. Second Vatican Council, "Dei Verbum," Vatican Website, November 18, 1965, no. 8, https://www.vatican.va/archive/hist_councils/ii_vatican_council/documents/vat-ii_const_19651118_dei-verbum_en.html.

8. Ormond Rush, *Still Interpreting Vatican II: Some Hermeneutical Principles* (Paulist Press, 2004), 82–83.

9. Second Vatican Council, "Lumen Gentium," no. 12.

10. Richard R. Gaillardetz, *The Church in the Making: Lumen Gentium, Christus Dominus, Orientalium Ecclesiarum* (Paulist Press, 2006), 49; International Theological Comission, "Synodality in the Life and Mission of the Church," Vatican Website, March 2, 2018, no. 2, https://www.vatican.va/roman_curia/congregations/cfaith/cti_documents/rc_cti_20180302_sinodalita_en.html; Ormond Rush, "The Church as a Hermeneutical Community and the Eschatological Function of the Sensus Fidelium," in *Learning from All the Faithful: A Contemporary Theology of the Sensus Fidei*, ed. Bradford E. Hinze and Peter C. Phan (Pickwick Publications, 2016), 145–46.

11. Gaillardetz, *The Church in the Making*, 49.
12. Gaillardetz, *The Church in the Making*, 53.
13. Second Vatican Council, "Dei Verbum," no. 10.
14. This is evidenced in the repeated firings of LGBTQ+ educators as well as the silencing of theological dissenting voices as discussed in chapter 3.
15. Second Vatican Council, "Dei Verbum," no.10.
16. John W. O'Malley, *What Happened at Vatican II* (Belknap Press, 2010), 178.
17. Francis, "Evangelii Gaudium," Vatican Website, November 24, 2013, no. 119, https://www.vatican.va/content/francesco/en/apost_exhortations/documents/papa-francesco_esortazione-ap_20131124_evangelii-gaudium.html.
18. Francis, "General Audience," Vatican Website, June 26, 2013, https://www.vatican.va/content/francesco/en/audiences/2013/documents/papa-francesco_20130626_udienza-generale.html.
19. Francis, "Address of His Holiness Pope Francis during the Meeting on the Family," Vatican Website, October 4, 2014, https://www.vatican.va/content/francesco/en/speeches/2014/october/documents/papa-francesco_20141004_incontro-per-la-famiglia.html.
20. The synod of bishops operates as a smaller less authoritative version of a council. Synod meetings are convened by the pope to discuss a particular topic and advice the pope on how to proceed on particular pressing matters. Pope Paul VI first instituted the Synod of Bishops to aid the implementation of Vatican II. See "The Synod of Bishops: An Introduction," Vatican Website, accessed November 19, 2023, https://www.vatican.va/roman_curia/synod/documents/rc_synod_01011995_profile_en.html#.
21. Francis, "Address of His Holiness Pope Francis at the Ceremony Commemorating the 50th Anniversary of the Institution of the Synod of Bishops," Vatican Website, October 17, 2015, https://www.vatican.va/content/francesco/en/speeches/2015/october/documents/papa-francesco_20151017_50-anniversario-sinodo.html.
22. Francis, "Address of His Holiness Pope Francis."
23. Francis, "Letter of the Holy Father to Card. Marc Ouellet, President of the Pontifical Commission for Latin America," March 19, 2016, https://www.vatican.va/content/francesco/en/letters/2016/documents/papa-francesco_20160319_pont-comm-america-latina.html.
24. "Through synodality, the Church reveals and configures herself as the pilgrim People of God and as the assembly convoked by the risen lord." See International Theological Commission, "Synodality in the Life and Mission of the Church," Vatican Website, March 2, 2018, no. 42, https://www.vatican.va/roman_curia/congregations/cfaith/cti_documents/rc_cti_20180302_sinodalita_en.html.
25. "Synodality in the Life and Mission of the Church," no. 58.
26. "Synodality in the Life and Mission of the Church," no. 64.
27. According to the ITC, "A synodal Church is a Church of participation and co-responsibility." See "Synodality in the Life and Mission of the Church," no. 67.
28. "Synodality in the Life and Mission of the Church," no. 77.
29. "Synodality in the Life and Mission of the Church," no. 100.
30. Faggioli, "From Collegiality to Synodality," no. 15.

31. Pneumatology refers to the theological study of the third person in the Trinity, the Holy Spirit.

32. Amanda C. Osheim, "Stepping toward a Synodal Church," *Theological Studies* 80, no. 2 (June 1, 2019): 371–72, https://doi.org/10.1177/0040563919836225.

33. Bradford Hinze, "Can We Find a Way Together? The Challenge of Synodality in a Wounded and Wounding Church," *Irish Theological Quarterly* 85, no. 3 (August 1, 2020): 228, https://doi.org/10.1177/0021140020926595.

34. Grzegorz Strzelczyk, "Synodality: An Epiphany of the Spirit," *Studia Teologii Dogmatycznej* 5 (March 28, 2020): 143, https://doi.org/10.15290/std.2019.05.12.

35. Hinze, "Can We Find a Way Together?," 215–16.

36. Strzelczyk, "Synodality," 141.

37. Francis, "The God of Surprises: Morning Meditation in the Chape; of the Domus Sanctae Marthae," Vatican Website, October 13, 2014, https://www.vatican.va/content/francesco/en/cotidie/2014/documents/papa-francesco-cotidie_20141013_the-god-of-surprises.html.

38. Rush, "The Church as a Hermeneutical Community and the Eschatological Function of the Sensus Fidelium."

39. Francis, "Making Room for Voices of Peace," *L'Osservatore Romano*, September 1, 2023, https://www.osservatoreromano.va/en/news/2023-09/ing-035/making-room-for-voices-of-peace.html. Emphasis in original.

40. Ruiz, "Synodality in the Catholic Church."

41. For two examples, see Salvatore Cordileone and Michael Barber, "The Body-Soul Unity of the Human Person," Archdiocese of San Francisco, September 29, 2023, https://sfarchdiocese.org/the-body-soul-unity-of-the-human-person/?fbclid=IwAR0nEaUfM87eif-Q8KV14ELb3kOh2x_nOtOak_wB7Gg3TIccZKzCiqyJATE; Chaput Charles, "Father James Martin and Catholic Belief," Catholic Philly, September 19, 2019, https://catholicphilly.com/2019/09/archbishop-chaput-column/father-james-martin-and-catholic-belief/.

42. Perhaps these people identify as gay or as trans, for example, but would seek to live lives as close to heterosexual and cisgender lifestyles as possible. San Francisco gay activist Cleve Jones famously brings up this question several times in his memoir, "Are gay people the same as straight people except for what we do in the bedroom? Or are we different in other ways?" See Cleve Jones, *When We Rise: My Life in the Movement* (Hachette Books, 2016).

43. Queer theology, as an emerging field, is defined in many ways and theologians often disagree on the definition and scope of the field. Some theologians would disagree with the way I engage in the field.

44. The concept of the Queer God is beyond the scope of this project but has been developed by other queer theologians before. See Marcella Althaus-Reid, *The Queer God* (Routledge, 2003); Patrick S. Cheng, *Radical Love: Introduction to Queer Theology* (Seabury Books, 2011); Miguel H. Díaz, *Queer God de Amor* (Fordham University Press, 2022).

45. Roberto Che Espinoza, who offers an intersectional theological analysis of queer and Latinx identity, describes queerness as an ontological, epistemological, and ethical reality. Ontologically, he believes human nature is inherently queer because

we often seek to *create* outside of "the box." Epistemologically, Espinoza argues that we are capable of recognizing and challenging underlying cultural norms. Ethically, he argues we have a responsibility as queer persons to transgress against them. See Robyn Henderson-Espinoza, "Queer Theory and Latina/o Theologizing," in *The Wiley Blackwell Companion to Latino/a Theology*, ed. Orlando O. Espin (Wiley Blackwell, 2015), 329–46. [Note: This author is a trans person who published this article prior to transitioning, hence the use of his "dead name" on the citation.]

46. Marcella Althaus-Reid, *Indecent Theology: Theological Perversions in Sex, Gender and Politics* (Routledge, 2000).

47. Craig A. Ford Jr., "Transgender Bodies, Catholic Schools, and a Queer Natural Law Theology of Exploration," *Journal of Moral Theology* 7, no. 1 (January 1, 2018): 97–98, https://jmt.scholasticahq.com/article/11382-transgender-bodies-catholic-schools-and-a-queer-natural-law-theology-of-exploration.

48. Craig A. Ford Jr., "Black Queer Natural Law: On Brownness and Disidentification," Political Theology Network, November 11, 2022, https://politicaltheology.com/black-queer-natural-law-on-brownness-and-disidentification/.

49. Ish Ruiz, "Queering Synodality," *Go, Rebuild My House* (blog), July 14, 2023, https://sacredheartuniversity.typepad.com/go_rebuild_my_house/2023/07/queering-synodality-.html.

50. Ruiz, "Queering Synodality."

51. For my detailed argument about the connection between queerness and synodality, see Ish Ruiz, "Queer Theology and a Synodal Catholic Church," *Feminist Theology*, April 18, 2024, https://doi.org/10.1177/09667350241233585.

52. Thomas Groome, *Educating for Life: A Spiritual Vision for Every Teacher and Parent* (Herder & Herder, 2001), 59–60.

53. By utilizing the concept of "virtue," I am retrieving a classical (Aristotelian) Catholic (Thomistic) understanding of virtues. According to this account, a virtue is a good habit that can be developed through practice. Humans are born with a capability for goodness, but that potential is gradually fulfilled through habituation. As persons practice these different good habits, they become virtuous. According to Aristotle and Aquinas, a life of virtue reflects a life of flourishing. In a secular sense, according to Aristotle, this flourishing is experienced as *eudaimonia*, or happiness. In a theological sense, according to Aquinas, flourishing is connected not only to happiness on earth, but also to salvation. For a comprehensive treatment of classical and theological virtue ethics, see *Aristotle, Aristotle's Nicomachean Ethics*, trans. Robert C. Bartlett and Susan D. Collins, Repr. ed. (University of Chicago Press, 2012); Thomas Aquinas, "Summa Theologiae," trans. Fathers of the English Dominican Province, New Advent, 2017, I–II, II–II, https://www.newadvent.org/summa/3064.htm.

54. Groome, *Educating for Life*, 289–90.

55. The concept of spiritual wrestling is discussed by Richard Gaillardetz in the *Jesuitical* podcast. See Jesuitical, "When Catholic Doctrine Can Change—and When It Can't," accessed November 11, 2023, https://www.americamagazine.org/faith/2023/10/25/jesuitical-richard-gaillardetz-doctrine-change-246368.

56. Various religious orders articulate this concept. For example, the Jesuits have an understanding of *curia personalis* that involves the care for the whole person,

the Vincentian Daughters of Charity speak of holistic education which does the same thing, and the Marianists articulate an integral education as a Characteristic of Marianist Education. See Andy Otto, "Cura Personalis," *Ignatian Spirituality* (blog), August 15, 2013, https://www.ignatianspirituality.com/cura-personalis/; Louise Sullivan, "The Core Values of Vincentian Education," *Vincentian Heritage Journal* 16, no. 2 (October 1, 1995), https://via.library.depaul.edu/vhj/vol16/iss2/3; "Marianist Characteristics," Marianist Website, accessed November 19, 2023, https://www.marianist.com/characteristics/.

57. Hinze, "Can We Find a Way Together?," 215–16.

58. Groome, *Educating for Life*, 289–90.

59. Groome, *Educating for Life*, 252.

60. Apostolic succession refers to the theological understanding of bishops as the direct descendants of the twelve apostles and, therefore, possessors of spiritual authority by virtue of their full ordination. See Second Vatican Council, "Christus Dominus," Vatican Website, October 28, 1965, no. 2, https://www.vatican.va/archive/hist_councils/ii_vatican_council/documents/vat-ii_decree_19651028_christus-dominus_en.html.

61. Regina Bechtle, "Spirit Guides and Table Companions: Saints as Models for Lay Ecclesial Ministers," in *Lay Ecclesial Ministry: Pathways toward the Future*, ed. Zeni Fox (Rowman & Littlefield, 2010), 128.

62. Paulo Freire, *Pedagogy of the Oppressed* (Penguin, 2017).

63. bell hooks, *Teaching to Transgress* (Routledge, 2014).

64. Parker J. Palmer, *The Courage to Teach: Exploring the Inner Landscape of a Teacher's Life*, 20th ed. (Jossey-Bass, 2017).

65. "Code of Canon Law," Vatican Website, nos. 800–806, accessed December 30, 2022, https://www.vatican.va/archive/cod-iuris-canonici/eng/documents/cic_lib3-cann793-821_en.html#CHAPTER_I.

66. Christopher White, "Pope Francis Blasts Reactionary American Catholics Who Oppose Church Reform," *National Catholic Reporter*, August 28, 2023, https://www.ncronline.org/vatican/vatican-news/pope-francis-blasts-reactionary-american-catholics-who-oppose-church-reform.

67. Hinze, "Can We Find a Way Together?," 228.

68. Ish Ruiz and Mark Guevara, eds., *Cornerstones: Sacred Stories of LGBTQ+ Employees in Catholic Institutions* (New Ways Ministry, 2024).

69. Ruiz and Guevara, *Cornerstones*.

Chapter 5

Catholic Social Teaching and Human Rights

Giving Catholic School LGBTQ+ Educators Their Due

In 2014, I was preparing to teach a course in Catholic Church History to tenth grade students in San Francisco. In an attempt to better understand what my students would need and hope to get from that class, I decided to conduct a preliminary survey of their relationship with the Catholic Church. The assignment asked students to quickly research some news headlines that represented their impression of the Church and their relationship with it. The vast majority of students highlighted issues of financial corruption, abuse of minors, and exclusion of LGBTQ+ persons and women; all of which adversely colored their experience of the Church. Dismayed by this response (since I hoped to find a "door" to discuss what a life-giving relationship with the institutional Church could look like), I prompted the students to dig deeper for some positive news sources. The students struggled to find a place to start but eventually produced some headlines about the Church speaking out in favor of immigrant rights, the abolition of the death penalty, and overall services to the poor. Interestingly, the students were also positively shocked to learn that Church doctrine, specifically Catholic social teaching, has sided with the plight of the oppressed in many of these cases. After learning this, several students expressed optimism for the future of the Church and their relationship with it with statements along the lines of: "If the Church truly stands for the rights of immigrants, that is a Church I would be interested in being a part of."

This activity, which I facilitated each of the eight years I was at that school, taught me two important things about our youth's relationship with the Church. First, and most importantly, their relationship with the Church often hinges on how they perceive Catholic institutions' participation in the public sphere. Present-day youth are suspicious of institutions in general, but they are particularly resistant, or at least apathetic, to institutions they perceive to be unjust or corrupt. Second, and perhaps more obvious, the Catholic Church in the United States has done a poor job of showcasing Catholic social teaching through word and deed to young people, further contributing to young Catholics' perception that the Church solely operates as an exclusive, unjust, and corrupt institution.[1] I suspect that the increasing focus on the abortion debate, which has overshadowed other components of Catholic social teaching, contributes to this apathy toward the Church in the United States.[2] For this reason, I invoke Catholic social teaching in this chapter to argue that Catholic schools should take great care to ensure their policies and practices uphold these social doctrines and model for students the doctrines of the Church that are aimed at building a just Kingdom of God on Earth. Unfortunately, the repeated firings of LGBTQ+ educators in Catholic schools present a challenge to this vision because such firings impress upon the youth an image of the Church as exclusive and solely concerned with policing sexual morality at the expense of social justice.

Catholic social teaching, broadly defined, refers to the social justice doctrines of the Church. This body of teachings can be interpreted through a threefold lens. The first part is relational and communal. Through this lens, Catholic social teaching is concerned with right relationships between persons. Here I invoke the traditional conception of *justice* as "giving others what is their due."[3] Therefore, Catholic social teaching is concerned with social structures that foster communities where all persons receive what they deserve or are entitled to. Distributive and commutative justice, which are concerned with the allocation of goods and the adequate reciprocity between entities respectively, are a part of this process.[4] The main goal of this lens is to protect the inherent dignity of all human persons as beings created in the *Imago Dei*, in the Image of God. The second part is *eudemonic*, which means that the Church is concerned with the *flourishing* of all persons.[5] Under this lens, Catholic social teaching seeks to promote the *common good*, which refers to a social vision whereby all members of the society participate in, contribute to, and benefit from the "goods" of our society and can become the best versions of themselves (i.e., *eudaimonia*). The third part is eschatological. Eschatology is the study of the end of the world. Under this lens, Catholic social teaching is at the service of God's Kingdom which is mysteriously both "at hand" in the present and also still to fully unfold in the future. The Kingdom of God is made manifest in our present society when right relationships and the common good are attained. For this reason, all persons are called to actively "build" this Kingdom here on Earth.

When we succeed at this, at any point in time, we experience a version of this Kingdom in that present moment. Conversely, the future-Kingdom refers to God's plan that slowly unfolds. The virtue of hope is associated with this as Catholics are called to place hope-filled trust in God's unfolding plan. The future-Kingdom of God refers to the perfection of society, but can also be interpreted as the Second Coming of Christ and the Kingdom of God in heaven, all of which point to a society where perfect justice reigns. Responding to Jesus's call to help bring about this Kingdom on Earth, the magisterium has outlined the Catholic social tradition through a set of key principles that apply to political, economic, and other societal structures.[6] Among these principles is a conception of human rights, which the magisterium eventually developed in the 1960s as a response to the global political climate of the time. Finally, I note that while there is both a moral law and a civil law component to some Catholic social teachings like religious liberty, this chapter focuses on the *moral* exercise of the key principles of Catholic social teaching regardless of the legal codification of a right or principle in American jurisprudence. While laws can hinder or help promote Catholic social teaching, I am not making civil law arguments in this chapter but will rather speak to the moral obligation of Catholic leaders and Catholic institutions to live up to the precepts of the Catholic social tradition despite what civil law allows. Catholic institutions have a moral responsibility in our society to not only meet basic legal requirements (presupposing that they are moral laws) but to surpass them and strive toward the common good, that is, toward the preservation of all human rights and the promotion of human flourishing for all. I also argue that they have the obligation to disregard or disobey civil laws that are unjust. This would help bring about the Kingdom of God on Earth.

In this chapter, I retrieve the Catholic social tradition to argue that the way US Catholic school leaders have deployed the moral right to religious liberty to bar LGBTQ+ educators from employment in Catholic schools (as discussed in chapter 1) represents a serious problematic violation of key principles of Catholic social teaching and an unjustified violation of the dignity of the LGBTQ+ employees. In other words, I argue that the firing of LGBTQ+ persons is unjust, detrimental to our communities, and antithetical to the Kingdom of God. After arguing that probabilism makes room for LGBTQ+ theological perspectives in the Church (see chapter 3) and that a synodal model of Catholic education would seek to celebrate the presence and the gifts of LGBTQ+ persons (see chapter 4), in this final chapter, I contend that—even though Catholic leaders do possess a legally protected civil right to religious liberty—there is no moral or theological justification for exercising this right by firing LGBTQ+ educators from Catholic schools. The dismissals represent a serious disregard for the employee's right to religious liberty, right to work, the preferential option for the poor and vulnerable (henceforth: preferential option for the vulnerable), and—therefore—their dignity as human beings. For these reasons, the firings must stop.

To explore how the controversy of LGBTQ+ educators in Catholic schools pertains to the Catholic social tradition, I divided this chapter into four parts. The first part will offer a brief historical overview of Catholic social teaching on human rights as reflected in the tradition of papal encyclicals.[7] The second part will demonstrate that US Catholic leaders' use of religious liberty to dismiss LGBTQ+ employees from Catholic Schools is morally problematic. The third part will affirm several rights of LGBTQ+ Catholic school employees as outlined in the key principles of Catholic social teaching. And the fourth part will propose a new way for Catholic schools to exercise their religious liberty, in light of probabilism and synodality, in a way that upholds Catholic social teaching with particular attention to the dignity of the vulnerable. The conclusion will reflect on the impact such emphasis on Catholic social teaching would have on Catholic school students.

HUMAN RIGHTS AND THE CATHOLIC CHURCH

Genesis of Catholic Social Teaching

After centuries of Catholic influence in a theocratic medieval Europe, during which the Church dictated many matters of political and spiritual life, a new political reality emerged following the Enlightenment whereby the Catholic hierarchy began to lose its foothold on the political sphere of the Western world. The various economic, political, philosophical, and artistic revolutions of the seventeenth, eighteenth, and nineteenth centuries brought about a shift away from theocentric politics and toward a secularized liberal notion of society.[8] Furthermore, the Industrial Revolution brought about significant challenges to the lives of average citizens, who now faced new economic struggles at the hands of an increasingly capitalistic market. In this context, at the end of the nineteenth century, the Church began to develop a deeper social conscience with the publication of the first social papal encyclical by Pope Leo XIII in 1891.

The Catholic social tradition finds its official doctrinal genesis in Pope Leo XIII's *Rerum Novarum*, which defined Church teaching on labor, private property, wages, unions, and the conditions of work.[9] Similarly, the second social encyclical in this series on labor,[10] *Quadragesimo Anno* (published in 1931 and commemorating forty years after *Rerum Novarum*), established important teachings that defend workers, condemn the income gap, call for duties between rich and poor, and propose reforms to the social order.[11] However, while these initial encyclicals articulated a justice-based Catholic mission, they did not develop a conception of human rights as we know them; rather they appealed to theology on human dignity and the common good as a basis for justice.[12]

Incorporating Human Rights Language into Catholic Social Teaching

Despite these advances in social justice, the Catholic social tradition resisted the concept of human rights during the first half of the twentieth century. While secular discourse on human rights advanced quickly in the international political sphere, particularly after the atrocities of the Holocaust and the subsequent United Nation's Universal Declaration of Human Rights in 1948,[13] the Catholic hierarchy was hesitant to adopt the language and methodology of human rights due the growing secular liberalism in the post-Enlightenment era that limited the political power of the Church.[14] Catholic leaders were worried that such liberal secularized language would undermine the teaching authority of the Church on social matters by separating questions of morality and justice from religious dogma and doctrine. The most poignant rejection of the language of human rights is seen in Pope Pius IX's 1864 encyclical titled *Quanta Cura* and its appendix, the *Syllabus of Errors*, which—among other things—condemned any notion that a secular and rational understanding of human rights has more authority than the theologically grounded teachings of the Church.[15]

However, as human rights language became more popular in the international political sphere in the mid-twentieth century, high-ranking members of the Catholic hierarchy eventually began to consider its framework. One of those figures was Cardinal Angelo Roncalli, who eventually became Pope John XXIII in 1958.[16] As pope, he convened the Second Vatican Council to guide the Church into a better relationship with the modern world. He also published an encyclical titled *Pacem in Terris*, which—in response to the nuclear crisis of the 1960s—adopted a language of human rights to advocate for international peace and disarmament.[17] This encyclical brought forth a new era in the Catholic social tradition through which the Church was better positioned to advocate for justice for all persons regardless of their political or religious affiliation.

Similar to the Universal Declaration on Human Rights, *Pacem in Terris* grounded human rights in human dignity, which is ever present regardless of the spiritual or social status of a person. Pope John XXIII clarifies, "A man who has fallen into error does not cease to be a man. He never forfeits his personal dignity."[18] Therefore, *Pacem in Terris* declares human rights "universal and inviolable, and therefore altogether inalienable."[19] A Catholic language of rights as seen in *Pacem in Terris* is grounded in the common good because it emphasizes that "human beings are persons among and with other persons, not just individuals with claims on one another, and that their full flourishing takes place in community where all flourish together."[20] Most importantly, the encyclical links human rights to previous notions of the common good by stating, "The common good is best safeguarded when personal rights and duties are guaranteed."[21]

Analyzing the Catholic Grammar of Human Rights

William O'Neill refers to human rights as a "grammar," which means that they operate as a "language" with a particular methodology and a particular set of rules.[22] Simply defined, from a secular standpoint, human rights are a set of entitlements all persons must be able to enjoy in order to live a human life of dignity, meaning, and respect.[23] Although a Catholic conception of human rights shares many similarities with a secular notion of rights, in a Catholic context, human rights also function theologically. Considering Catholic anthropology that emphasizes human flourishing, a Catholic grammar of human rights connects rational notions of human dignity with a theological understanding of flourishing through virtue, community, and a relationship with God. In other words, from a Catholic standpoint, human rights are a set of basic entitlements that all persons must be able to enjoy in order to live lives of dignity and flourish through relationships with God and community. Thus, the contemporary Church believes that the right to religious liberty remains crucial to humanity because it fosters a relationship with God through community.

Crucially, with the adoption of human rights language in *Pacem in Terris* and subsequent social encyclicals, Catholic social teaching elevates the well-being of each person as an essential component of the common good. Because human rights are tied to a person's humanity, which Catholic teaching argues cannot be lost or renounced, they are inviolable and must be respected to the greatest extent possible. Furthermore, this inviolability implies that authority figures have a *duty* to preserve human rights as a means to protect the dignity of all persons and the common good.[24]

Unfortunately, despite this idyllic vision of a world where everyone's rights are protected, the grammar of human rights faces significant obstacles in daily life. For the sake of brevity, I will remark on two obstacles that are relevant the dismissals of LGBTQ+ educators in Catholic schools. First, it is hard to determine whether something classifies as an inviolable human right or simply an individual's desire, which can nonetheless be legally protected as a civil right (e.g., being able to purchase alcohol after the age of twenty-one is a legal right, but not a human right). Regarding the right to marry, some people in the United States believe that marrying a person you love is a human right that should be available to all humans regardless of sexual orientation while others do not consider it a right but rather a vocational call (and therefore favor limiting marriage to heterosexual couples). Pertaining to employment, some argue that, while people have a right to employment, that doesn't guarantee that they have a right to work in a particular institution. For example, there is no such thing as a human right to work in a Catholic school. In cases where there are conflicting accounts on whether something classifies as a human right or not, from a Catholic standpoint, an advocate for a particular human right must first demonstrate how that "right" is central to human flourishing, community, and a relationship with God. After that, the advocate must then explain how persons or institutions in charge of upholding human rights are duty-bound to defend said particular right. As this chapter will showcase, this question of "what classifies as a right?" plays a key role in the dispute involving LGBTQ+ educators in Catholic schools.

Second, a person's human rights often conflict with another's human rights, making the process of adjudication difficult. As the popular phrase states, "My right to swing my arms ends when your right to not have your nose broken begins." In these cases, human authorities often have to determine the scope of each right in conflict and articulate what a reasonable limitation of an individual right might look like when it enters into conflict with the other. For this adjudication to happen, one must first examine whether the rights in conflict are on the same level playing field or whether one right has supremacy over the other and demands an automatic limitation of the less important right. For example, while human beings possess a right to free speech, a person cannot use speech to make up a false rumor that can cause psychological or financial harm to another person (i.e., slander or libel). In these cases, it would be reasonable to say that the first individual's right to free speech should be limited for the sake of the second person's right to psychological and financial well-being. Obviously, these adjudications are incredibly complicated (both in the legal and moral spheres) and must be approached with caution.

Applying a Catholic grammar of human rights to the conflict of LGBTQ+ employees in Catholic schools, I observe various dynamics at play. First, Catholic leaders are invoking their moral right to religious liberty, via the civil law recognition of the *ministerial exception*, to fire these teachers. Second, LGBTQ+ educators in Catholic schools, as human beings, can claim a set of basic rights such as employment, nondiscrimination, and privacy. Third, Catholic doctrine supports both of these sets of rights. Fourth, the rights appear to conflict with each other—thus necessitating adjudication. Finally, in light of previous chapters, this adjudication should transpire in the context of a synodal Church. What follows is an analysis of the set of rights claimed by the warring parties in this conflict.

CATHOLIC INSTITUTIONS AND RELIGIOUS LIBERTY

As discussed in chapter 1, religious liberty functions as the operating moral principle that enables the firing of LGBTQ+ educators from Catholic schools. As such, these firings fall in the realm of Catholic social teaching because religious liberty, legally manifested in the *ministerial exception* that frees Catholic institutions from having to abide by legal nondiscrimination policies, is deployed in a social context and affects community, flourishing, and the overall Kingdom of God reflected in social structures. These dismissals of LGBTQ+ educators are not contained to the internal workings of the Catholic institution but rather have financial, personal, and political consequences in the lives of the fired employees and the overall society they occupy. For this reason, I consider the exercise of religious liberty in the United States as a moral exercise and not merely a legal one. Furthermore, Catholic doctrine on the human right to religious liberty, which was recognized at the Second Vatican Council, has significant theological importance as it contains insights into the relationship between the faith of the individual believer and the universal faith expressed by the institution through doctrine.

The Origins of Religious Liberty in the Catholic Church

Prior to the Second Vatican Council in the 1960s, the official position of the Church on religious liberty was to deny that persons had a right to freedom of religion. This position rested on the assumption that "error has no rights." In other words, since the Catholic hierarchy considered the Catholic Church to be the one true faith, they refused to recognize a person's "right" to practice an "erroneous" religion. Furthermore, the magisterium held that the state had a moral obligation to promote the true religion, which was Catholicism.[25] During Vatican II, however, US Catholic leaders advocated for a doctrine on religious liberty since Catholics often faced discrimination and persecution in countries like the United States where they were a minority.[26] Thus, the council fathers began exploring the possibility of such a doctrine and eventually crafted a declaration on religious liberty titled *Dignitatis Humanae*.[27]

John Courtney Murray, a Vatican II *periti* (i.e., an expert invited by the bishops or the pope to the council) from the United States, offered some significant contributions to this conversation. Highly influenced by the conceptualization of religious liberty in the US Constitution, Murray's work provided a theological basis for *Dignitatis Humanae*. In his book, *We Hold These Truths*, Murray argued that Catholic doctrines on natural law and freedom are perfectly compatible with the First Amendment of the US Constitution and should guide Catholics and Protestants alike to support religious liberty.[28]

In his book, *The Problem of Religious Freedom*, Murray offered two significant contributions that helped the Council fathers promote a doctrine of religious freedom at Vatican II. First, he argued in favor of a separation of Church and state, claiming that the state has no competence to participate in theological discourse. According to Murray, the state's only competence related to religion is limited to protecting the religious freedom of the people and the freedom of religious organizations to exist and freely articulate and live out their beliefs.[29] Therefore, religious freedom serves as an immunity from civil or secular coercion or interference with regard to the beliefs, practices, and internal polity of the Church unless such practices violate the public order.[30] And, second, Murray rejects the entire framework that yielded the question of "Does error have rights or not?"[31] He considers religious liberty to be a human right that is inalienable regardless of the person's understanding of truth. In other words, the state should allow people to pursue faith and practice religion as they wish regardless of whether that religion is "the correct" religion or not.

These two theological insights were crucial to the discussions on religious liberty at the Second Vatican Council. After various disputes, and with the support of the pope, the Second Vatican Council approved the declaration on religious liberty, *Dignitatis Humanae*. The new declaration justified the right to religious liberty by grounding it on "human dignity" and not on the correctness of the person's conscientious judgment of truth. The council fathers recognized that a relationship with God, which is crucial to flourishing and the common good, can only take place genuinely if the person has full freedom to pursue it. Therefore, human dignity merits freedom.

The Insights of *Dignitatis Humanae*

Grounded in human dignity, the declaration on religious liberty, *Dignitatis Humanae*, defends the human right to religious freedom at two levels. The first level is individual: "This Vatican Council declares that the human person has a right to religious freedom."[32] Considering the freedom that is a prerequisite for a genuine relationship with God, *Dignitatis Humanae* condemns any attempts from the Church or the state to coerce a person's conscience on matters of faith and morals.[33] This bestows upon each person the freedom to pursue truth (which is a part of the natural law, according to the document) and to worship. Other persons, therefore, have a duty to respect individual religious liberty. Even missionaries tasked with evangelization must be careful not to engage in coercive practices that force someone into conversion or into practicing a particular faith.[34] Thus, each person, because of their inherent dignity,[35] possesses this human right to religious liberty and is entitled to freedom from coercion on matters of faith and morals.

The second application of religious liberty is communal, or ecclesial. As the document explains, "The freedom or immunity from coercion in matters religious which is the endowment of persons as individuals is also to be recognized as their right when they act in community. Religious communities are a requirement of the social nature both of man and of religion itself."[36] Unless a religious group is violating public order, civil authorities must protect this ecclesial corporate right to operate and proclaim its teachings publicly. Furthermore, "Religious communities also have the right not to be hindered, either by legal measures or by administrative action on the part of government, in the selection, training, appointment, and transferral of their own ministers."[37] Thus, the document charges governments with the protection of religious liberty for communities and with fostering environments where religious expression can thrive.

The Rights to Individual and Corporate Religious Liberty

At first glance, the individual and communal rights to religious freedom may appear intricately interconnected. As the document explains, the *communal* right to religious liberty is an extended recognition of the *individual* right to religious freedom. However, I argue that, while they are related, individual and communal rights operate differently from each other. An individual right to religious freedom is grounded in a Catholic anthropology of personhood as free and capable of exercising a conscientious choice to pursue truth and express it through religion. This is part of what it means to be created in the *Imago Dei*. For this reason, individual religious liberty is a human right grounded in human anthropology. However, the communal right simply refers to a right for a religious organization to exist and to operate as a corporate entity in a state. This communal right is, therefore, akin to a corporate right to be civilly protected by the government. It is not a human right *per se*.

According to the grammar of human rights, as established by *Dignitatis Humanae* and by most contemporary human rights theorists, human rights are only bestowed upon individual persons. In the words of Jack Donnelly, "Human rights are literally the rights that one has simply because one is a human being."[38] In a moral sense (not a legal one), religious institutions, while they are comprised of human persons, are not human beings themselves and cannot possess a *human* right. Therefore, an ecclesial right to religious liberty is simply a civil corporate right protected legally by the state. John Courtney Murray explains that ecclesial or corporate religious freedom refers to "their immunity from the intervention of the public powers or of any social agency in the declaration of their own statute of corporate existence, in the determination of their own doctrine and polity, in their internal discipline and self-government, in the appointment of officials and in the definition of their functions, in the training and employment of ministers."[39] Though it may find some civil justification in the *human* right to religious freedom, the corporate right of religious institutions is distinct from an understanding of human rights.

Some may argue, in opposition to my argument, that protecting a communal right to religious freedom is simply a large-scale protection of the individual human rights of each human member of the group. In other words, objectors may raise the concept of "group human rights" to argue that the Catholic Church's right to religious liberty is a collective exercise of the *human rights* possessed by every individual Catholic member of the ecclesial group. I disagree, and, to explore this matter further, I return to Jack Donnelly's work on the question of group human rights.[40] Donnelly expresses significant skepticism about the validity of group human rights because he believes they are difficult to define and implement as human rights. Donnelly defines group rights as "rights held by a corporate entity that is not reducible to its individual members"[41] and argues that "few groups meet this test."[42] The claim to group human rights, as irreducible to individual human rights, is based on the idea that the individual members of the group can only exercise the individual human right in question together, in unison, through the group human right. Presumably, there would be a spokesperson for the group that would advocate and claim the group's human right for collective enjoyment. In the case of a religious group, such as Catholic institutions, the religious leaders (i.e., bishops) tend to operate as said spokespersons. Herein lies the inconsistency with the argument that the Catholic Church's corporate right to religious liberty is a group *human* right.

When a Catholic bishop mandates the firing of an LGBTQ+ educator from a Catholic school and justifies the firing as an exercise of the religious liberty of the Church, he is doing so against the wishes of the majority of individual Catholics in the United States, who support the inclusion of LGTBQ+ persons in the Church.[43] In other words, most US Catholics do not wish to exercise their human right to religious liberty in a way that results in the firing of an LGBTQ+ person. For this reason, these dismissals are simply an enforcement of a corporate policy mandated by an institution (i.e., Catholic doctrine on sexuality) and not a collective unified exercise of the human rights of each individual comprising the institution. Therefore, the right to religious liberty, manifested in the *ministerial exception* is a corporate right and not a human right.

As this case underscores, dissent in the Church is evidence of the distinction between the corporate civil right to religious liberty and the individual human right to religious freedom. Ladislas Orsy observes, "Good-faith conflict situations in the Church are arising with some frequency, and often with urgency."[44] To resolve these cases of dissent, Orsy believes that the preservation of one's integrity (i.e., their ability to form and follow their conscience freely and honestly) is paramount along with the protection of the basic beliefs of the community. The ability to freely live a life of integrity in a religious community is a constitutive element of the religious liberty of all individuals. He also cites the axiom I referenced in my discussion of probabilism, "Unity in all that is necessary; freedom in all that is doubtful; charity in all."[45] Thus, with these statements, Orsy distinguishes the legally protected corporate ecclesial right to religious liberty, which promotes the promulgation of doctrinal principles, from the individual human right to religious liberty, which is inviolable and takes precedence. He then advocates for a reasonable degree of theological disagreement on peripheral matters within the Church grounded in the integrity protected by the individual right to religious liberty. Orsy explains that *Dignitatis Humanae* established that "in the hierarchy of human and Christian values living human persons (imperfect as they are) have priority over abstract propositions (true as they may be). Humans have rights; propositions have meanings but no rights."[46] Here I briefly return to chapter 3 on the doctrine of probabilism to argue that this tool, in addition to facilitating synodality, also facilitates our moral understanding and implementation of the human right to religious freedom by freeing up a person's conscience to act in accordance with its dictates on matters of faith and morals.

Religious Liberty, the US Catholic Church, and LGBTQ+ Employees in Catholic Schools

Human beings have the right to form organized religious organizations. Therefore, the very existence of the Catholic Church itself can be considered an extension of human rights. Once the religious corporation exists, however, its activities are legally and morally protected under a corporate understanding of religious liberty but not under the classification of human rights. Therefore, since the ecclesial right to religious liberty is a corporate and civil right to operate, and not a human right *per se*, the human rights of individual Catholics have primacy over the institution's corporate right as long as these individual human rights do not prevent the Church from existing. In comparison to various other places throughout the world, where Christianity is persecuted and suppressed,[47] I argue that the presence of LGBTQ+ persons in Catholic institutions (even as ministerial employees) does not threaten the existence of the Church. On the contrary, as evidenced in chapter 2, it may enhance it. As history has and will demonstrate, the urgency with which some bishops issue warnings about the demise of the US Church due to same-sex marriages and gender-related transitions is simply baseless.[48]

More importantly, since a corporate ecclesial right should not trump a human right, which is inalienable and inviolable, the dismissals of LGBTQ+ employees who conscientiously disagree with doctrine on homosexuality constitute a problematic violation of that employee's human right to religious liberty. Based on *Dignitatis Humanae*, I argue that Catholic institutions have a moral obligation (regardless of their legal immunities), to uphold the dignity of LGBTQ+ persons by respecting their right to form their conscience as bestowed upon them by their right to religious liberty. Furthermore, synthesizing an individual's human right to religious freedom with a notion of probabilism, I argue that LGBTQ+ employees in Catholic schools have the moral human right to religious liberty to disagree with peripheral magisterial doctrine on sexuality and still be able to exercise their faith and ministry in the Church.

Considering that termination from employment exercises a significant amount of stress upon an individual (especially those who rely on employment to sustain themselves or their families, which is probably most employees in Catholic schools), I argue that threats of termination can constitute "coercion" of a person's conscience and a violation of their dignity. For this reason, I argue that the threat of dismissing LGBTQ+ employees from Catholic schools if they do not conform to Catholic doctrine on sexuality is a violation of their freedom of conscience, their religious liberty, and their human dignity.

A final objection one may raise against my argument is that, since all rights can be limited with due justification, an employee's violation of magisterial doctrine on homosexuality or gender may justifiably merit such a limitation of their human rights to religious liberty. Since, from a Catholic *eudemonic* standpoint, human rights also lead to flourishing through a relationship with God, and since sin (including sexual sin) breaks such a relationship, some may argue that it is morally justifiable to dismiss an LGBTQ+ educator who disagrees through word and deed with the doctrine of the Church. Thus, the firings would not only represent a justified limitation of a human right but also a promotion of the common good by preserving the traditional heteronormative family unit. In response to this objection, I retrieve my argument that the doctrine of homosexuality and gender is significantly credibly contested and does not provide an ironclad justification for such extreme measures as employment termination. Probabilism makes room for a reasonable degree of theological pluralism that includes LGBTQ+ persons' quest to flourish through same-sex relationships and gender-affirming transitions.

More importantly, in the context of a synodal Church, there should be an emphasis on walking together on a journey that may lead to a spiritual epiphany rather than a strict emphasis on doctrinal rigorism, especially on a doctrine that is so contested.

In sum, the way Catholic leaders have wielded their right to religious liberty via the ministerial exception to fire LGBTQ+ employees in Catholic schools is inconsistent with a Catholic grammar of human rights. It is self-defeating because it results in violations of human dignity, which is what human rights language tries to preserve. The disregard for the dignity of LGBTQ+ employees in the US Catholic school system reflects a broader disregard for the dignity of those who disagree with Catholic doctrine on sexuality. I call upon Catholic leaders to foster a genuine commitment to protecting the dignity of all through the preservation of the right to religious freedom of all individuals in Catholic institutions, including schools.

RETRIEVING KEY PRINCIPLES OF CATHOLIC SOCIAL TEACHING

In addition to the problematic and inconsistent exercise of the corporate right to religious liberty to dismiss LGBTQ+ educators from Catholic schools, the dismissals represent direct violations of the right to work, which is another human right long recognized by the Catholic Church, as well as other key principles of Catholic social teaching. In this section, I explore the right to work, the right to privacy (which has been significantly underdeveloped in the Church), and four principles of Catholic social teaching: the preferential option for the vulnerable, nondiscrimination, subsidiarity, and participation. Given the robustness of Catholic social teaching and all of its principles, I will devote more attention to the right to work and the underdeveloped right to privacy as I consider them to be more pertinent to the question of LGBTQ+ educators in Catholic schools. I will offer brief overviews of the other principles to demonstrate how, proportionally speaking, Catholic social teaching largely supports the retention and celebration of LGBTQ+ educators in Catholic schools.

Catholicism and Labor Rights

As discussed earlier, the Catholic social tradition finds its genesis in its advocacy for the rights of workers in *Rerum Novarum*. However, while previous encyclicals establish the centrality of work as crucial to a life of dignity,[49] labor rights were not understood as *human* rights until Pope John XXIII's publication of *Pacem in Terris*.[50] He explains, "In the economic sphere, it is evident that a man has the inherent right not only to be given the opportunity to work, but also to be allowed the exercise of personal initiative in the work he does."[51] He also quotes Pope Pius XII, "Nature imposes work upon man as a duty, and man has the corresponding natural right to demand that the work he does shall provide him with the means of livelihood for himself and his children. Such is nature's categorical imperative for the preservation of man."[52] Furthermore, John XXIII also lists several rights that are constitutive of the right to work, including wages and proper work conditions. Subsequent social encyclicals build upon this newly reformulated human right to work as tied to human dignity.

Perhaps the most comprehensive treatment of the right to work in a social encyclical is found in John Paul II's *Laborem Excercens*. From the onset, he states, "man's life is built up every day from work, from work it derives its specific dignity."[53] In line with previous encyclicals, Pope John Paul II acknowledges that, through work, a person "*achieves fulfilment* as a human being and indeed, in a sense, becomes 'more a human being.'"[54] Crucially, *Laborem Excercens* recognizes the threat of unemployment, which it calls "in all cases an evil."[55] Pope John Paul II asserts, "we must first direct our attention to a *fundamental issue:* the question of finding work, or, in other words, the issue of *suitable employment for all who are capable of it.* The opposite of a just and right situation in this field is unemployment, that is to say the lack of work for those who are capable of it."[56]

Several decades later, Pope Benedict XVI also addressed the threat to human dignity presented by unemployment in *Caritas in Veritate*, stating, "In comparison with the casualties of industrial society in the past, unemployment today provokes new forms of economic marginalization."[57] He further reflected upon the relation between unemployment and poverty, "No consideration of the problems associated with development could fail to highlight the direct link between *poverty and unemployment.* In many cases, poverty results from a *violation of the dignity of human work* . . . because work opportunities are limited (through unemployment or underemployment)."[58]

Unemployment has very real consequences in the lives of those who lose their jobs. In his encyclical, *Fratelli Tutti*, Pope Francis connects the human right to work with the quest toward human flourishing and the common good by stating,

> The biggest issue is employment. . . . For "there is no poverty worse than that which takes away work and the dignity of work." In a genuinely developed society, work is an essential dimension of social life, for it is not only a means of earning one's daily bread, but also of personal growth, the building of healthy relationships, self-expression and the exchange of gifts. Work gives us a sense

of shared responsibility for the development of the world, and ultimately, for our life as a people.[59]

As with all human rights, the right to work (and the right to not be unemployed) is not absolute. All rights have limits. An employer may have a justified cause for termination of an employee and, to uphold that person's dignity, such termination should only take place as a last resort.[60] Firing an employee for inconsequential reasons or for unjustified causes, even in states that legally permit at-will employment, represents a moral violation of the human right (therefore dignity) of that employee.

Employees in Catholic schools, whether they are to be considered ministers or not, participate in this theological vision whereby work is tied to dignity. While their labor is framed in terms of "vocation," for most laypersons, it is also how they build a life and sustain a family. Edward P. Hannengberg observes that, for lay ecclesial ministers, "their response to God's call is a life-orienting decision, one that profoundly impacts their faith, their families, and their future."[61] As human beings who labor, they are also entitled to the human right to employment.

With this robust understanding of the right to work, which applies to ministerial workers in Catholic institutions, I argue that Catholic schools should uphold the rights of LGBTQ+ educators to work. LGBTQ+ persons are human beings who live human lives. Their work is also a source of dignity, purpose, and vocational fulfillment. They may have families (with children), mortgages or rent, and other basic human needs. More importantly, they are a part of society and deserve to participate in the common good. For these reasons, their dignity should be upheld through the protection of their right to work.

Obviously, many US Catholic leaders argue that LGBTQ+ educators' disagreement with Church teaching constitutes just cause for termination. In their 2006 pastoral letter, "Ministry to Persons with a Homosexual Inclination," the USCCB stated, "the Church has a right to deny roles of service to those whose behavior violates her teaching. Such service may seem to condone an immoral lifestyle and may even be an occasion of scandal."[62] In response, I retrieve my argument from chapters 1 and 3 that "fear of scandal" on such a contested matter of human sexuality does not provide enough justification for terminating someone's employment. Giving in to these fears constitutes an opposite scandal by teaching students that it is permissible to violate LGBTQ+ persons' right to employment without just cause. Therefore, the inviolable and inalienable human right to work of the individual LGBTQ+ educator must be upheld through retention in Catholic schools.

The Right to Privacy: An Underdeveloped Teaching

I am hesitant to discuss the right to privacy in relation to LGBTQ+ inclusion in Catholic schools because this right may be translated into a "don't ask, don't tell" policy that promotes shame about sexual identity and activity. I would worry that some institutions would pressure LGBTQ+ educators to stay in the closet under the pretense of "privacy." This would be antithetical to my previous argument about celebrating the unique and indispensable gifts of LGBTQ+ educators. However, I recognize that some Catholic contexts are not yet affirming of the grace-filled life witnessed by LGBTQ+ persons and these institutions might benefit from a Catholic understanding of privacy to, at the very least, "do no harm" when they learn of the sexual identity or behavior of their staff. At best, however, I restate that Catholic institutions should be celebrating the identity and gifts of LGBTQ+ people.

As discussed in chapter 1, some LGBTQ+ educators who have been fired from Catholic schools are terminated after a community member investigates their private life and makes their marital status known to Catholic leaders (e.g., Shelly Fitzgerald was terminated after a community member found her marriage license). Furthermore, several bishops have attempted to include sexual morality clauses in employment contracts (e.g., Archbishop Cordileone introduced these clauses in San Francisco).[63] Given these efforts, it is important to address questions about the moral and social obligation of Catholic schools toward the right to privacy of their employees.[64] Here I argue that, on matters of sexual identity, marital status, genital appearance, or sexual behavior, Catholic school employees are entitled to privacy. Catholic schools are not entitled to this information about their employees and should refrain from acting upon information that was acquired through violations of the employee's privacy (e.g., through an investigation by a community member).

While the right to privacy is significantly underdeveloped from a theological standpoint, the Catechism of the Catholic Church, when discussing the eighth commandment, "thou shalt not lie," states that "the good and safety of others, respect for privacy, and the common good are sufficient reasons for being silent about what ought not be known or for making use of a discreet language. . . . No one is bound to reveal the truth to someone who does not have the right to know it."[65] Truth-telling is contingent upon the relationship between the possessor of truth and the receiver. It can be unjust and even sinful to reveal a truth about someone when that person does not want that truth revealed, especially if revealing such truth about matters of sexual orientation or gender identity can cause someone to lose their job. Ideally, LGBTQ+ educators would feel safe in their Catholic school environment and would voluntarily reveal their queer identity to the school. However, if they sense the school is not safe, they should be able to withhold this truth from the community should they wish to.

The Second Vatican Council refers to conjugal love (i.e., sexual activity) as an *intimate* act between married partners.[66] It also describes sexual activity as taking place between two people who know and love each other. While the Council's statements refer to heterosexual couples, I argue that, in a same-sex relationship, sexual activity (regardless of whether it is considered sinful or not) remains an *intimate* act. These declarations about the intimacy of sexual activity are inherently grounded in the sexual act itself and are not dependent upon the gender of the participants. Furthermore, I argue that this extends to the genital appearance of a person (i.e., to the physical appearance of a transgender person) since both involve intimate components of one's body. While Catholic leaders can make pronouncements about what makes sexual activity and medical interventions "good" to guide the faithful along a particular path, any invasive inquiry or investigation into another's sexual activity or genital appearance entails a serious violation of their privacy, their dignity, and the intimate nature of sexuality. All persons have the right to sexual privacy.

In light of this right to sexual privacy, which also applies to LGBTQ+ persons, school community members should refrain from investigating the private sexual, genital, or romantic lives of Catholic school employees. This extends to marriage licenses which, while they are technically public records, can only be found through an investigation that, realistically, most Catholic students would not know how to conduct (thus casting further doubt on the "scandal argument" claiming that LGBTQ+ educators in same-sex unions lead students to sin). Such investigations represent an extraordinary action fueled by a blatant disregard for privacy. Matters of sexual morality or gender identity are not under the purview of school administrators, bishops, parents, parishioners, or other community members. These Catholic leaders should desist in their efforts to include private matters of sexual behavior in professional documents. Because sexual activity belongs in the private domain, any inclusion of this language invites public investigation and is a violation of privacy. Furthermore, they should not act on any information about the sexual identity or behavior of an employee that was acquired by any community member through an investigation or even a breach of confidentiality.

Objectors to this argument might rehearse the scandal argument, stating that parents and administrators have the duty to ensure LGBTQ+ persons in violation of Catholic doctrine are not leading children to sin. In response, I retrieve the argument of the opposite scandal to argue that the invasion of privacy of LGBTQ+ persons is also a scandal that might lead students to believe they can scrutinize the sexual, marital, or genital behavior of their teachers. I also note that the Congregation for the Doctrine of the Faith's document against civil same-sex marriage is grounded in the assumption that the couple is sexually active or scandalizing others through their union. Therefore, if LGBTQ+ employees are dismissed due to their civil marriage, the underlying theological and ethical implication is that they are scandalizing children (which I already addressed in chapter 1 by stating that scandal is not a sufficient argument) or being sexually active with their spouse, which falls under the private domain and should not concern members of a Catholic school.[67] For this reason, I argue that the dismissal of LGBTQ+ educators from Catholic schools is unjust because it hinges on either the unfairly overemphasized assumption that these educators are scandalizing the students or upon an invasive assumption that these persons are engaging in same-sex sexual activity or have undergone a gender-affirming transition. Catholic school leaders who act upon such assumptions are violating their LGBTQ+ employees' right to privacy and scandalizing their school community toward sin against LGBTQ+ persons.

If a student or parent suspects, investigates, or "discovers" an educator's civil union to a same-sex partner, it does not automatically mean that there is evidence of sexual intercourse between the partners, nor does it give license for further investigation about the nature of their relationship. Furthermore, it does not give them the right to spread that information without the consent of the educator. Catholic leaders who dismiss LGBTQ+ educators based on information that was acquired through immoral practices give legitimacy to such reprehensible investigations.[68] This is problematic because it sends a message to the school community that the school's leadership will act on private sexual information even if it is illicitly acquired. Such actions can potentially open the doors for future violations of the employees' privacy if community members begin to conduct "witch hunts" to root out LGBTQ+ educators. In light of the hardships faced by LGBTQ+ people (especially youth), Catholic leaders should protect the right to privacy of their employees (including sexual privacy) by paying no attention to the information brought forth through immoral investigative practices. They should model to their community the importance of respecting all employee's privacy by not acting on this information and by imparting consequences to members of the community that engage in invasive investigative practices.

Crucially, the argument I am making here is that personal and private information about the homosexual sexual activity or genital appearance of particular individuals is not up for discussion by leaders in Catholic schools. I am not saying that sexual activity, including homosexual sexual activity, should not be talked about or should be repressed. Rather, I am arguing that disclosure about an individual or a couple's sexual activity or genital appearance must be done only with the consent of the person or persons involved. Discussion or even disciplinary action in a place of employment over illicitly acquired information about the sexual activity or genitalia of an educator is a violation of the educator's right to privacy and overall dignity. In my research of LGBTQ+ employees in Catholic schools, I have not found any employee publicly discussing graphic anecdotes of their own sexual behavior with students. Such discussions would be precarious because they may violate the professional boundaries between an adult educator and a student who is legally a minor. While sexual activity, including homosexual activity, can be discussed academically, personal disclosures of private intimate acts on behalf of any adult educator regardless of sexual orientation, which I have not seen from LGBTQ+ educators in Catholic schools, is inappropriate and should be subjected to disciplinary action.

Finally, I restate that my argument on the right to privacy operates as a "do no harm" policy. It should serve as a basic entitlement any educator (whether LGBTQ+ or not) can resort to in places that are hostile to them because of their sexual identity or behavior. However, the ideal situation, as I have discussed in previous chapters, would be one where LGBTQ+ educators feel safe in their Catholic school environments to willingly disclose their sexual identity, marital status, or gender identity without fear of dismissal. A "don't ask, don't tell" policy, even under the guise of the right to privacy, is oppressive and harmful for LGBTQ+ educators and the LGBTQ+ youth they serve. A safe environment where LGBTQ+ people can live authentically would enable them to exercise their gifts more fully as LGBTQ+ persons and bring forth a queer epistemology (as discussed in chapter 4) that can guide the Catholic community forward as it journeys together.

Retrieving Four Key Principles

The dismissal of LGBTQ+ educators from Catholic schools violates four other principles outlined in Catholic social teaching. The principles of the preferential option for the vulnerable, nondiscrimination, subsidiarity, and participation have all been recognized as central components of social justice, particularly in the workforce. Unfortunately, Catholic leaders who dismiss these educators often disregard these principles in favor of a narrow application of religious liberty with a distinguishability focus as discussed in previous chapters. In response, I argue that these four principles must be retrieved and restored. While the Catholic Church is a different "kind" of society and does not operate like a secular private or public institution, nor is it regulated by the state in the same way, I believe Catholic institutions should strive to model for the world the principles of Catholic social teaching. Furthermore, LGBTQ+ educators in Catholic schools rely on the institution for income, benefits, and other goods akin to the public secular sector. Therefore, I believe the social teachings of the Church, specifically teachings on nondiscrimination, subsidiarity, and participation, apply toward them as they are human beings providing their labor to the schools through their vocation.

The Preferential Option for the Vulnerable

The Gospels highlight how Jesus sides with the oppressed and identifies with them, "whatever you did for one of the least of these brothers and sisters of mine, you did for me" (cf. Matt. 25:40). Building upon this message, various encyclicals, apostolic exhortations, and other magisterial documents (especially from Pope Francis) have begun to emphasize the centrality of this charitable vision in the life and mission of the Church.[69] As a key principle of Catholic social thought, the preferential option for the vulnerable calls Catholics to pay special attention to those who are oppressed by society. By "preferential option," the Church is hoping to underscore Jesus' call to respond to the plight of the most vulnerable in our society.

Vulnerability in our society is a result of material and normative social conditions that place some individuals at risk of disenfranchisement, that is, at risk of being excluded from accessing the goods and benefits our society has to offer (i.e., the common good). As a result, these persons experience hardship, suffering, and violations of their dignity as being created in the *Imago Dei*. The preferential option for the vulnerable calls upon Catholics to be aware of this suffering and seek to restore these persons to their rightful place as equitable members of our society.

Considering the alarming statistics LGBTQ+ persons face in society, along with the disproportionate rates of discrimination (especially in religious institutions),[70] I argue that they qualify as "vulnerable" and the Church must pay special attention to caring for them pastorally, materially, and politically. This means that Catholics must strive to ensure their economic and social well-being in addition to their spiritual flourishing.[71] Applying this principle to Catholic education should compel Catholic leaders to retain LGBTQ+ employees in Catholic schools. Furthermore, the preferential option for the vulnerable connects the retention of LGBTQ+ employees with the care of LGBTQ+ students who could benefit from adult LGBTQ+ role models to thrive. Therefore, the retention of LGBTQ+ educators in Catholic schools should not only aim to protect these vulnerable employees from spiritual, economic, and political harm but should also seek to apply their gifts toward the flourishing of vulnerable LGBTQ+ youth.

Nondiscrimination

In addition to the sexual morality component, Catholic doctrine on homosexuality contains a social teaching about discrimination. The Congregation for the Doctrine of the Faith (CDF) affirms that people with homosexual tendencies "must be accepted with respect, compassion and sensitivity. Every sign of unjust discrimination in their regard should be avoided."[72] Key in this statement is the word "unjust," which implies that there are some forms of *just* discrimination. In a 1992 letter, the CDF decried the violence many homosexuals have faced,[73] but argued that it is moral and licit to discriminate against homosexuals on matters of employment, housing, adoption, and other aspects of civil life because protecting the right to be homosexual, which the document invalidates, would endorse lifestyles that can ultimately harm society by harming the heteronormative family.[74]

Despite this document endorsing some forms of discrimination against LGBTQ+ persons as "just," I argue that the *injustice* lies in the disproportionate targeting of LGBTQ+ persons in Catholic institutions while ignoring other violations of Catholic doctrine that are more central to the faith. James Martin advances this argument in *Building a Bridge* when he lists other forms of dissent in faith and doctrine. In his words,

> If adherence to church teaching is going to be a litmus test for employment in Catholic institutions, then dioceses and parishes need to be consistent. Do we fire a straight man or woman who gets divorced and then remarries without an annulment? Divorce and remarriage of that sort are against church teaching. In fact, divorce is something Jesus himself forbade. Do we fire women who bear children out of wedlock? How about those living together before being married? Do we give pink slips to those who practice birth control? Those actions are against church teaching too. And what about employees who are not Catholic? . . . Requiring church employees to adhere to church teaching means, at the more fundamental level, adhering to the Gospel. To be consistent, shouldn't we fire people for not helping the poor, for not being forgiving, or for not being loving? . . . These commands of Jesus are the most essential "church teachings."[75]

By itself, I don't consider this argument on nondiscrimination to be ironclad since one cannot really justify (so-called) wrong-doing by pointing out other (so-called) wrong-doing. As the popular phrase goes, "two *wrongs* do not make a *right*." However, when combined with other arguments about the human rights of LGBTQ+ persons and in light of probabilism and the diversity of moral conscientious viewpoints, the way LGBTQ+ employees in Catholic schools have been singled out by the Church underscores a very sinister pervasive heterosexist and cisnormative culture in the Church leadership that is indeed *unjust*. Catholic leaders should become aware of this bias and, at the very least, cease the dismissals of LGBTQ+ educators from Catholic schools.

Subsidiarity

The Church defined the principle of subsidiarity in the encyclical on Labor, *Quadragessimo Anno*, which celebrated forty years since the publication of the first encyclical on labor, *Rerum Novarum*. Subsidiarity refers to a governance practice whereby leaders delegate particular governance decisions to the lowest levels of authority first. A "higher-up" leader should not be concerned with micromanaging decisions that fall more directly under the purview of a subordinate manager. Pope Pius XI states, "it is an injustice and at the same time a grave evil and disturbance of right order to assign to a greater and higher association what lesser and subordinate organizations can do."[76] The principle, therefore, calls for delegating the task of government and decision-making to the most local level possible. Applied to the issue of LGBTQ+ educators in Catholic schools, subsidiarity should encourage bishops to delegate the task of managing employment issues to the local school community. When a bishop interferes with Catholic schools at such a granular level to dismiss an LGBTQ+ employee, he is depriving the school of the ability to discern and determine how to best fulfill its particular mission. This is problematic because bishops who mandate the firing of LGBTQ+ educators often operate from a legalistic standpoint without showing concern for the particular Catholic culture and needs of the school which, through probabilism, may be more accepting of people who dissent on matters of sexual morality yet may be effective at bringing up the students in light of the Gospels. The examples discussed in chapter 1, in Indianapolis and San Francisco, both involve a bishop overstepping by mandating a particular employment practice without really considering the needs of the individual school communities. Subsidiarity would call upon those bishops to trust the discretion of the school administrators in deciding who is a suitable minister in their particular context.

Participation

In addition to Vatican II's call for "active participation" of all Catholics in liturgy and the life of the Church, Catholic social teaching also calls for participation in other aspects of daily life. According to the *Compendium of the Social Doctrine of the Church*,

> [Participation] is expressed essentially in a series of activities by means of which the citizen, either as an individual or in association with others, whether directly or through representation, contributes to the cultural, economic, political and social life of the civil community to which he [sic] belongs. Participation is a duty to be fulfilled consciously by all, with responsibility and with a view to

the common good. This cannot be confined or restricted to only a certain area of social life.[77]

The principle of participation, combined with the principle of subsidiarity, tasks all persons with actively contributing to the common good. As discussed in chapter 2, LGBTQ+ educators, especially those serving in ministerial roles, can offer unique and indispensable contributions to Catholic education.[78] Dismissing them from Catholic schools prevents them from participating by placing their gifts at the service of the institution. According to Catholic social teaching, this is an injustice because human dignity requires a participatory outlet through which persons can actively contribute to the common good.

RENEWING SYNODAL CATHOLIC SCHOOLS' COMMITMENT TO CATHOLIC SOCIAL TEACHING

So far, in this chapter, I have analyzed the various principles of Catholic social teaching that are at play in the controversy surrounding LGBTQ+ educators in Catholic schools. On one hand, Catholic leaders justify dismissals of LGBTQ+ educators from Catholic schools by claiming the right to religious liberty and exercising it by firing ministerial employees whose lives run contrary to Catholic doctrine on sexual morality. On the other hand, the fired LGBTQ+ employees can claim rights to employment, nondiscrimination, and privacy and could appeal to Catholic social teaching principles of the preferential option for the vulnerable, subsidiarity, and participation to justify their belonging in Catholic education. In light of synodality, probabilism, and the key principles of Catholic social teaching, I argue that the dismissals of LGBTQ+ educators are unjust and must stop.

Adjudicating the Conflict of Rights

The first order of business is the adjudication of a conflict of human rights between religious liberty versus the rights to employment, nondiscrimination, and privacy. As before, I argue that the rights in conflict are not on the same level because Catholic social teaching, reinforced by the magisterium for over a century, recognizes the right to employment as a human right whereas the right to religious liberty as exercised by Catholic leaders who fire LGBTQ+ educators is a corporate right to be protected by the state. Furthermore, Catholic social teaching attributes nondiscrimination as a component of the right to employment. I believe that the right to privacy, while underdeveloped in the magisterium, would also operate as a human right possessed by individuals. Because a corporate right can never be used to justify the violation of an inviolable and inalienable human right, I argue that the individual LGBTQ+ educator's rights to employment, nondiscrimination, and privacy hold supremacy in this conflict. Therefore, the right to corporate religious liberty through the ministerial exception does not morally justify the dismissal of LGBTQ+ educators from Catholic schools. In addition to this argument, I also argue that probabilism further subtracts credibility to Catholic leaders who are willing to violate LGBTQ+ persons' human rights to protect a doctrine that is credibly contested at all levels of the Church. Such dismissals represent an unjust disregard for human rights.

Religious liberty is meant to protect the free exercise of religion in the face of social, political, or cultural threats and LGBTQ+ people do not pose such threats to the exercise of the Catholic faith. The way many US bishops are raising an alarm about the demise of the Church at the hands of LGBTQ+ individuals is unfounded and insensitive to the more serious threats faced by the Church in many other places in the world where religious liberty is not recognized.[79] While LGBTQ+ Catholics present a tension or a challenge (based on their queer epistemology) to Catholic doctrine, this small percentage of the Catholic population hardly represents a real threat to the Church. More importantly, the tension in the Church on questions of homosexuality and transgender identities is not so much caused by LGBTQ+ Catholics themselves but rather is a result of the clash between the increasing number of Catholics recognizing the grace present in LGBTQ+ persons and relationships versus traditionalist Catholics who fear change in the Church's understanding of human sexuality. Realistically, when placing the current state of the debate in the broader historical context of the doctrines of homosexuality and gender, one can clearly see that the Church as a whole is developing on the matter by moving slowly in a direction of welcoming LGBTQ+ persons. Catholic leaders who exercise the right to religious liberty to fire LGBTQ+ educators are not protecting their ability to exist as a Church (which is what the corporate right to religious liberty is meant to protect) but rather are trying to prevent the Church from evolving. Unfortunately, many of them seem willing to violate human rights to prevent this change while raising false alarms about LGBTQ+ people tearing the fabric of society and the Church.

Finally, because religious liberty seeks to protect a particular good (i.e., the practice of religion), its moral exercise is dependent upon fealty to the substance of that good. For religious liberty to be morally exercised, it must abide by the faith it seeks to protect. Religious leaders claiming to exercise religious liberty in the name of Catholicism should first formulate a realistic picture of where the faith is. A bishop wielding religious liberty to defend a pre-Vatican II version of Catholicism is exercising the corporate right to religious liberty incorrectly by remaining faithful to an unrealistic conception of Catholicism. The responsible exercise of the corporate right to religious liberty must be honest about where the corporate entity (i.e., the Catholic community) is at with the matters at hand. On matters of homosexuality and gender identity, the Church is still figuring out its way forward; therefore, wielding religious liberty to preserve a contested or outdated doctrine is a morally irresponsible act on behalf of these religious leaders. For this reason, I retrieve the model of synodality to call religious leaders toward unity and I retrieve the doctrine of probabilism to call religious leaders toward humility.

The Right to a Vocation in Catholic Schools: A Place at the Table

Human rights apply in a legal sphere and in a moral one. Legally, the state is responsible for creating laws and enforcement structures that preserve human rights. The state should offer basic protections for these rights to ensure that, at least, the bare minimum duties conferred by a right are being met. This is what Henry Shue refers to as a "morality of the depths."[80] Through the lens of the Catholic social tradition, however, human rights should become more than just a list of bare minimum basic entitlements but rather should strive toward flourishing. For this reason, Catholic social teaching infuses the doctrine of human rights with a doctrine of the common good. In this sense, human rights become a "morality of the heights," since they point toward flourishing.

From a moral standpoint, considering the spiritual nature of the work of educators in Catholic schools, the human right to employment must be reconceived as a right to vocation. In other words, all human beings are called by God to contribute to the common good and the flourishing of all and should have the right to answer that call through their work. The Church must respect and promote the vocational call of all persons, including LGBTQ+ ones who wish to serve in Catholic schools.

Living a life of vocation allows people to gradually experience the Kingdom of God as they labor to build it on Earth. Building the Kingdom encompasses personal growth and development, which occurs through community and the work of social justice in our daily lives. More importantly, this act of building God's Kingdom on Earth involves both a "here and now" and a "future yet to come." Herein lies a degree of uncertainty about what the Kingdom looks like and, according to probabilism and synodality, the Church must stand united and be ready to be surprised by God throughout the process. For these reasons, I argue that all humans should have the ability to pursue this journey and must be allowed, encouraged, and guided by Catholic leaders in the process. This is the substance of the right to a vocation, which allows all persons to build this Kingdom through their labor.

LGBTQ+ persons should be able to enjoy this moral right to a vocation. God calls each of us, whether LGBTQ+ or not, to contribute to this Kingdom. While this right to a vocation is not legally enforceable in the United States, as this would require that the state develop a spiritual or theological competence that the government is not equipped for, I believe Catholic institutions have a moral obligation to protect and preserve such a right to a vocation. As evidence in chapter 2, LGBTQ+ educators in Catholic schools are capable, willing, and enthusiastic about this mission. Many of them feel called to build God's Kingdom through their work in Catholic education—a task they can excel at. To dismiss them is to place obstacles on God's work through them and to stall the building of the Kingdom of God. The just thing to do would be to foster a Catholic school environment where the vocation and gifts of LGBTQ+ educators can contribute to the building of the Kingdom.

Reenvisioning Justice in Synodal Catholic Schools

A synodal Catholic school is one that journeys together, listening to the Holy Spirit through the diverse lives of the faithful. It allows the *sensus fidelium* to guide the community along God's plan. In other words, a synodal Church trusts that God is the ultimate architect of the Kingdom and that all hands are called to help construct it. Individuals, who come from diverse backgrounds, in their uniqueness offer significant and indispensable contributions to this Kingdom. While everyone is imperfect and susceptible to sin and temptation, synodality calls for mutual accompaniment as the community discerns its way forward together.

Catholic social teaching has developed as a blueprint of the Kingdom of God—one that needs continual revisions. LGBTQ+ people play a part in it. Synodal Catholic schools should renew their commitment to Catholic social teaching and should seek justice (i.e., to give all persons their due) within their community and in the broader society. Doing so would help bring about the Kingdom of God on earth. Catholic leaders who dismiss LGBTQ+ educators from Catholic schools are acting against this Kingdom, therefore, I assert that these dismissals are unjust and must cease. The Church's commitment to human dignity should guide its efforts to include LGBTQ+ persons and their beautiful vocations into the life of the school and the broader Church.

LGBTQ+ educators, because of their queer epistemologies, offer unique contributions to Catholic schools, the Church, and the Kingdom of God. Queerness, as discussed in chapter 4, can question, challenge, and transgress against some underlying norms in the Church and in our world that are oppressive. Queerness, therefore, presents a unique opportunity to uphold the dignity of all persons by destabilizing norms that violate it. Our call to build this Kingdom where the dignity of all is upheld should inspire Catholic leaders to renew their commitment to Catholic social teaching and to make this vision a reality.

CONCLUSION

In this chapter I invoked key principles of Catholic social teaching to argue that the dismissals of LGBTQ+ educators from Catholic schools are unjust and must cease. The firings are unjust because they break the relationship between the Catholic community and a vulnerable population they are called to care for, because they place obstacles to the flourishing of LGBTQ+ persons, and because they exclude LGBTQ+ people from participating in the common good and the impending Kingdom of God. In light of the Catholic tradition's adoption of human rights language, I argued that said language operates as a methodology (i.e., a grammar) with a set of rules. In examining the firings, I observed inconsistent applications of human rights language in a way that promotes a politicized ideology while sacrificing the human dignity of LGBTQ+ persons. For this reason, I call upon the leaders of the Catholic Church to reevaluate and recommit to the mission of LGBTQ+ inclusion in Catholic schools.

Catholic institutions have a responsibility in our society to not only meet basic legal requirements (if they are moral) but to surpass them and strive toward the common good, that is, toward the preservation of all human rights and the promotion of human flourishing for all. This includes protecting the human rights to individual religious liberty, employment, nondiscrimination, privacy, and vocation. Furthermore, Catholic institutions should operate in accordance with their own principles of subsidiarity, participation, and the preferential option for the vulnerable. Such efforts must be carried out *ad intra* (within the Church) and *ad extra* (outside of the Church in the broader society). Applied to the *ad intra* controversy of LGBTQ+ educators in Catholic schools, I argued that the Catholic Church must, at minimum, respect their basic human rights. At best, however, Catholic leaders should incorporate the vocational gifts of LGBTQ+ persons into the community and should place their gifts at the service of the Kingdom of God. This vision of God's Kingdom makes room for LGBTQ+ persons, including students, and promotes their flourishing.

From a pragmatic standpoint, I also observe that the way Catholic institutions engage in the practices of Catholic social teaching, including religious liberty, affects how Catholics relate to the Church, especially younger generations who are already resistant or apathetic to it in light of the Church's numerous public controversies. Most importantly, however, I argue that Catholic social teaching in relation to LGBTQ+ Catholics reflects an opportunity to evangelize by bringing our youth into a closer relationship with God and the Church. For this reason, I believe the Church is in a unique position with regard to its LGBTQ+ educators to model for the students the wonders of the Kingdom of God.

If Catholic schools live up to this vision, they would be a witness to all Catholics—especially young ones—of God's justice manifested on Earth. I dream of a Church that serves as a beacon to all nations, modeling the Kingdom of God that is at hand. As a gay man who has been blessed with a queer Catholic community in San Francisco for many years, I can attest to the inspiring power LGBTQ+ people have to create Catholic communities of love and justice. I have also seen the power of queer communities outside of the Church through social and political activism. I have experienced the Kingdom of God through the lives of my queer Catholic friends and colleagues as well as my non-Catholic queer friends and colleagues, and I am convinced that we have a key role to play in this synodal journey toward the coming Kingdom of God.

NOTES

1. SJ Thomas Massaro, *Living Justice: Catholic Social Teaching in Action*, 3rd ed. (Rowman & Littlefield, 2015), 10.

2. US Conference of Catholic Bishops, "Forming Consciences for Faithful Citizenship," USCCB.org, 2019, 6, https://www.usccb.org/issues-and-action/faithful-citizenship/upload/forming-consciences-for-faithful-citizenship.pdf.

3. This definition was developed in classical literature, including the work of Thomas Aquinas, and is adopted by the contemporary Church. See *Aristotle, Aristotle's Nicomachean Ethics*, trans. Robert C. Bartlett and Susan D. Collins, Repr. ed. (University of Chicago Press, 2012), Book V, sec. III; Thomas Aquinas, "*Summa Theologiae*," trans. Fathers of the English Dominican Province, New Advent, 2017, II–II, q. 58, preprint 1, https://www.newadvent.org/summa/3064.htm; "Compendium of the Social Doctrine of the Church," Vatican Website, no. 201, accessed December 23, 2023, https://www.vatican.va/roman_curia/pontifical_councils/justpeace/documents/rc_pc_justpeace_doc_20060526_compendio-dott-soc_en.html#Work,%20the%20right%20to%20participate.

4. For a classical overview of these types of justice, see *Aristotle, Aristotle's Nicomachean Ethics*, Book V; Thomas Aquinas, "*Summa Theologiae*," II–II, Q. 67; "Compendium of the Social Doctrine of the Church," no. 201.

5. Aquinas discusses justice as part of the natural law, which guides humans toward flourishing. See Thomas Aquinas, "*Summa Theologiae*," II–II, q. 57, preprint 3–4.

6. See "Compendium of the Social Doctrine of the Church."

7. Encyclicals are papal letters responding to a contemporary matter of social concern. While popes have written many encyclicals on different issues, as I will discuss

in this chapter, the first social encyclical was written in 1891 and was titled *Rerum Novarum*.

8. In this sense, the word "liberal" refers to "liberty" or "freedom" and not partisan liberalism (usually associated with being progressive as opposed to conservative).

9. Leo XIII, "Rerum Novarum," Vatican Website, May 15, 1891, https://www.vatican.va/content/leo-xiii/en/encyclicals/documents/hf_l-xiii_enc_15051891_rerum-novarum.html; Thomas A Shannon, "Commentary on Rerum Novarum," in *Modern Catholic Social Teaching: Commentaries and Interpretations*, ed. Kenneth R. Himes (Georgetown University Press, 2005), 127–50.

10. While there is no official list from the Catholic hierarchy on which encyclicals are part of the official social teaching on labor, popes have a tradition of publishing encyclicals about labor on milestone anniversaries of the first one. Other documents, such as the constitutions of Vatican II and other papal encyclicals, also address matters of labor. See Leo XIII, "Rerum Novarum"; Pius XI, "Quadragesimo Anno," Vatican Website, May 15, 1931, https://www.vatican.va/content/pius-xi/en/encyclicals/documents/hf_p-xi_enc_19310515_quadragesimo-anno.html; John XXIII, "Mater et Magistra," Vatican Website, May 15, 1961, https://www.vatican.va/content/john-xxiii/en/encyclicals/documents/hf_j-xxiii_enc_15051961_mater.html; John Paul II, "Laborem Exercens," Vatican Website, September 14, 1981, https://www.vatican.va/content/john-paul-ii/en/encyclicals/documents/hf_jp-ii_enc_14091981_laborem-exercens.html; John Paul II, "Centesimus Annus," May 1, 1991, https://www.vatican.va/content/john-paul-ii/en/encyclicals/documents/hf_jp-ii_enc_01051991_centesimus-annus.html.

11. Christine Frierer Hinze, "Commentary on Quadragesimo Anno," in *Modern Catholic Social Teaching: Commentaries and Interpretations*, ed. Kenneth R. Himes (Georgetown University Press, 2005), 151.

12. Since its origin, the Catholic social tradition teaches that, because humans are made in the image of God, every person possesses intrinsic dignity. Furthermore, since we are relational, social, and political beings, we have the right to benefit from and participate in the goods of society (i.e., the common good). See Leo XIII, "Rerum Novarum," no. 20, 34.

13. Jack Donnelly, *Universal Human Rights in Theory and Practice*, 3rd ed. (Cornell University Press, 2013), 25–29; United Nations, "Universal Declaration of Human Rights," (December 10, 1948), https://www.un.org/en/about-us/universal-declaration-of-human-rights.

14. These political philosophies placed more emphasis on separation of Church and state, opting to grant more freedoms to individual citizens. In other words, the political sphere shifted toward liberalism. According to Richard Gaillardetz, these political shifts toward liberalism caused the Church to move "from a confident . . . engagement with society to a growing siege mentality" and seeking to combat the growing secularism that permeated the political sphere. See Richard R. Gaillardetz, "The Ecclesiological Foundations of Modern Catholic Social Teaching," in *Modern Catholic Social Teaching: Commentaries and Interpretations*, ed. Kenneth R. Himes (Georgetown University Press, 2005), 73.

15. Pius IX, "The Syllabus of Errors," Papal Encyclicals, 1864, https://www.papalencyclicals.net/pius09/p9syll.htm.
16. Drew Christiansen, "Commentary on Pacem in Terris," in *Modern Catholic Social Teaching: Commentaries and Interpretations*, ed. Kenneth R. Himes (Georgetown University Press, 2005), 236.
17. John XXIII, "Pacem in Terris," Vatican Website, April 11, 1963, https://www.vatican.va/content/john-xxiii/en/encyclicals/documents/hf_j-xxiii_enc_11041963_pacem.html.
18. John XXIII, "Pacem in Terris," no. 158.
19. John XXIII, "Pacem in Terris," no. 9.
20. Christiansen, "Commentary on Pacem in Terris," 226.
21. John XXIII, "Pacem in Terris," no. 60.
22. William O'Neill, *Catholic Social Teaching: A User's Guide* (Orbis, 2021), xiii, 129.
23. Donnelly, *Universal Human Rights in Theory and Practice*, 97; Henry Shue, *Basic Rights: Subsistence, Affluence, and U.S. Foreign Policy*, 3rd ed. (Princeton University Press, 2020), 18–19.
24. John XXIII, "Pacem in Terris," nos. 24–30, 34–36.
25. Julio L. Martínez, "Teología de la libertad," *Estudios Eclesiásticos. Revista de investigación e información teológica y canónica* 81, no. 317 (2006): 392, https://revistas.comillas.edu/index.php/estudioseclesiasticos/article/view/9540.
26. This was particularly true in the United States, which is a predominantly protestant nation. For this reason, Noonan refers to religious liberty as "an American invention." See John T. Noonan, *The Lustre of Our Country: The American Experience of Religious Freedom* (University of California Press, 1998), 2.
27. For a comprehensive discussion on this history, see Leslie Griffin, "Commentary on Dignitatis Humanae," in *Modern Catholic Social Teaching: Commentaries and Interpretations*, ed. Kenneth R. Himes, 2nd ed. (Georgetown University Press, 2017).
28. John Courtney Murray and Peter Augustine Lawler, *We Hold These Truths: Catholic Reflections on the American Proposition* (Sheed & Ward, 2005), 61–66, 268–69, 299.
29. John Courtney Murray, *The Problem of Religious Freedom* (Newman, 1965), 32–41.
30. Murray, *The Problem of Religious Freedom*, 43.
31. Murray, *The Problem of Religious Freedom*, 21.
32. Second Vatican Council, "Dignitatis Humanae," Vatican Website, December 7, 1965, no. 2, https://www.vatican.va/archive/hist_councils/ii_vatican_council/documents/vat-ii_decl_19651207_dignitatis-humanae_en.html.
33. "Dignitatis Humanae," nos. 3, 10–11.
34. "Dignitatis Humanae," no. 14.
35. "Dignitatis Humanae," no. 1.
36. "Dignitatis Humanae," no. 4.
37. "Dignitatis Humanae," no. 4.
38. Donnelly, *Universal Human Rights in Theory and Practice*, 10.

39. Murray, *The Problem of Religious Freedom*, 25.
40. Donnelly, *Universal Human Rights in Theory and Practice*, 46.
41. Donnelly, *Universal Human Rights in Theory and Practice*, 48.
42. Donnelly believes that an acceptable use of group human rights is seen, for example, in the group human rights of indigenous people. In this case, the rights of the corporate entity of "indigenous people" cannot be reduced to individual rights of individual indigenous persons, for the violations they face to their human dignity are deployed against them as a whole. Furthermore, the group rights they claim to land and autonomy can only be exercised communally and are irreducible to the individual's rights. See Donnelly, *Universal Human Rights in Theory and Practice*, 48–49.
43. Jeff Diamant, "How Catholics around the World See Same-Sex Marriage, Homosexuality," Pew Research Center, November 2, 2020, https://www.pewresearch.org/fact-tank/2020/11/02/how-catholics-around-the-world-see-same-sex-marriage-homosexuality/.
44. Ladislas Orsy, "The Divine Dignity of Human Persons in Dignitatis Humanae," *Theological Studies* 75, no. 1 (March 1, 2014): 18, https://doi.org/10.1177/0040563913519565.
45. Orsy, "The Divine Dignity of Human Persons in Dignitatis Humanae," 18.
46. Orsy, "The Divine Dignity of Human Persons in Dignitatis Humanae," 12.
47. For examples, see Kevin Clarke, "Jesuits Banned in Nicaragua by Ortega Regime," *America Magazine*, August 24, 2023, https://www.americamagazine.org/politics-society/2023/08/24/jesuits-expelled-nicaragua-ortega-245924; Tyler Arnold, "Here's Where Christians Continued to Face Persecution in 2023," Catholic News Agency, December 30, 2023, https://www.catholicnewsagency.com/news/256408/here-s-where-christians-continued-to-face-persecution-in-2023.
48. Candida Moss, in her excellent analysis of the discourse of persecution and martyrdom of the early Church, argues that Christians have adopted a victim mentality about being persecuted by the dominant culture since its origin. Furthermore, this mentality is synthesized with an idealization of martyrdom and zeal for faith in the face of such persecution. For this reason, many contemporary Christians, even those who oppress others, retrieve this victim mentality that paints them as persecuted when the state, social, or religious entities push back against their oppressive doctrines. See Candida Moss, *The Myth of Persecution: How Early Christians Invented a Story of Martyrdom*, Repr. ed. (HarperOne, 2014).
49. In *Mater et Magistra*, just prior to publishing *Pacem in Terris*, Pope John XXIII recognizes, "In the majority of cases a man's work is his sole means of livelihood. Its remuneration, therefore, cannot be made to depend on the state of the market. It must be determined by the laws of justice and equity." See John XXIII, "Mater et Magistra," 18.
50. While Pope Leo XIII uses the language of rights loosely in this encyclical, he does enumerate several key principles that are now commonly referred to as "worker rights." Because this encyclical does not offer an extensive theoretical treatment of modern human rights, it is not considered the first formal adoption of rights language by the magisterium. The encyclical is largely grounded Catholic doctrine on natural

law. See Shannon, "Commentary on Rerum Novarum," 134; Leo XIII, "Rerum Novarum," no. 2.

51. John XXIII, "Pacem in Terris," no. 18.
52. Pius XII qtd. in John XXIII, no. 20.
53. John Paul II, "Laborem Exercens," no. 1.
54. John Paul II, "Laborem Exercens," no. 18.
55. John Paul II, "Laborem Exercens," no. 18.
56. John Paul II, "Laborem Exercens," no. 18. Italics in original.
57. Benedict XVI, "Caritas in Veritate," Vatican Website, June 29, 2009, no. 25, https://www.vatican.va/content/benedict-xvi/en/encyclicals/documents/hf_ben-xvi_enc_20090629_caritas-in-veritate.html.
58. Benedict XVI, "Caritas in Veritate," no. 63.
59. Francis, "Fratelli Tutti," Vatican Website, October 3, 2020, no. 162, https://www.vatican.va/content/francesco/en/encyclicals/documents/papa-francesco_20201003_enciclica-fratelli-tutti.html.
60. Congregation for Catholic Education, "The Identity of the Catholic School for a Culture of Dialogue," Vatican Website, January 25, 2022, no. 80, https://www.vatican.va/roman_curia/congregations/ccatheduc/documents/rc_con_ccatheduc_doc_20220125_istruzione-identita-scuola-cattolica_en.html.
61. Edward P. Hahnenberg, "Theology of Lay Ecclesial Ministry: Future Trajectories," in *Lay Ecclesial Ministry: Pathways Toward the Future*, ed. Zeni Fox (Rowman & Littlefield, 2010), 73.
62. US Conference of Catholic Bishops, "Ministry to Persons with a Homosexual Inclination: Guidelines for Pastoral Care," USCCB.org, November 14, 2006, 17, https://www.usccb.org/resources/ministry-to-persons-of-homosexual-iInclination_0.pdf.
63. Dan Guernsey and Denize Donohue, "Faith and Morals Language in Catholic School Teacher Employment Documents: Best Practices Brief," Cardinal Newman Society, June 25, 2015, https://cardinalnewmansociety.org/faith-morals-language-catholic-school-teacher-employment-documents-best-practices-brief/.
64. For examples of other educators fired after being unwittingly discovered to be in a same-sex civil marriage, see Jeremy P. Kelly, "Gay Catholic School Teacher Ousted; Alter Principal Calls It 'Unfortunate,'" *Dayton Daily News*, April 28, 2020, https://www.daytondailynews.com/news/local-education/gay-catholic-school-teacher-ousted-alter-principal-calls-unfortunate/Y1hK2VgRGomfGNY7NxStBK/; Vic Ryckaert, Holly V. Hays, and Crystal Hill, "Roncalli High School Can Legally Fire Counselor over Same-Sex Marriage, Expert Says," *The Indianapolis Star*, August 13, 2018, https://www.indystar.com/story/news/politics/2018/08/13/roncalli-defends-firing-counselor-shelly-fitzgerald-gay-same-sex-marriage-catholic-faith/974581002/; Keira Wingate, "A Gay Teacher in New York Was Fired from a Catholic School after Marrying His Partner," *USA Today*, October 27, 2021, https://www.usatoday.com/story/news/education/2021/10/27/gay-new-york-teacher-fired-catholic-school-over-marriage/8567547002/; Victor Fiorillo, "Parents Outraged Over Firing of Lesbian Teacher at Waldron Mercy Academy," *Philadelphia Magazine*

(blog), July 8, 2015, https://www.phillymag.com/news/2015/07/08/gay-teacher-fired-waldron-mercy-academy-margie-winters/.

65. "Catechism of the Catholic Church," Vatican Website, no. 2489, accessed June 7, 2023, https://www.vatican.va/archive/ENG0015/_INDEX.HTM.

66. Second Vatican Council, "Gaudium et Spes," Vatican Website, October 7, 1965, nos. 48–51, https://www.vatican.va/archive/hist_councils/ii_vatican_council/documents/vat-ii_const_19651207_gaudium-et-spes_en.html.

67. The doctrinal prohibition against same-sex civil marriage is simply a prudential application of the teaching on sexual activity, and not defensible if it is independent of the homosexual sexual activity itself. In other words, if a same-sex couple enters a civil marriage but does not engage in sexual activity, they are—according to Church doctrine—not in a state of sin. Their civil marriage is only condemned by the Church if it promotes homosexual sexual activity privately (between the couple) or publicly (in a way that gives scandal). When an LGBTQ+ person is fired from a Catholic school for being married, they are really being held accountable for their sexual activity or for promoting sexual activity in the context of the marriage. In light of the right to privacy applied to the intimate sexual activity of the couple, I argue that such firings infringe upon the LGBTQ+ person's right to privacy. I draw these insights from the Congregation for the Doctrine of the Faith's 2003 prohibiting the legalization of same-sex civil marriage. The document was prefaced by a statement indicating that there was no new doctrine but rather an application of previous doctrine. Same-sex civil unions, therefore, are condemned because they promote same-sex sexual activity and not because they are evil in and of themselves. See Congregation for the Doctrine of the Faith, "Considerations Regarding Proposals to Give Legal Recognition to Unions between Homosexual Persons," Vatican Website, June 3, 2003, nos. 1, 4–5, https://www.vatican.va/roman_curia/congregations/cfaith/documents/rc_con_cfaith_doc_20030731_homosexual-unions_en.html.

68. An example of this involves the firing of Matt Tedeschi, who I reference earlier. He was discovered and blackmailed by students on a dating app and then outed to the school's administration, resulting in his dismissal. See Matt Tedeschi, "'Men and Women for Others,' But Not You: My Time as a Teacher at St. Ignatius," *Medium* (blog), March 5, 2019, https://medium.com/@MrTee/https-medium-com-my-time-as-a-teacher-at-st-ignatius-d596c8ee17d0.

69. See Francis, "Querida Amazonia," Vatican Website, February 2, 2020, nos. 7–8, 26–27, 60, 63, 106, 110, https://www.vatican.va/content/francesco/en/apost_exhortations/documents/papa-francesco_esortazione-ap_20200202_querida-amazonia.html; Francis, "Fratelli Tutti," Vatican Website, October 3, 2020, nos. 56, 73, 162, https://www.vatican.va/content/francesco/en/encyclicals/documents/papa-francesco_20201003_enciclica-fratelli-tutti.html; Francis, "Evangelii Gaudium," Vatican Website, November 24, 2013, 186–216, https://www.vatican.va/content/francesco/en/apost_exhortations/documents/papa-francesco_esortazione-ap_20131124_evangelii-gaudium.html.

70. James Martin, "Why Should the Church Reach out to L.G.B.T.Q. People? Some Shocking Statistics Can Answer That," *America Magazine*, August 2, 2021,

https://www.americamagazine.org/faith/2021/08/02/james-martin-lgbtq-catholics-statistics-241139.

71. Richard Peddicord argued that LGBTQ+ issues in the United States should be treated as a matter of social justice and not just sexual morality. See Richard Peddicord, *Gay and Lesbian Rights: A Question: Sexual Ethics or Social Justice?* (Sheed and Ward, 1996).

72. Congregation for the Doctrine of the Faith, "Considerations Regarding Proposals to Give Legal Recognition to Unions between Homosexual Persons," no. 4.

73. Congregation for the Doctrine of the Faith, "Some Considerations Concerning the Response to Legislative Proposals on the Non-Discrimination of Homosexual Persons," Vatican Website, July 24, 1992, no. 7, https://www.vatican.va/roman_curia/congregations/cfaith/documents/rc_con_cfaith_doc_19920724_homosexual-persons_en.html.

74. Congregation for the Doctrine of the Faith, "Some Considerations Concerning the Response to Legislative Proposals on the Non-Discrimination of Homosexual Persons."

75. James Martin, *Building a Bridge: How the Catholic Church and the LGBT Community Can Enter into a Relationship of Respect, Compassion, and Sensitivity*, 2nd ed. (HarperOne, 2018), 47–49.

76. Pius XI, "Quadragesimo Anno," Vatican Website, May 15, 1931, 79, https://www.vatican.va/content/pius-xi/en/encyclicals/documents/hf_p-xi_enc_19310515_quadragesimo-anno.html.

77. "Compendium of the Social Doctrine of the Church," Vatican Website, no. 189, accessed December 23, 2023, https://www.vatican.va/roman_curia/pontifical_councils/justpeace/documents/rc_pc_justpeace_doc_20060526_compendio-dott-soc_en.html#Work,%20the%20right%20to%20participate.

78. For a treatment of the principle of participation related to LGBTQ+ educators in Catholic schools, see Matt Tedeschi, "Catholic Schools Are Called to Form a Culture of LGBTQ Participation," *New Ways Ministry* (blog), February 2, 2021, https://www.newwaysministry.org/2021/02/02/catholic-schools-are-called-to-form-a-culture-of-lgbtq-participation/.

79. See note 47.

80. Henry Shue, *Basic Rights: Subsistence, Affluence, and U.S. Foreign Policy*, 3rd ed. (Princeton University Press, 2020), 18.

Conclusion

In 2023, I was giving a lecture to undergraduates at Emory University on the intersection of Catholicism, Latinx identity, and LGBTQ+ identity. I began my remarks with a statement akin to my introductory line in this book: I come to this conversation as a gay Puerto Rican Catholic educator seeking to better understand the interplay between identities that appear to be in tension with each other. After the lecture, and the ensuing discussion that followed it, a student stayed behind to talk to me individually. She thanked me for the lecture and said, "I have never met someone like you." I asked her, "Had you never met a theologian before?" and she said that she had met plenty of theologians, but not one that was openly Latinx and queer and could harness the power of those identities to gain insight about God. She then disclosed that she is a queer Latina and that this lecture opened her eyes to a new possibility for her academic trajectory. Witnessing the story of an integrated queer Latinx Catholic painted a new horizon of potentiality for her. That was the *power* of "showing up" as my authentic self. This was one of the proudest moments of my career as an educator, one that I am not sure I can replicate in a Catholic high school to the same extent.

At the university level, I have worked with many fellow queer professors who similarly impact their students through their open and authentic life witness in the classroom. However, in the high school setting, we don't always have access to our full power due to the fear of dismissal. Nevertheless, I also have worked with queer high school educators who, despite the limitations they face, have found ways to assert their authenticity in small ways that also impacted their students. All of these LGBTQ+ educators are a gift to ministry and education, especially theological education. They have a unique perspective that is desperately needed in our Catholic institutions. I have learned invaluable lessons from my fellow LGBTQ+ colleagues, from LGBTQ+ activists, and from our allies about what the Kingdom of God looks like. I am proud to be a gay Catholic teacher and am committed to building God's Kingdom in Catholic education.

My hope with this book is that it provides theological, moral, and justice-based tools that can propel the Church forward toward a new vision for Catholic education that is inclusive of the gifts of LGBTQ+ educators. I call upon Catholic leaders to discern how synodality, probabilism, and Catholic social teaching apply in their institutions; and to foster a school environment that welcomes and cherishes the gifts of LGBTQ+ persons. However, through our Baptism, all Catholics are called to "Catholic leadership," so I call upon all readers to engage in this conversation with your local bishop and Catholic school community. The *sensus fidelium* is manifested in our lives and, through it, we are called to voice to the Church where we discern the Spirit is calling us and engage in a process of joint communal discernment. Through my research and ministry, I long to see a Church that fully embraces and promotes the dignity of all persons, especially those who are LGTBQ+.

I will conclude with a message to LGBTQ+ educators in Catholic schools: I wish you peace and happiness through your beautiful vocation. I understand that some of you must find other ways to plant your seeds of love and I fully support you, but if you are capable of staying in Catholic education despite the daily struggles you face, please stay! You are a gift to Catholic schools and to your students, especially to the LGBTQ+ ones. Young LGBTQ+ people need models who will affirm their place in the Church as beloved children of God, made in the *Imago Dei*. Even cisgender heterosexual students need you: they also need welcoming Catholic schools. Your commitment to Catholic education and the larger Church makes the Church a brighter, more loving place. Your life witness is a model of radical love and transgressive justice that is transformative in society. Without you, the Church would not be the same. You are the Church! I pray Catholic leaders learn to walk a synodal path, embrace your gifts in all their fullness, and commit to journeying together with you as full members of the People of God. May it be so.

Bibliography

Aldana, Ursula. "Moving Beyond the College-Preparatory High School Model to a College-Going Culture in Urban Catholic High Schools." *Journal of Catholic Education* 17, no. 2 (April 10, 2014): 131–53. https://doi.org/10.15365/joce.1702092014.

Althaus-Reid, Marcella. *Indecent Theology: Theological Perversions in Sex, Gender and Politics.* Routledge, 2000.

Anzaldúa, Gloria. *Borderlands / La Frontera: The New Mestiza,* 5th ed. Aunt Lute Books, 2022.

Aquino, Jorge A. "No Queer Aggiornamento This Time: Resubscribing to the Philosophy of Natural Law, Pope Francis Forecloses Reforms of Catholic Teaching on Sexuality." *Politics and Religion Journal* 11, no. 2 (2017): 217–33. https://doi.org/10.54561/prj1102217a.

Archdiocese of Denver. "Guidance for Issues Concerning the Human Person and Sexual Identity," n.d. https://www.documentcloud.org/documents/23218852-guidance-for-issues-concerning-the-human-person-and-sexual-identity.

Archdiocese of Milwaukee. "Catechesis and Policy on Questions Concerning Gender Theory," January 18, 2022. https://www.archmil.org/ArchMil/attachments/2022GenderTheoryfinal.pdf?utm_source=sendgrid&utm_medium=email&utm_campaign=website.

Aristotle. "Nicomachean Ethics." Translated by W. D. Ross. The Internet Classics Archive, 350AD. https://classics.mit.edu/Aristotle/nicomachaen.html.

Arnold, Tyler. "Here's Where Christians Continued to Face Persecution in 2023." Catholic News Agency, December 30, 2023. https://www.catholicnewsagency.com/news/256408/here-s-where-christians-continued-to-face-persecution-in-2023.

Aron, Hillel. "Ninth Circuit Blocks Discrimination Suit by Black Principal against Catholic School | Courthouse News Service." *Courthouse News Services,* November 23, 2021. https://www.courthousenews.com/ninth-circuit-blocks-discrimination-suit-by-black-principal-against-catholic-school/.

Associated Press. "Germany's Catholic Bishops Vote to Approve Blessings for Same-Sex Couples." *National Catholic Reporter,* March 10, 2023. https://www.ncronline.org/news/germanys-catholic-bishops-vote-approve-blessings-same-sex-couples.

———. "Ohio Catholic School Teacher Claims She Was Fired over Pregnancy." *The News Herald*, December 31, 2012. https://www.news-herald.com/2012/12/31/ohio-catholic-school-teacher-claims-she-was-fired-over-pregnancy/.

Bakshi, Kaustav. "Writing the LGBTIHQ+ Movement in Bangla: Emergence of Queer Epistemologies in Kolkata in the Early Days of Queer Political Mobilizations." *South Asian History and Culture* 13, no. 2 (April 3, 2022): 231–45. https://doi.org/10.1080/19472498.2022.2067636.

Barnard, Cornell. "Hundreds Protest Morality Clause for Teachers Proposed by SF Archbishop." *ABC7 San Francisco*, February 8, 2015. https://abc7news.com/morality-clause-teachers-san-franciscos-archdioceses/524464/.

Bechtle, Regina. "Spirit Guides and Table Companions: Saints as Models for Lay Ecclesial Ministers." In *Lay Ecclesial Ministry: Pathways toward the Future*, edited by Zeni Fox. Rowman & Littlefield, 2010.

Benedict XVI. "Caritas in Veritate." Vatican Website, June 29, 2009. https://www.vatican.va/content/benedict-xvi/en/encyclicals/documents/hf_ben-xvi_enc_20090629_caritas-in-veritate.html.

Binnie, Jon. "Coming out of Geography: Towards a Queer Epistemology?" *Environment and Planning D: Society and Space* 15, no. 2 (April 1, 1997): 223–37. https://doi.org/10.1068/d150223.

Boff, Leonardo, and Clodovis Boff. *Introducing Liberation Theology*. Translated by Paul Burns. Orbis Books, 1987.

Bruni, Frank. "Catholicism Undervalues Women." *New York Times*, May 6, 2015, sec. Opinion. https://www.nytimes.com/2015/05/06/opinion/frank-bruni-catholicism-undervalues-women.html.

Bryk, Anthony S., Valerie E. Lee, and Peter B. Holland. *Catholic Schools and the Common Good*. Harvard University Press, 1993.

Cahill, Lisa Sowle. *Sex, Gender, and Christian Ethics*. Cambridge University Press, 1996.

Carson, Sophie. "Milwaukee Catholic Archdiocese Transgender Policy Harmful, Critics Say." *Milwaukee Journal Sentinel*, 2022. https://www.jsonline.com/story/news/local/2022/05/10/milwaukee-catholic-archdiocese-policy-hurts-trans-teens-critics-say-lgbtq/7231737001/.

Catholic News Agency. "Archbishop Cordileone Thankful for San Francisco Teacher Contract Agreement," August 23, 2015. https://www.catholicnewsagency.com/news/32507/archbishop-cordileone-thankful-for-san-francisco-teacher-contract-agreement.

———. "Pope Francis: Synodality Is Not a 'Search for Majority Consensus,'" January 3, 2022. https://www.catholicnewsagency.com/news/250094/pope-francis-synodality-is-not-a-search-for-majority-consensus.

Catholic San Francisco. "Archdiocese Releases Q&A; on Union Contract Proposals," February 4, 2015. https://web.archive.org/web/20150206080928/http://www.catholic-sf.org/ns.php?newsid=25&id=63174.

———. "Archdiocese Releases Statement on Church Teachings, Practice in High Schools," February 4, 2015. https://web.archive.org/web/20150211095801/http://www.catholic-sf.org/ns.php?newsid=25&id=63175.

Catholic Theological Ethics in the World. "Michael G. Lawler." Accessed June 7, 2023. https://catholicethics.com/ethicists/michael-g-lawler/.
Charles, Chaput. "Father James Martin and Catholic Belief." Catholic Philly, September 19, 2019. https://catholicphilly.com/2019/09/archbishop-chaput-column/father-james-martin-and-catholic-belief/.
Chasan, Aliza. "New Jersey Supreme Court Rules in Favor of Catholic School That Fired Unwed Pregnant Teacher." *CBS News*, August 15, 2023. https://www.cbsnews.com/news/victoria-crisitello-new-jersey-supreme-court-pregnant-unwed-catholic-school-teacher-st-theresa-school/.
Christiansen, Drew. "Commentary on Pacem in Terris." In *Modern Catholic Social Teaching: Commentaries and Interpretations*, edited by Kenneth R. Himes, 217–43. Georgetown University Press, 2005.
City News Services. "Black Teacher Sues Playa Del Rey Catholic School over Alleged Discrimination, Grading Disputes." *Daily News*, July 12, 2022. https://www.dailynews.com/2022/07/12/black-teacher-sues-playa-del-rey-catholic-school-over-alleged-discrimination-grading-disputes/.
Clarke, Kevin. "Jesuits Banned in Nicaragua by Ortega Regime." *America Magazine*, August 24, 2023. https://www.americamagazine.org/politics-society/2023/08/24/jesuits-expelled-nicaragua-ortega-245924.
Cohoat, Matt, and Rob Bridges. "Dear Cathedral Family," June 23, 2019. https://www.gocathedral.com/about/news-marketing/school-news/news-post/~board/homepagenews/post/dear-cathedral-family.
Conferencia Episcopal Argentina. "Sínodo de la Sinodalidad: Síntesis de Argentina," 2022. https://episcopado.org/assetsweb/cont/3469/argentina_sintesis_final_sinodo_21-23.pdf.
Conferencia Episcopal Española. "Síntesis sobre la Fase Diocesana del Sínodo sobre la Sinodalidad de la Iglesia que Peregrina en España." conferenciaepiscopal.es, June 11, 2022. https://www.conferenciaepiscopal.es/wp-content/uploads/2022/06/SINTESIS-FINAL-FASE-DIOCESANA-DEL-SINODO.pdf.
Congregation for Catholic Education. "'Male and Female He Created Them'—Toward a Path of Dialogue on the Question of Gender Theory in Education." Vatican Website, 2019. https://www.vatican.va/roman_curia/congregations/ccatheduc/documents/rc_con_ccatheduc_doc_20190202_maschio-e-femmina_en.pdf.
———. "Criteria for the Discernment of Vocation for Persons with Homosexual Tendencies." Vatican Website, November 4, 2005. https://www.vatican.va/roman_curia/congregations/ccatheduc/documents/rc_con_ccatheduc_doc_20051104_istruzione_en.html.
———. "Educational Guidance in Human Love: Outlines for Sex Education." Vatican Website, November 1, 1983. https://www.vatican.va/roman_curia/congregations/ccatheduc/documents/rc_con_ccatheduc_doc_19831101_sexual-education_en.html.
———. "The Catholic School." Vatican Website, March 19, 1977. https://www.vatican.va/roman_curia/congregations/ccatheduc/documents/rc_con_ccatheduc_doc_19770319_catholic-school_en.html.

———. "The Identity of the Catholic School for a Culture of Dialogue." Vatican Website, January 25, 2022. https://www.vatican.va/roman_curia/congregations/ccatheduc/documents/rc_con_ccatheduc_doc_20220125_istruzione-identita-scuola-cattolica_en.html.

———. "The Religious Dimension of Education in a Catholic School: Guidelines for Reflection and Renewal." Vatican Website, April 7, 1988. https://www.vatican.va/roman_curia/congregations/ccatheduc/documents/rc_con_ccatheduc_doc_19880407_catholic-school_en.html.

Congregation for the Doctrine of the Faith. "Considerations Regarding Proposals to Give Legal Recognition to Unions between Homosexual Persons." Vatican Website, June 3, 2003. https://www.vatican.va/roman_curia/congregations/cfaith/documents/rc_con_cfaith_doc_20030731_homosexual-unions_en.html.

———. "Notification on the Book Just Love. A Framework for Christian Sexual Ethics by Sr. Margaret A. Farley, R.S.M." Vatican Website, March 30, 2012. https://www.vatican.va/roman_curia/congregations/cfaith/documents/rc_con_cfaith_doc_20120330_nota-farley_en.html.

———. "Persona Humana—Declaration on Certain Questions Concerning Sexual Ethics." Vatican Website, December 29, 1975. https://www.vatican.va/roman_curia/congregations/cfaith/documents/rc_con_cfaith_doc_19751229_persona-humana_en.html.

Cordileone, Salvatore, and Michael Barber. "The Body-Soul Unity of the Human Person." Archdiocese of San Francisco, September 29, 2023. https://sfarchdiocese.org/the-body-soul-unity-of-the-human-person/?fbclid=IwAR0nEaUfM87eif-Q8KV14ELb3kOh2x_nOtOak_wB7Gg3TIccZKzCiqyJATE.

Cordileone, Salvatore. "Archbishop's Letter to Catholic High School Teachers." Catholic San Francisco, February 4, 2015. https://web.archive.org/web/20150209114456/http://www.catholic-sf.org/ns.php?newsid=25&id=63177.

———. "Draft of Revised Faculty Handbooks for San Francisco Archdiocese," May 29, 2015. https://www.scribd.com/document/267577184/Draft-of-revised-faculty-handbooks-for-San-Francisco-archdiocese.

———. "Knowledge, Virtue, and Holiness." Catholic Culture, February 6, 2015. https://www.catholicculture.org/culture/library/view.cfm?recnum=10849.

Cox, Daniel, Juhem Navarro-Rivera, and Robert P. Jones. "A Shifting Landscape: A Decade of Change in American Attitudes about Same-Sex Marriage and LGBT Issues." Public Religion Research Institute. Accessed April 7, 2023. https://www.prri.org/research/2014-lgbt-survey/.

Crary, David. "Rejection or Welcome: Transgender Catholics Encounter Both." *AP News*, February 26, 2022. https://apnews.com/article/lifestyle-religion-united-states-gender-identity-marquette-368a622737d78df1f1f254a1e8e68aaf.

Creighton University Website. "Salzman, Todd A." Accessed June 7, 2023. https://www.creighton.edu/campus-directory/salzman-todd.

Cupich, Blase J. "The Development of Doctrine Is the Tradition." Chicago Catholic, September 13, 2023. https://www.chicagocatholic.com/cardinal-blase-j.-cupich/-/article/2023/09/13/the-development-of-doctrine-is-the-tradition.

D'Alfonso, Sean. "Exploring the Experiences of Black Students in a Predominantly White, All-Male, Suburban Catholic High School: A Critical Narrative Qualitative Study." EdD Diss., Seton Hall University, 2021. https://scholarship.shu.edu/dissertations/2853.

Damian, Chris. "'Dear Alana,' Hit No. 1 on Apple Podcasts. Are Church Leaders Listening?" *National Catholic Reporter*, September 14, 2023. https://www.ncronline.org/culture/dear-alana-hit-no-1-apple-podcasts-are-church-leaders-listening.

DeBernardo, Francis, and Robert Shine. "Employees of Catholic Institutions Who Have Been Fired, Forced to Resign, Had Offers Rescinded, or Had Their Jobs Threatened Because of LGBT Issues." New Ways Ministry, September 21, 2021. https://www.newwaysministry.org/issues/employment/employment-disputes/.

DeCosse, David E., Thomas A. Nairn, and Lisa Fullam, eds. "Dealing with Doubt: Epikeia, Probabilism, and the Formation of Medical Conscience." In *Conscience and Catholic Health Care: From Clinical Contexts to Government Mandates*. Orbis Books, 2017.

Diamant, Jeff. "How Catholics around the World See Same-Sex Marriage, Homosexuality." Pew Research Center, November 2, 2020. https://www.pewresearch.org/fact-tank/2020/11/02/how-catholics-around-the-world-see-same-sex-marriage-homosexuality/.

Diaz, Miguel H. "The Word That Crosses: Life-Giving Encounters with the Markan Jesus and Guadalupe." In *The Word Became Culture*, edited by Miguel H. Diaz, 1–24. Orbis Books, 2021.

Donnelly, Jack. *Universal Human Rights in Theory and Practice*. 3rd ed. Cornell University Press, 2013.

Dulles, Avery. *Models of the Church*. Expanded ed. Doubleday, 1987.

Erickson, Mandy. "Catholic Teachers Narrowly Vote to Accept Union Agreement with SF Archdiocese." National Catholic Reporter, August 20, 2015. https://www.ncronline.org/news/parish/catholic-teachers-narrowly-vote-accept-union-agreement-sf-archdiocese.

———. "Hundreds Attend Forum Opposed to San Francisco Handbook Changes." *National Catholic Reporter*, March 17, 2015. https://www.ncronline.org/news/parish/hundreds-attend-forum-opposed-san-francisco-handbook-changes.

Everitt, James. "The Experience of Catholic Gay and Lesbian Catholic Secondary School Teachers within Northern California: A Participatory Action Research Study." EdD Diss., University of San Francisco, 2010. https://repository.usfca.edu/diss/376.

Faggioli, Massimo. "From Collegiality to Synodality: Promise and Limits of Francis's 'Listening Primacy.'" *Irish Theological Quarterly* 85, no. 4 (November 1, 2020): 352–69. https://doi.org/10.1177/0021140020916034.

Farley, Margaret. *Just Love: A Framework for Christian Sexual Ethics*. Continuum, 2008.

Fathers of the English Dominican Province, trans. "Summa Theologiae," 2017. https://www.newadvent.org/summa/.

Figueroa, Christian. "Coming out as a Gay Catholic Teenager." Outreach, April 15, 2023. https://outreach.faith/2023/04/coming-out-as-a-gay-catholic-teenager/.

Fiorillo, Victor. "Parents Outraged Over Firing of Lesbian Teacher at Waldron Mercy Academy." *Philadelphia Magazine* (blog), July 8, 2015. https://www.phillymag.com/news/2015/07/08/gay-teacher-fired-waldron-mercy-academy-margie-winters/.

First Vatican Council. "Dei Filius." Vatican Website, April 28, 1870. https://www.vatican.va/content/pius-ix/la/documents/constitutio-dogmatica-dei-filius-24-aprilis-1870.html.

Fitzgerald vs. Roncalli High School and Roman Catholic Archdiocese of Indianapolis, no. 1:19-cv-04291-RLY-TAB (Southern District of Indiana 9/30).

Fitzgibbon, Éamonn. "Together on the Way—Pope Francis and Synodality." *The Furrow* 68, no. 10 (October 2017): 532–39. https://thefurrow.ie/product/together-way-pope-francis-synodality/.

Fleming, Julia. *Defending Probabilism: The Moral Theology of Juan Caramuel*. Georgetown University Press, 2006.

Ford Jr., Craig A. "Black Queer Natural Law: On Brownness and Disidentification." Political Theology Network, November 11, 2022. https://politicaltheology.com/black-queer-natural-law-on-brownness-and-disidentification/.

———. "Blackness, Queerness, and the New Galileo Moment in Magisterial Authority," 2021.

———. "Transgender Bodies, Catholic Schools, and a Queer Natural Law Theology of Exploration." *Journal of Moral Theology* 7, no. 1 (January 1, 2018): 70–98. https://jmt.scholasticahq.com/article/11382-transgender-bodies-catholic-schools-and-a-queer-natural-law-theology-of-exploration.

Foucault, Michel. *The History of Sexuality, Vol. 1: An Introduction*. Vintage, 1990.

Fox59. "Roncalli Counselor Suspended for Same-Sex Marriage Files Second Discrimination Charge," *The Indianapolis Star*, March 1, 2019. https://www.indystar.com/story/news/fox59/2019/03/01/shelly-fitzgerald-files-second-charge-against-roncalli-archdiocese-same-sex-marriage-case/3028812002/.

Francis. "Address of His Holiness Pope Francis at the Ceremony Commemorating the 50th Anniversary of the Institution of the Synod of Bishops." Vatican Website, October 17, 2015. https://www.vatican.va/content/francesco/en/speeches/2015/october/documents/papa-francesco_20151017_50-anniversario-sinodo.html.

———. "Address of His Holiness Pope Francis during the Meeting on the Family." Vatican Website, October 4, 2014. https://www.vatican.va/content/francesco/en/speeches/2014/october/documents/papa-francesco_20141004_incontro-per-la-famiglia.html.

———. "Address of Pope Francis to Students of Jesuit Schools of Italy and Albania." Vatican Website, June 7, 2013. https://www.vatican.va/content/francesco/en/speeches/2013/june/documents/papa-francesco_20130607_scuole-gesuiti.html#:~:text=Dear%20Young%20People%2C,home%E2%80%9D%20with%20all%20of%20you.

———. "Amoris Laetitia." Vatican Website, March 19, 2016. https://www.vatican.va/content/dam/francesco/pdf/apost_exhortations/documents/papa-francesco_esortazione-ap_20160319_amoris-laetitia_en.pdf.

———. "Evangelii Gaudium." Vatican Website, November 2013. https://www.vatican.va/evangelii-gaudium/en/files/assets/basic-html/../../../index.html.

———. "Fratelli Tutti." Vatican Website, October 3, 2020. https://www.vatican.va/content/francesco/en/encyclicals/documents/papa-francesco_20201003_enciclica-fratelli-tutti.html.

———. "General Audience." Vatican Website, June 26, 2013. https://www.vatican.va/content/francesco/en/audiences/2013/documents/papa-francesco_20130626_udienza-generale.html.

———. "Letter of the Holy Father to Card. Marc Ouellet, President of the Pontifical Commission for Latin America," March 19, 2016. https://www.vatican.va/content/francesco/en/letters/2016/documents/papa-francesco_20160319_pont-comm-america-latina.html.

———. "Praedicate Evangelium: Apostolic Constitution on the Roman Curia and Its Service to the Church and to the World." Vatican Website, March 19, 2022. https://www.vatican.va/content/francesco/en/apost_constitutions/documents/20220319-costituzione-ap-praedicate-evangelium.html#General_Norms.

———. "Querida Amazonia." Vatican Website, February 2, 2020. https://www.vatican.va/content/francesco/en/apost_exhortations/documents/papa-francesco_esortazione-ap_20200202_querida-amazonia.html.

———. "The God of Surprises: Morning Meditation in the Chape; of the Domus Sanctae Marthae." Vatican Website, October 13, 2014. https://www.vatican.va/content/francesco/en/cotidie/2014/documents/papa-francesco-cotidie_20141013_the-god-of-surprises.html.

Frierer Hinze, Christine. "Commentary on Quadragesimo Anno." In *Modern Catholic Social Teaching: Commentaries and Interpretations*, edited by Kenneth R. Himes, 151–74. Georgetown University Press, 2005.

Fullam, Lisa. "'Giving Scandal' in 'The Call of the Catholic Citizen: Theologians and Other Scholars Respond to Cathleen Kaveny.'" *America Magazine*, November 1, 2010. https://www.americamagazine.org/issue/753/100/call-catholic-citizen.

———. "Civil Same-Sex Marriage: A Catholic Affirmation." New Ways Ministry. Accessed September 19, 2023. https://www.newwaysministry.org/issues/marriage-equality/civil-sex-marriage-catholic-affirmation/.

———. "Transgender Students in Catholic Schools, Probabilism, and Reciprocity of Conscience." In *Conscience and Catholic Education: Theology, Administration, and Teaching*, edited by Kevin C. Baxter and David E. DeCosse, 133–49. Orbis, 2022.

Fung, Simon K. "Dear Alana." Accessed September 14, 2023. https://dearalana.com/.

Gaillardetz, Richard R. "The Ecclesiological Foundations of Modern Catholic Social Teaching." In *Modern Catholic Social Teaching: Commentaries and Interpretations*, edited by Kenneth R. Himes, 72–98. Georgetown University Press, 2005.

———. "The Theological Reception of Coworkers in the Vineyard of the Lord." In *Lay Ecclesial Ministry: Pathways toward the Future*, edited by Zeni Fox, 17–31. Rowman & Littlefield, 2010.

———. *By What Authority?: Foundations for Understanding Authority in the Church*. 2nd ed. Liturgical Press, 2018.

———. *The Church in the Making: Lumen Gentium, Christus Dominus, Orientalium Ecclesiarum*. Paulist Press, 2006.

General Secretariat of the Synod. "Enlarge the Space of Your Tent: Working Document for the Continental Stage." synod.va, October 2022. https://www.synod.va/content/dam/synod/common/phases/continental-stage/dcs/Documento-Tappa-Continentale-EN.pdf.

———. "The Ordinary General Assembly of the Synod of Bishops." synod.va, April 17, 2023. https://www.synod.va/content/dam/synod/news/2023-04-26_punto_stampa/2024.04.26_EN_FAQ_Partecipanti_Assemblea.pdf.

Gramick, Jeanine. "Pope Francis Has Condemned LGBTQ Criminalization. Now What?" *National Catholic Reporter*, February 27, 2023. https://www.ncronline.org/opinion/guest-voices/pope-francis-has-condemned-lgbtq-criminalization-now-what.

Gray, Kathleen. "Music, Marriage, a Happy Life in the Church. Now, Harder Times." *New York Times*, June 24, 2020, sec. U.S. https://www.nytimes.com/2020/06/24/us/politics/church-lgbtq-workplace-rights.html.

Griffin, Leslie. "Commentary on Dignitatis Humanae." In *Modern Catholic Social Teaching: Commentaries and Interpretations*, edited by Kenneth R. Himes. 2nd ed. Georgetown University Press, 2017.

Groome, Thomas H. "What Makes a School Catholic?" In *The Contemporary Catholic School: Context, Identity And Diversity*, edited by Terence McLaughlin and Joseph O'Keefe, 107–25. Routledge, 1996.

———. *Educating for Life: A Spiritual Vision for Every Teacher and Parent*. Herder & Herder, 2001.

Guernsey, Dan, and Denize Donohue. "Faith and Morals Language in Catholic School Teacher Employment Documents: Best Practices Brief." Cardinal Newman Society, June 25, 2015. https://cardinalnewmansociety.org/faith-morals-language-catholic-school-teacher-employment-documents-best-practices-brief/.

Gutierrez, Gustavo. *A Theology of Liberation: History, Politics, and Salvation*. Translated by Caridad Inda and John Eagleson. Rev. ed. Orbis Books, 1988.

Hahnenberg, Edward P. "Theology of Lay Ecclesial Ministry: Future Trajectories." In *Lay Ecclesial Ministry: Pathways toward the Future*, edited by Zeni Fox, 67–84. Rowman & Littlefield, 2010.

Herbert Jr., Henry. "I'm a Catholic High School Student Who Came Out. It's Time for Catholic Schools to Come Out, Too." Outreach, May 13, 2022. https://outreach.faith/2022/05/im-a-catholic-high-school-student-who-came-out-its-time-for-catholic-schools-to-come-out-too/.

Hernandez, Elizabeth. "Denver Archdiocese's LGBTQ Guidance to Local Catholic Schools." *The Denver POst*, November 7, 2022. https://www.denverpost.com/2022/11/07/denver-catholic-archdiocese-lgbtq-guidance-transgender-gay-students/.

———. "Family Blames Religious Conversion Therapy for Alana Chen's Death, Looks to Spark Hope with New Foundation." *The Denver Post*, January 6, 2020. https://www.denverpost.com/2020/01/06/alana-chen-conversion-therapy-suicide/.

Herndon, Astead W. "Catholic School, Gay Man Settle Discrimination Lawsuit." *Boston Globe*, May 9, 2016. https://www.bostonglobe.com/metro/2016/05/09/

dorchester-man-settles-with-catholic-school-discrimination-lawsuit/tCU2x8z18V-lhcVQXk3H1TP/story.html.
Herron, Arika. "Brebeuf Jesuit Appeals Split with Catholic Church, Barred from Holding All-School Mass." *The Indianapolis Star*, August 5, 2019. https://www.indystar.com/story/news/education/2019/08/05/brebeuf-jesuit-appeals-split-catholic-church-barred-holding-mass/1920187001/.
———. "Cathedral Fired a Gay Teacher. Brebeuf Protected One. They Are Married to Each Other, Lawyer Says." *The Indianapolis Star*, July 10, 2019. https://www.indystar.com/story/news/education/2019/07/10/cathedral-teacher-fired-same-sex-marriage-sues-indianapolis-archdiocese-identifies-himself/1694669001/.
———. "Catholic School Controversy: Rainbow Streamers Welcome Back Cathedral Students." *The Indianapolis Star*, August 8, 2019. https://www.indystar.com/story/news/education/2019/08/08/catholic-school-controversy-rainbow-streamers-welcome-back-cathedral-students/1952923001/.
Hill, Crystal. "Another Roncalli Guidance Counselor Alleges Discrimination over Sexual Orientation." *The Indianapolis Star*, November 16, 2018. https://www.indystar.com/story/news/2018/11/16/roncalli-guidance-counselor-files-federal-complaint-against-school-archdiocese/2029962002/.
Hinze, Bradford. "Can We Find a Way Together? The Challenge of Synodality in a Wounded and Wounding Church." *Irish Theological Quarterly* 85, no. 3 (August 1, 2020): 215–29. https://doi.org/10.1177/0021140020926595.
hooks, bell. *Teaching to Transgress*. Routledge, 2014.
Horan, Daniel P. "US Bishops' Document against Transgender Health Care Is a Disaster." National Catholic Reporter, March 23, 2023. https://www.ncronline.org/opinion/guest-voices/us-bishops-document-against-transgender-health-care-disaster.
International Theological Commission. "Sensus Fidei in the Life of the Church." Vatican Website, 2014. https://www.vatican.va/roman_curia/congregations/cfaith/cti_documents/rc_cti_20140610_sensus-fidei_en.html.
———. "Synodality in the Life and Mission of the Church." Vatican Website, March 2, 2018. https://www.vatican.va/roman_curia/congregations/cfaith/cti_documents/rc_cti_20180302_sinodalita_en.html.
Jesuitical. "When Catholic Doctrine Can Change—and When It Can't." *American Magazine*. Accessed November 11, 2023. https://www.americamagazine.org/faith/2023/10/25/jesuitical-richard-gaillardetz-doctrine-change-246368.
Jiménez Del Toro, Emanuel, Andrés Cruz Santos, and Adam Rosario Rodríguez. "Escala de masculinidad hegemónica en una muestra de adultos gais de Puerto Rico: Desarrollo y validación." *Revista Puertorriqueña de Psicología* 34, no. 1 (May 17, 2023): 14–27. https://doi.org/10.55611/reps.3401.02.
John Paul II. "Laborem Exercens." Vatican Website, September 14, 1981. https://www.vatican.va/content/john-paul-ii/en/encyclicals/documents/hf_jp-ii_enc_14091981_laborem-exercens.html.
———. *Man and Woman He Created Them: A Theology of the Body*. 2nd ed. Pauline Books and Media, 2006.

John XXIII. "Mater et Magistra." Vatican Website, May 15, 1961. https://www.vatican.va/content/john-xxiii/en/encyclicals/documents/hf_j-xxiii_enc_15051961_mater.html.
———. "Pacem in Terris." Vatican Website, April 11, 1963. https://www.vatican.va/content/john-xxiii/en/encyclicals/documents/hf_j-xxiii_enc_11041963_pacem.html.
Jones, Cleve. *When We Rise: My Life in the Movement*. Hachette Books, 2016.
Jonsen, Albert R., and Stephen Toulmin. *The Abuse of Casuistry: A History of Moral Reasoning*. University of California Press, 1990.
Jovel, Jesse, and Brandi Lucas. "Transformation from Within: Grounded Practice of Teachers amidst Cultural Change." *Journal of Catholic Education* 19, no. 1 (September 24, 2015): 243–50. https://doi.org/10.15365/joce.1901122015.
Keenan, James. *A History of Catholic Theological Ethics*. Paulist Press, 2022.
Kellerman SJ, Christopher J. *All Oppression Shall Cease: A History of Slavery, Abolitionism, and the Catholic Church*. Orbis, 2022.
Kelly, Jeremy P. "Gay Catholic School Teacher Ousted; Alter Principal Calls It 'Unfortunate.'" *Dayton Daily News*, April 28, 2020. https://www.daytondailynews.com/news/local-education/gay-catholic-school-teacher-ousted-alter-principal-calls-unfortunate/Y1hK2VgRGomfGNY7NxStBK/.
Kirchgaessner, Stephanie. "Vatican: Pope's Only 'audience' Was with Gay Former Student—Not Kim Davis." *The Guardian*, October 2, 2015, sec. World news. https://www.theguardian.com/world/2015/oct/02/pope-francis-kim-davis-audience-gay-student.
Knox, Liam. "Survey Details Obstacles to Black Student Attainment." Inside Higher Ed. Accessed November 25, 2023. https://www.insidehighered.com/news/2023/02/10/cost-discrimination-pose-challenges-black-students.
Kosnik, Anthony, William Carroll, Agnes Cunningham, Ronald Modras, and James Schulte. *Human Sexuality: New Directions in American Catholic Thought: A Study*. Paulist Pr, 1977.
Kouveglo, Emile. "La Sinodalidad En La Actualidad, a La Luz Del Concilio Vaticano II." *Revista de Investigación de La Cátedra Internacional Conjunta Inocencio III* 1, no. 7 (October 30, 2018): 279–97. https://vergentis.ucam.edu/index.php/vergentis/article/view/93.
Larson, Joseph. "I Am a Queer Graduate of an Elite Catholic High School. And I Am Tired of the Homophobia." Outreach, July 7, 2023. https://outreach.faith/2023/07/i-am-a-queer-graduate-of-an-elite-catholic-high-school-and-i-am-tired-of-the-homophobia/.
Levada, William. "Dissent and the Catholic Religion Teacher." In *Readings in Moral Theology No. 6: Dissent in the Church*, edited by Charles E. Curran and Richard A. McCormick, 133–51. Paulist Press, 1987.
Leo XIII. "Rerum Novarum." Vatican Website, May 15, 1891. https://www.vatican.va/content/leo-xiii/en/encyclicals/documents/hf_l-xiii_enc_15051891_rerum-novarum.html.

Lipka, Michael. "Young U.S. Catholics Overwhelmingly Accepting of Homosexuality." Pew Research Center, October 6, 2014. https://www.pewresearch.org/fact-tank/2014/10/16/young-u-s-catholics-overwhelmingly-accepting-of-homosexuality/.

Maher, Michael. *Being Gay and Lesbian in a Catholic High School: Beyond the Uniform*. Routledge, 2001.

Mahowald, Lindsay. "Hispanic LGBTQ Individuals Encounter Heightened Discrimination." Center for American Progress, July 29, 2021. https://www.americanprogress.org/article/hispanic-lgbtq-individuals-encounter-heightened-discrimination/.

Mannion, Gerard. "Sensus Fidelium and the International Theological Commission—Has Anything Changed between 2012 and 2014?" In *Learning from All the Faithful: A Contemporary Theology of the Sensus Fidei*, edited by Bradford E. Hinze and Peter C. Phan. Pickwick Publications, 2016.

Marcos-Mendez, Eva. "Exploratory Case Study: Key Factors Influencing the Academic and Social-Emotional Success of Black and Latinx Students." ProQuest Dissertations Publishing, 2022. https://search.proquest.com/docview/2696824040?pq-origsite=primo.

Mares, Courtney. "Pope Francis Announces Decision to Extend Synod on Synodality to 2024." Catholic News Agency, October 16, 2022. https://www.catholicnewsagency.com/news/252560/pope-francis-announces-decision-to-extend-synod-on-synodality-to-2024.

Marianist LGBTQ+ Initiative Team. "Living Our Marianist Charism: Embracing the LGBTQ+ Community Video." Marianist Social Justice Collaborative, July 2020. https://marianistsjc.net/lgbtq-initiative.

Martin, James. "Why Should the Church Reach Out to L.G.B.T.Q. People? Some Shocking Statistics Can Answer That." *America Magazine*, August 2, 2021. https://www.americamagazine.org/faith/2021/08/02/james-martin-lgbtq-catholics-statistics-241139.

———. *Building a Bridge: How the Catholic Church and the LGBT Community Can Enter into a Relationship of Respect, Compassion, and Sensitivity*. 2nd ed. HarperOne, 2018.

Martínez, Julio L. "Teología de la libertad." *Estudios Eclesiásticos. Revista de investigación e información teológica y canónica* 81, no. 317 (2006): 383–419. https://revistas.comillas.edu/index.php/estudioseclesiasticos/article/view/9540.

Massaro, SJ Thomas. *Living Justice: Catholic Social Teaching in Action*. 3rd ed. Rowman & Littlefield, 2015.

Massingale, Bryan N. "Beyond 'Who Am I to Judge?' The Sensus Fidelium, LGBT Experience, and Truth-Telling in the Church." In *Learning from All the Faithful: A Contemporary Theology of the Sensus Fidei*, edited by Bradford E. Hinze and Peter C. Phan. Pickwick Publications, 2016.

McCarty, Robert J., and John M. Vitek. *Going, Going, Gone: The Dynamics in Disaffiliation in Young Catholics*. Saint Mary's Press, 2018.

McCoy, Mary. "Thriving in the Multicultural Classroom: Principles and Practices for Effective Teaching, by Mary Dilg." *Journal of Catholic Education* 11, no. 3 (March 1, 2008): 408–10. https://doi.org/10.15365/joce.1103122013.

McEown, Jonah. "U.S. Bishops Say Religious Freedom Protections in Same-Sex Marriage Bill Are 'Insufficient.'" *Catholic News Agency*, November 17, 2022. https://www.catholicnewsagency.com/news/252849/us-bishops-religious-freedom-same-sex-marriage.

———. "Teacher Fired for Abortion Rights Social Media Posts Sues Catholic School in SC." *Catholic News Agency*. Accessed November 25, 2023. https://www.catholicnewsagency.com/news/41769/teacher-fired-for-abortion-rights-social-media-posts-sues-catholic-school-in-sc.

McNeill, John J. *The Church and the Homosexual: Fourth Ed.* 4th ed. Beacon Press, 1993.

Medina, Eduardo. "School's Catholic Title in Peril Over Pride and Black Lives Matter Flags." *New York Times*, June 18, 2022, sec. U.S. https://www.nytimes.com/2022/06/18/us/bishop-catholic-school-black-lives-matter-pride-flags.html.

Moloney, Anastasia. "LGBT+ Murders at 'Alarming' Levels in Latin America—Study." *Reuters*, August 8, 2019, sec. everythingNews. https://www.reuters.com/article/us-latam-lgbt-killings-idUSKCN1UY2GM.

Morey, Melanie M., and John J. Piderit. *Catholic Higher Education: A Culture in Crisis*. Oxford University Press, 2006.

Morris-Young, Dan. "Archbishop Salvatore Cordileone Takes Divisive Action in San Francisco Archdiocese," May 22, 2015. https://www.ncronline.org/news/parish/archbishop-salvatore-cordileone-takes-divisive-action-san-francisco-archdiocese.

———. "Influential Catholics Call for Removal of San Francisco Archbishop in Full-Page Ad." *National Catholic Reporter*, April 16, 2015. https://www.ncronline.org/news/parish/influential-catholics-call-removal-san-francisco-archbishop-full-page-ad.

———. "New Faculty Handbooks in San Francisco to Include Statement Developed by Archbishop." National Catholic Reporter, February 4, 2025. https://www.ncronline.org/news/parish/new-faculty-handbooks-san-francisco-include-statement-developed-archbishop.

———. "Teachers Union: Revised Faculty Handbook Could Reduce San Francisco Legal Protections." National Catholic Reporter, June 3, 2015. https://www.ncronline.org/news/parish/teachers-union-revised-faculty-handbook-could-reduce-san-francisco-legal-protections.

Moss, Candida. *The Myth of Persecution: How Early Christians Invented a Story of Martyrdom*. Repr. ed. HarperOne, 2014.

Muñoz, José Esteban, Joshua Chambers-Letson, Tavia Nyong'o, and Ann Pellegrini. *Cruising Utopia: The Then and There of Queer Futurity*. 2nd ed. New York University Press, 2019.

Murray, John Courtney, and Peter Augustine Lawler. *We Hold These Truths: Catholic Reflections on the American Proposition*. Sheed and Ward, 2005.

———. *The Problem of Religious Freedom*. Newman, 1965.

Narea, Nicole. "Nearly 2,000 Children Were Sexually Abused in the Illinois Catholic Church." Vox, May 24, 2023. https://www.vox.com/2023/5/24/23736234/illinois-catholic-church-child-sex-abuse.

New Ways Ministry. "Employees of Catholic Institutions Who Have Been Fired, Forced to Resign, Had Offers Rescinded, or Had Their Jobs Threatened Because of LGBT Issues." New Ways Ministry. Accessed December 6, 2022. https://www.newwaysministry.org/issues/employment/employment-disputes/.

Newman, John Henry. *Essay on the Development of Christian Doctrine*. Word on Fire Classics, 2017.

Niebuhr, H. Richard. *Christ and Culture*. Harper & Row, 1975.

Noonan, John T. *Church That Can and Cannot Change: The Development of Catholic Moral Teaching*. University of Notre Dame Press, 2005.

———. *The Lustre of Our Country: The American Experience of Religious Freedom*. University of California Press, 1998.

O'Loughlin, Michael J. *Hidden Mercy: AIDS, Catholics, and the Untold Stories of Compassion in the Face of Fear*. Broadleaf Books, 2021.

O'Malley, John W. *What Happened at Vatican II*. Belknap Press, 2010.

O'Neill, William. *Catholic Social Teaching: A User's Guide*. Orbis, 2021.

Orsy, Ladislas. "The Divine Dignity of Human Persons in Dignitatis Humanae." *Theological Studies* 75, no. 1 (March 1, 2014): 8–22. https://doi.org/10.1177/0040563913519565.

Osheim, Amanda C. "Stepping toward a Synodal Church." *Theological Studies* 80, no. 2 (June 1, 2019): 370–92. https://doi.org/10.1177/0040563919836225.

Otto, Andy. "Cura Personalis." *Ignatian Spirituality* (blog), August 15, 2013. https://www.ignatianspirituality.com/cura-personalis/.

Palmer, Parker J. *The Courage to Teach: Exploring the Inner Landscape of a Teacher's Life, 20th Anniversary Ed*. 20th ed. Jossey-Bass, 2017.

Park, Peter. "Knowledge and Participatory Research." In *Handbook of Action Research: Participative Inquiry and Practice*, edited by Peter Reason and Hilary Bradbury. Sage, 2005.

Paul VI. "Humanae Vitae." Vatican Website, July 25, 1968. https://www.vatican.va/content/paul-vi/en/encyclicals/documents/hf_p-vi_enc_25071968_humanae-vitae.html.

Peddicord, Richard. *Gay and Lesbian Rights: A Question: Sexual Ethics or Social Justice?* Sheed & Ward, 1996.

Pelikan, Jaroslav. *The Christian Tradition: A History of the Development of Doctrine, Vol. 5: Christian Doctrine and Modern Culture*. University of Chicago Press, 1991.

Pena, Jorge, John Reyes, and Michael O'Connor. "Catholic Theological and Equity Framework to Champion Hispanic Representation in Catholic Schools." *Journal of Catholic Education* 25, no. 2 (January 1, 2022): 94–115. https://doi.org/10.15365/joce.2502062022.

Phillips, Peter. "Synodality and The Gift of Authority." *Theology* 103, no. 815 (September 1, 2000): 323–30. https://doi.org/10.1177/0040571X0010300502.

Pius IX. "The Syllabus of Errors." Papal Encyclicals, 1864. https://www.papalencyclicals.net/pius09/p9syll.htm.

Pius X. "Vehementer Nos." Vatican Website, February 11, 1906. https://www.vatican.va/content/pius-x/en/encyclicals/documents/hf_p-x_enc_11021906_vehementer-nos.html.

Pius XI. "Quadragesimo Anno." Vatican Website, May 15, 1931. https://www.vatican.va/content/pius-xi/en/encyclicals/documents/hf_p-xi_enc_19310515_quadragesimo-anno.html.

Porter, Jean. *Nature as Reason: A Thomistic Theory of the Natural Law*. Wm. B. Eerdmans-Lightning Source, 2004.

Reese, Thomas. "Vatican Financial Scandals: Corruption, Stupidity or Both?" National Catholic Reporter. Accessed November 25, 2023. https://www.ncronline.org/opinion/guest-voices/vatican-financial-scandals-corruption-stupidity-or-both.

Rodríguez-Madera, Sheilla L., Mark Padilla, Nelson Varas-Díaz, Torsten Neilands, Ana C. Vasques Guzzi, Ericka J. Florenciani, and Alíxida Ramos-Pibernus. "Experiences of Violence among Transgender Women in Puerto Rico: An Underestimated Problem." *Journal of Homosexuality* 64, no. 2 (January 28, 2017): 209–17. https://doi.org/10.1080/00918369.2016.1174026.

Romney, Lee. "S.F. Archbishop's Imposition of Morality Clause at Schools Outrages Many." *Los Angeles Times*, February 12, 2015, sec. California. https://www.latimes.com/local/california/la-me-san-francisco-archbishop-20150212-story.html.

Ruiz, Ish, and Jane Bleasdale. "Mixed Blessings: Understanding the Experience of LGBTQIA+ Educators in Catholic Schools." *Journal of Homosexuality* 69, no. 12 (October 15, 2022): 2148–66. https://doi.org/10.1080/00918369.2021.1984787.

Ruiz, Ish, and Mark Guevara, eds. *Cornerstones: Sacred Stories of LGBTQ+ Employees in Catholic Institutions*. New Ways Ministry, 2024.

Ruiz, Ish. "Latino/a/x Theology." *Proceedings of the Catholic Theological Society of America* 77 (September 8, 2023): 140–41. https://ejournals.bc.edu/index.php/ctsa/article/view/17033.

———. "Queering Synodality." *Go, Rebuild My House* (blog), July 14, 2023. https://sacredheartuniversity.typepad.com/go_rebuild_my_house/2023/07/queering-synodality-.html.

———. "Synodality in the Catholic Church: Toward a Conciliar Ecclesiology of Inclusion for LGBTQ+ Persons." *Journal of Moral Theology* 12, no. 2 (July 18, 2023): 55–77. https://doi.org/10.55476/001c.84391.

———. "The Stones That Have Been Rejected: Contributions of Queer Educators in Catholic Schools." In *The Human in a Dehumanizing World: Reexamining Theological Anthropology and Its Implications*, 67:128–40. College Theology Society Annual Volume. Orbis Books, 2022.

Rush, Ormond. "Inverting the Pyramid: The Sensus Fidelium in a Synodal Church." *Theological Studies* 78, no. 2 (June 1, 2017): 299–325. https://doi.org/10.1177/0040563917698561.

———. "Sensus Fidei: Faith 'Making Sense' of Revelation." *Theological Studies* 62, no. 2 (May 1, 2001): 231–61. https://doi.org/10.1177/004056390106200201.

———. "The Church as a Hermeneutical Community and the Eschatological Function of the Sensus Fidelium." In *Learning from All the Faithful: A Contemporary Theology of the Sensus Fidei*, edited by Bradford E. Hinze and Peter C. Phan. Pickwick Publications, 2016.

———. *Still Interpreting Vatican II: Some Hermeneutical Principles*. Paulist Press, 2004.

Ryckaert, Vic. "A Second Roncalli Counselor Has Been Told She Will Lose Her Job over Same-Sex Marriage." *The Indianapolis Star*, March 25, 2019. https://www.indystar.com/story/news/2019/03/25/roncalli-counselor-losing-job-same-sex-marriage-shelly-fitzgerald-lynn-starkey/3265868002/.

Ryckaert, Vic, and Holly V. Hays. "'My Faith Hasn't Been Shaken,' Says Roncalli School Counselor Whose Job Is on the Line." *The Indianapolis Star*, August 14, 2018. https://www.indystar.com/story/news/2018/08/14/roncalli-high-school-counselor-catholic-school-same-sex-marriage-conflict/986631002/.

Ryckaert, Vic, Holly V. Hays, and Crystal Hill. "Roncalli High School Can Legally Fire Counselor over Same-Sex Marriage, Expert Says." *The Indianapolis Star*, August 13, 2018. https://www.indystar.com/story/news/politics/2018/08/13/roncalli-defends-firing-counselor-shelly-fitzgerald-gay-same-sex-marriage-catholic-faith/974581002/.

Salzman, Todd A., and Michael G. Lawler. *The Sexual Person: Toward a Renewed Catholic Anthropology*. Georgetown University Press, 2008.

Schlag, Martin. "Social Justice or Preferential Option for the Poor?" *Studia Moralia* 58, no. 2 (July 2020): 355–71. https://login.proxy.library.emory.edu/login?url=https://search.ebscohost.com/login.aspx?direct=true&db=a9h&AN=147349903&site=ehost-live&scope=site.

Second Vatican Council. "Christus Dominus." Vatican Website, October 28, 1965. https://www.vatican.va/archive/hist_councils/ii_vatican_council/documents/vat-ii_decree_19651028_christus-dominus_en.html.

———. "Dei Verbum." Vatican Website, November 18, 1965. https://www.vatican.va/archive/hist_councils/ii_vatican_council/documents/vat-ii_const_19651118_dei-verbum_en.html.

———. "Gaudium et Spes." Vatican Website, October 7, 1965. https://www.vatican.va/archive/hist_councils/ii_vatican_council/documents/vat-ii_const_19651207_gaudium-et-spes_en.html.

———. "Gravissimum Educationis." Vatican Website, October 28, 1965. https://www.vatican.va/archive/hist_councils/ii_vatican_council/documents/vat-ii_decl_19651028_gravissimum-educationis_en.html.

———. "Lumen Gentium," November 21, 1964. https://www.vatican.va/archive/hist_councils/ii_vatican_council/documents/vat-ii_const_19641121_lumen-gentium_en.html.

———. "Sacrosanctum Concilium." Vatican Website, December 4, 1963. https://www.vatican.va/archive/hist_councils/ii_vatican_council/documents/vat-ii_const_19631204_sacrosanctum-concilium_en.html.

Shannon, Thomas A. "Commentary on Rerum Novarum." In *Modern Catholic Social Teaching: Commentaries and Interpretations*, edited by Kenneth R. Himes, 127–50. Georgetown University Press, 2005.

Shaughnessy, John. "Archbishop Encourages Christ-Centered Approach to Move Forward in Unity (July 12, 2019)," July 12, 2019. https://www.archindy.org/criterion/local/2019/07-12/archbishop.html.

"Shelly's Voice." Accessed June 7, 2023. https://shellysvoice.org/.

Shine, Robert. "After Colorado Shooting, Bishops' Responses Muted, Other Catholic Leaders Speak Out." *New Ways Ministry, Bondings 2.0* (blog), November 23, 2022. https://www.newwaysministry.org/2022/11/23/after-colorado-shooting-bishops-responses-muted-other-catholic-leaders-speak-out/.

———. "Anti-LGBTQ Criminalization & the Catholic Church: A Chronology." New Ways Ministry, July 14, 2019. https://www.newwaysministry.org/resources/catholic-responses-criminalization/.

———. "As Global Synod Progresses, LGBTQ+ Inclusion a Prominent Issue in National Reports." *New Ways Ministry* (blog), August 25, 2022. https://www.newwaysministry.org/2022/08/25/as-global-synod-progresses-lgbtq-inclusion-a-prominent-issue-in-national-reports/.

Shine, Robert. "As Global Synod Progresses, LGBTQ+ Inclusion a Prominent Issue in National Reports." New Ways Ministry. *Bondings 2.0* (blog), Sutust 2022. https://www.newwaysministry.org/2022/08/25/as-global-synod-progresses-lgbtq-inclusion-a-prominent-issue-in-national-reports/.

———. "Catholic School Backs Away from Banning Transgender Students." *New Ways Ministry* (blog), March 29, 2016. https://www.newwaysministry.org/2016/03/29/catholic-school-backs-away-from-banning-transgender-students/.

———. "From 'A' to 'D-': How Catholic LGBTQ+ Leaders Grade Pope Francis at Ten Years, Part I." *New Ways Ministry, Bondings 2.0* (blog), March 14, 2023. https://www.newwaysministry.org/2023/03/14/from-a-to-d-how-catholic-lgbtq-leaders-grade-pope-francis-at-ten-years-part-i/.

———. "New USCCB Document Seeks to Stop Transgender Healthcare at Catholic Institutions." *New Ways Ministry, Bondings 2.0* (blog), March 22, 2023. https://www.newwaysministry.org/2023/03/22/new-usccb-document-seeks-to-stop-transgender-healthcare-at-catholic-institutions/.

———. "U.S. Bishops' Conference Elects President with Anti-LGBTQ Record." *New Ways Ministry* (blog), November 16, 2022. https://www.newwaysministry.org/2022/11/16/u-s-bishops-conference-elects-president-with-anti-lgbtq-record/.

Shue, Henry. *Basic Rights: Subsistence, Affluence, and U.S. Foreign Policy*. 3rd ed. Princeton University Press, 2020.

Simonds, Thomas, Carin Appleget, Timothy Cook, Ronald Fussell, Kelsey Philippe, Alexander Rödlach, and Renzo Rosales. "Understanding the Latino/a Student Experience in Catholic High Schools in a United States Diocese." *International Studies in Catholic Education* 1 (2023): 1–16. https://doi.org/10.1080/19422539.2022.2164005.

Sims, Katherine, Nina Tran, Rachel Lam, and RadioActive Youth Media. "Seattle Catholic Students Form Underground Clubs For LGBTQ Youth." *National Public Radio*, October 24, 2018. https://www.kuow.org/stories/seattle-catholic-students-form-underground-clubs-lgbtq-youth.

Smith, Christian, and Melina Lundquist Denton. *Soul Searching: The Religious and Spiritual Lives of American Teenagers*. Repr. ed. Oxford University Press, 2009.

Southern Africa Catholic Bishops Conference. "SACBC Synod Synthesis Report." SACBC.org, June 9, 2022. https://sacbc.org.za/sacbc-submitted-a-synod-synthesis-report/.

St. Norbert's College Website. "Craig A. Ford, Jr." Accessed June 7, 2023. https://www.snc.edu/academics/faculty/craig.ford.html.

Stahel, Thomas H. "Interview: Andrew Sullivan on Being Openly Gay and Catholic." *America Magazine*, November 10, 2022. https://www.americamagazine.org/faith/2022/11/10/vantage-point-america-andrew-sullivan-244119.

Starkey v. Roman Catholic Archdiocese of Indianapolis and Roncalli High School, no. 21-2524 (7 Circuit Court July 28, 2022).

Steidl-Jack, Jason. *LGBTQ Catholic Ministry: Past and Present*. Paulist Press, 2022.

Stockbridge, Kevin. "Queer Teachers in Catholic Schools: Cosmic Perceptions of an Easter People." PhD Diss., Chapman University, 2017. https://doi.org/10.36837/chapman.000032.

Strzelczyk, Grzegorz. "Synodality: An Epiphany of the Spirit." *Studia Teologii Dogmatycznej* 5 (March 28, 2020): 139–48. https://doi.org/10.15290/std.2019.05.12.

Sullivan, Louise. "The Core Values of Vincentian Education." *Vincentian Heritage Journal* 16, no. 2 (October 1, 1995). https://via.library.depaul.edu/vhj/vol16/iss2/3.

Synod.va. "Synodal Process." Accessed November 25, 2023. https://www.synod.va/en/synodal-process.html.

Tanner, Norman P. *The Church and the World: Gaudium et Spes, Inter Mirifica*. Paulist Press, 2005.

Tedeschi, Matt. "'Men and Women for Others,' But Not You: My Time as a Teacher at St. Ignatius." *Medium* (blog), March 5, 2019. https://medium.com/@MrTee/https-medium-com-my-time-as-a-teacher-at-st-ignatius-d596c8ee17d0.

———. "Catholic Schools Are Called to Form a Culture of LGBTQ Participation." *New Ways Ministry* (blog), February 2, 2021. https://www.newwaysministry.org/2021/02/02/catholic-schools-are-called-to-form-a-culture-of-lgbtq-participation/.

The Pillar. "Cardinal Tobin Asked to Mediate Indy High School Standoff." January 27, 2021. https://www.pillarcatholic.com/cardinal-tobin-asked-to-mediate-indy/.

The Trevor Project. "Facts about LGBTQ Youth Suicide." December 15, 2021. https://www.thetrevorproject.org/resources/article/facts-about-lgbtq-youth-suicide/.

———. "National Survey on LGBTQ Youth Mental Health 2021." 2021. https://www.TheTrevorProject.org/survey-2021/.

———. "Religiosity and Suicidality among LGBTQ Youth." April 14, 2020. https://www.thetrevorproject.org/research-briefs/religiosity-and-suicidality-among-lgbtq-youth/.

———. "The Trevor Project Research Brief: Accepting Adults Reduce Suicide Attempts among LGBTQ Youth." The Trevor Project, June 2019. https://www.thetrevorproject.org/wp-content/uploads/2019/06/Trevor-Project-Accepting-Adult-Research-Brief_June-2019.pdf.

Thomas Aquinas. "Summa Theologiae." Translated by Fathers of the English Dominican Province. New Advent, 2017. https://www.newadvent.org/summa/3064.htm.

Thomas, Daniel J., Marcus W. Johnson, Langston Clark, and Louis Harrison. "When the Mirage Fades: Black Boys Encountering Antiblackness in a Predominantly

White Catholic High School." *Race Ethnicity and Education* 25, no. 7 (November 10, 2022): 958–77. https://doi.org/10.1080/13613324.2020.1798376.

Thompson, Charles C. "Key Facts and Answers to Frequently Asked Questions." Archdiocese of Indianapolis Website, June 27, 2019. https://www.archindy.org/archbishop/press-2019-faq.html.

Tinner-Williams, Nate. "'Personal Passion for HBCUs Overshadowed Support for the School Mission': Black Teacher Abruptly Fired from Georgia Catholic School." *Black Catholic Messenger*, June 6, 2022. https://www.blackcatholicmessenger.com/hicks-firing-decatur/.

Tutino, Stefania. *Uncertainty in Post-Reformation Catholicism: A History of Probabilism*. Oxford University Press, 2017.

UNCF. "K–12 Disparity Facts and Statistics." *UNCF* (blog). Accessed November 25, 2023. https://uncf.org/pages/k-12-disparity-facts-and-stats.

United Nations. "Universal Declaration of Human Rights," December 10, 1948. https://www.un.org/en/about-us/universal-declaration-of-human-rights.

United States Catholic Conference. *To Teach as Jesus Did: A Pastoral Message on Catholic Education*. United States Catholic Conference, 1972.

United States Conference of Catholic Bishops. "Co-Workers in the Vineyard of the Lord: A Resource for Guiding the Development of Lay Ecclesial Ministry." USCCB.org, 2005. https://www.usccb.org/upload/co-workers-vineyard-lay-ecclesial-ministry-2005.pdf.

———. "Discrimination against Catholic Adoption Services." Accessed April 9, 2023. https://www.usccb.org/committees/religious-liberty/discrimination-against-catholic-adoption-services.

———. "Doctrinal Note on the Moral Limits to Technological Manipulations of the Hhuman Body." USCCB.org, March 20, 2023. https://www.usccb.org/resources/Doctrinal%20Note%202023-03-20.pdf.

———. "Forming Consciences for Faithful Citizenship." USCCB.org, 2019. https://www.usccb.org/issues-and-action/faithful-citizenship/upload/forming-consciences-for-faithful-citizenship.pdf.

———. "Inadequacies in the Theological Methodology and Conclusion of the Sexual Person: Toward a Renewed Catholic Anthropology by Todd A. Salzman and Michael G. Lawler." USCCB.org, September 15, 2010. https://www.usccb.org/resources/inadequacies-theological-methodology-and-conclusion-sexual-person-toward-renewed-catholic.

———. "Ministry to Persons with a Homosexual Inclination: Guidelines for Pastoral Care." USCCB.org, November 14, 2006. https://www.usccb.org/resources/ministry-to-persons-of-homosexual-iInclination_0.pdf.

———. "U.S. National Synthesis 2021-2023 Synod." USCCB.org, 2022. https://www.usccb.org/resources/US%20National%20Synthesis%202021-2023%20Synod.pdf.

Vatican Website. "Catechism of the Catholic Church." Accessed June 7, 2023. https://www.vatican.va/archive/ENG0015/_INDEX.HTM.

———. "Code of Canon Law." Accessed December 30, 2022. https://www.vatican.va/archive/cod-iuris-canonici/eng/documents/cic_lib3-cann793-821_en.html#CHAPTER_I.

———. "Compendium of the Social Doctrine of the Church." Accessed December 23, 2023. https://www.vatican.va/roman_curia/pontifical_councils/justpeace/documents/rc_pc_justpeace_doc_20060526_compendio-dott-soc_en.html#Work,%20the%20right%20to%20participate.

———. "The Synod of Bishops: An Introduction." Accessed November 19, 2023. https://www.vatican.va/roman_curia/synod/documents/rc_synod_01011995_profile_en.html#.

Verbryke, Bill. "Update from Brebeuf Jesuit President, Fr. Bill Verbryke, S.J." Brebeuf Jesuit Preparatory School, February 25, 2019. https://web.archive.org/web/20210225032948/https://brebeuf.org/update-from-brebeuf-jesuit-president-fr-bill-verbryke-s-j-2/.

Vogt, Christopher P. "The Inevitability of Scandal: A Moral and Biblical Analysis of Firing Gay Teachers and Ministers to Avoid Scandal." In *The Bible and Catholic Theological Ethics*, edited by Yiu Sing Lucas Chan, James Keenan, and Ronaldo Zacharias, 262–72. Orbis Books, 2017.

Wex Definitions Team. "Affirmative Defense." Legal Information Institute, June 2022. https://www.law.cornell.edu/wex/affirmative_defense.

White, Christopher. "Pope Francis Blasts Reactionary American Catholics Who Oppose Church Reform." *National Catholic Reporter*, August 28, 2023. https://www.ncronline.org/vatican/vatican-news/pope-francis-blasts-reactionary-american-catholics-who-oppose-church-reform.

Whitehead, Evelyn, and James D. Whitehead. *Fruitful Embraces: Sexuality, Love, and Justice*. True Directions, 2014.

Williams, Mará Rose. "In Court, Diocese Blasts Fired Catholic School Teacher Who Was Pregnant and Unmarried." *The Kansas City Star*, August 30, 2019. https://www.kansascity.com/news/local/article234560777.html.

Wimmer, AC. "Vatican Warns Threats of Germany's 'Synodal Way' to the Church." Catholic News Agency, July 21, 2022. https://www.catholicnewsagency.com/news/251841/vatican-warns-of-threat-to-the-unity-germany-synodal-way.

Winfield, Nicole. "Francis Becomes 1st Pope to Endorse Same-Sex Civil Unions." *AP News*, October 21, 2020, sec. Religion. https://apnews.com/article/pope-endorse-same-sex-civil-unions-eb3509b30ebac35e91aa7cbda2013de2.

———. "Pope Francis Meets Transgender Guests of Rome Church." *Associated Press*, August 11, 2022. https://apnews.com/article/pope-francis-religion-rome-208b6a50c4872fde0e04335868b9d9e8.

Wingate, Keira. "A Gay Teacher in New York Was Fired from a Catholic School after Marrying His Partner." *USA Today*, October 27, 2021. https://www.usatoday.com/story/news/education/2021/10/27/gay-new-york-teacher-fired-catholic-school-over-marriage/8567547002/.

Wolfram Smith, Nicholas. "Study Shows Young Adults Leaving Church Start Down That Path at Age 13." National Catholic

Reporter, December 11, 2018. https://www.ncronline.org/news/study-shows-young-adults-leaving-church-start-down-path-age-13.

Yale Divinity School Website. "Margaret A. Farley." Accessed June 7, 2023. https://divinity.yale.edu/faculty-and-research/yds-faculty/margaret-farley.

Yurcaba, Jo. "Catholic Diocese Says Gay and Trans People Can't Be Baptized or Receive Communion." *NBC News*, December 10, 2021. https://www.nbcnews.com/nbc-out/out-news/catholic-diocese-says-gay-trans-people-cant-baptized-receive-communion-rcna8217.

Index

access, to Catholic education, 70–71, 117
affirmative defense, religious liberty and, 8–9, 25n28, 26n35
Althaus-Reid, Marcella, 105
Amoris Laetitia (Pope Francis), 75–76, 85
apathy, 42; evangelization and, 33; injustice and, 124; students and, 32, 87
archbishops: Cordileone, 4–5, 14–16, 27n49, 38, 104; ministerial employees and, 3–4; Thompson, 6–8, 16
authenticity, 52, 57, 116–18; secrecy and, 1–2, 53
authority: of Catholic Church, 69, 85–86; disagreement and, 99; synodality and, 114
autonomy, of conscience, 39–41, 43, 72–73

baptism, 98–100, 104–5, 160; ministry and, 11
Bechtle, Regina, 112
belonging, 19, 83–84, 86; communities and, 43; LGBTQ+ students and, 21–22, 28n65; mentorship and, 49–50; secular culture and, 58n5; synodality and, 106–7
Benedict XVI (pope), 137
bishops, 20, 22, 122n59; Catholic culture and, 13–15; dismissals and, 2–3, 133; doctrine and, 82–83; scandal and, 15–16; schools and, 25n30, 76, 110, 145; synodal schools and, 113–14; Synod of, 74, 100–101, 119n20; USCCB and, 10–11, 33, 42–44, 54, 138
Bleasedale, Jane, xvi, 45
blessings, 78–79, 83–84
Brebeuf Jesuit Preparatory school, 6–8, 10, 25n23

California (CA), San Francisco, 3–5, 14–15, 22
cardinals, 7; Levada, 16
casuistry, 73; probabilism and, 68–69
Catechism, 16, 59n6, 139
Catholic Church, 123–24; authority of, 69, 85–86; global, 23, 70–71, 95–97, 117; inclusion and, 34–35; participation in, 12, 42, 97–100, 138, 145–46, 150, 152n12; as People of God, 87–88, 98, 101–2, 160; threats to, 134–35, 147

Catholic culture, 22–23, 27n48; bishops and, 13–15; distinguishability and, 16–18; diversity and, 40
Catholic education: access to, 70–71, 117; distinguishability and, 13–15; doctrine and, 65–66; mission of, 38–41, 60n26. *See also* schools; synodal schools
Catholic identity, 41, 44–47; of schools, 10, 13–14, 16–18, 53–55, 83, 108–10; threats to, 2–4, 7–8, 15–16, 27n48, 83
Catholic leaders, 66–67, 113–14, 160; laity and, 71, 85–86, 96–97; morality and, 125; privacy and, 140; suicide and, 35
Catholic tradition, 13–15, 20–21, 40–41, 43, 111–12; contradiction of, 11, 53–54; probabilism and, 61n36, 74, 79, 82–83, 85; transmission of, 108–10
CCE. *See* Congregation for Catholic Education
CDF. *See* Congregation for the Doctrine of the Faith
change: doctrine and, 84–85, 89n26, 147; fear of, 7, 147; freedom and, 72
Code of Cannon Law, 25n30
collaboration, 17, 50, 100–103
communal discernment, 103, 107, 160; probabilism and, 86–87
communalism, 38, 61n39; evangelization and, 40
communities, 41–43, 108, 117, 132, 151; conscience and, 134; disaffiliation and, 95–96; faith and, 18; harm to, 12–13; isolation from, 54–57; Latinx, 57n1; LGBTQ+ people and, 70–71; morality and, 19–20; needs of, 22, 145; religious liberty and, 128; role models and, 49–50; schools as, 16–17; transgression and, 115–16
confession, 65; morality and, 68–69

Congregation for Catholic Education (CCE), 7, 13, 16–17, 26n37, 26n41, 27n56, 76–77
Congregation for the Doctrine of the Faith (CDF), 77–78, 93n72, 143–44, 156n67
conscience, 83, 85–86, 103; autonomy of, 39–41, 43, 72–73; communities and, 134; disagreement and, 87
consistency, 144; ministerial employees and, 11–13, 26n39; theological, 22
contestation, doctrine and, 83, 135–36, 147–48
contradiction, of Catholic tradition, 11, 53–54
controversy, 21–22, 150–51
Cordileone, Salvatore (archbishop), 4–5, 14–16, 27n49, 38, 104
corporate religious liberty, 132–34, 146–48
critical thinking: doctrine and, 43; freedom and, 66
cultural context, xviii, 5, 38; diversity and, 16–17; educators and, 44–45; human nature and, 70; revelation and, 88n11; of students, 109
cultural strategies, for dismissal, 2–3, 13–21

DDF. *See* Dicastery for the Doctrine of the Faith
"Dear Alana," 35
Dei Verbum, 98–99
dialogue, 19–20, 114; communities and, 41; diversity and, 18, 34–35, 39; morality clauses and, 17; *sensus fidelium* and, 102–3; synodality and, 85
Dicastery for Culture and Education, 38. *See also* Congregation for Catholic Education
Dicastery for the Doctrine of the Faith (DDF), 76–78, 91n41. *See also* Congregation for the Doctrine of the Faith

Dignitatis Humanae, 130–32, 134–35
dignity, 54, 124, 160; dismissals and, 125; freedom and, 131; justice and, 127, 152n12; labor and, 20, 137–38; queerness and, 149–50
disaffiliation, 33–34; communities and, 95–96
disagreement, 84, 88, 111; authority and, 99; conscience and, 87; disaffiliation and, 34; ministry and, 48; probabilism and, 110; respect and, 42, 97
discernment: communal, 86–87, 103, 107, 160; diversity and, 86, 144; doctrine and, 109–10; laity and, 101; LGBTQ+ educators and, 86–87; students and, 109–12
discrimination, xvi, 2–3, 12, 143–44, 146; doctrine and, 55, 78–79; pastoral care and, 36; religious liberty and, 8–9, 125; same-sex marriage and, 6, 8–9; social teaching and, 19; theology and, 26n35
dis-integration, identity and, 36, 96
dismissals, 4, 22–23, 115, 119n14; bishops and, 2–3, 133; cultural strategies for, 2–3, 13–21; dignity and, 125; doctrine and, 66; fear of, xv–xvii, 1–2, 142, 159; human rights and, 134–36; legal strategies for, 2–3, 8–13; opposite scandal and, 18–20, 138, 140; privacy and, 141, 156n68; probabilism and, 83–84; risk of, xvi–xvii, 45–46, 53–54, 159; same-sex marriage and, xixn4, 5–10, 28n65; subsidiarity and, 145–46; vocation and, 2, 149–50
dissent, 84, 119n14; from magisterial doctrine, 2, 26n36, 65–67, 82; religious liberty and, 133–34
distinguishability, 13, 15; Catholic culture and, 16–18; morality clauses and, 14
diversity, 22, 32–33, 149; Catholic culture and, 40; cultural context and, 16–17; dialogue and, 18, 34–35, 39; discernment and, 86, 144; faith and, 109; probabilism and, 87–88; role models and, 11–12; synodality and, 110–11; theology and, 23, 65–66, 69; witness and, 41–42
doctrine, xviii, 12, 43; bishops and, 82–83; Catholic education and, 65–66; change and, 84–85, 89n26, 147; contestation and, 83, 135–36, 147–48; discernment and, 109–10; discrimination and, 55, 78–79; dismissal and, 66; gender and, 74–75; ministerial employees and, 17; personal lives and, xvi–xvii; role models in, 45–48; same-sex marriage and, 156n67; scandal and, 15–16, 27n49; teaching of, 42; transgender identity and, 76–77
Donnelly, Jack, 132–33, 154n42

ecclesiology, inclusive, 96, 101–5
educators, 41–43; cultural context and, 44–45; non-Catholic, 11, 47; safe spaces and, 32; students and, 15–16; studies of, 44–56; synodality and, 112–13. *See also* LGBTQ+ educators
empathy, for students, 49–50, 116
employment disputes, 3–8, 22, 129
encyclicals, 127–28, 152n10; *Humanae Vitae*, 77, 93n72; *Rerum Novarum*, 20, 126, 136–37, 145, 151n7, 154n50; *Vehementer Nos*, 98
epiphany, 102–3, 107, 111; synodality and, 135–36
epistemology, 58n4, 69–70; queer, 32–33, 106–7, 115–17, 149
eschatology, 124
Espinoza, Roberto Che, 121n45
eudaimonia, 81, 121n52, 124
Evangelii Gaudium (Pope Francis), 100
evangelization, 9–10, 35, 58n5, 131; apathy and, 33; communalism and, 40; LGBTQ+ educators and, 47–48; protests and, 21; safe spaces and, 32;

secular culture and, 40–41; social teaching and, 150–51
Everitt, James, 44–49, 51–53, 55
evil, 16, 77–79, 84, 156n67
exclusion, 40–41; spiritual harm and, 31–32
extrinsic probabilism, 71–72; magisterial doctrine and, 82–83

faith, 38; communities and, 18; diversity and, 109; justice and, 45–46; morality and, 98–99; transmission of, 15–16, 21, 42, 108–10
families, LGBTQ+ youth and, 35, 59n14
Farley, Margaret, 80–81
fear, 36, 53–54; of change, 7, 147; of dismissal, xv–xvii, 1–2, 142, 159; of scandal, 19, 138
Fiducia Supplicans, 71, 78, 83–84, 86
First Vatican Council, 84
Fitzgerald, Shelly, xixn4, 5–6, 8–9
Fleming, Julia, 67
flourishing, 124, 128, 135; human rights and, 148, 150
Ford, Craig A., Jr., 70, 81–82, 92n66, 106
Francis (pope), xviii, 8, 42, 86; *Amoris Laetitia*, 75–76, 85; *Evangelii Gaudium*, 100; *Fratelli Tutti*, 137; synodality and, 23, 71, 100–101, 103
Fratelli Tutti (Pope Francis), 137
freedom, 66; change and, 72; dignity and, 131; human rights and, 127, 152n14; probabilism and, 69; secularism and, 126, 152n8; teaching and, 109–10; truth and, 131–32
Fullam, Lisa, 19, 71–73

Gaillardetz, Richard R., 11, 86, 98–99, 109–10, 152n14
Gaudium et Spes, 69, 98
gay straight alliance clubs (GSAs), 36, 49

gender: doctrine and, 74–75; human nature and, 81; theology on, 75–77
gender-affirming surgery, 66, 76, 88n1
gender ideology, 75–77, 81
gender transition, xvi–xvii, 66, 76, 88n1, 141
gifts, of LGBTQ+ educators, 33, 44–45, 86, 117, 160
global Church, 23, 70–71, 95, 97; local communities and, 96, 117
governance, schools and, 4, 7, 10, 25n23
Gravissimum Educationis, 60n26
Groome, Thomas H., 33, 39–44, 97, 108–10
group human rights, 133–34, 154n42
GSAs. *See* gay straight alliance clubs

Hannengberg, Edward P., 138
harm: to communities, 12–13; spiritual, xviii–xix, 21, 31–32, 95–96
hierarchy, 69, 126–27; local communities and, 95–103, 145
Hinze, Bradford, 102, 109, 114
Holy Spirit, 71, 99, 101, 113–14, 117, 149; teaching and, 102–3, 107
homosexuality, 65–67; doctrine and, 77–79; natural law and, 74–75, 77, 79; pastoral care and, 77–78; theology and, 79–82
hooks, bell, 112–13
hope, 124–25; struggle and, 56; synodality and, 96
Horan, Dan, 77
hostility, 50; LGBTQ+ people and, 31, 57n1
Humanae Vitae (Pope Paul VI), 77, 93n72
human nature, 58n2, 80–82, 106, 121n45; cultural context and, 70
human rights, xviii, 78, 132; dismissal and, 134–36; flourishing and, 148, 150; freedom and, 127, 152n14; group, 133–34, 154n42; LGBTQ+ educators and, 128–29, 144; religious

liberty and, 20–21, 23, 133–34, 146–48; social teaching and, 127–29

identity, 105, 120n42, 159–60; disintegration and, 36, 96; Latinx, 121n45; natural law and, 106; pathologized, 77–78, 81, 104; sacraments and, 47; spiritual crisis and, 31, 56–57; transgender, 75–77; vocation and, xv. *See also* Catholic identity
IN. *See* Indiana
inclusion, 70–71, 150; Catholic Church and, 34–35; LGBTQ+, xviii–xix, 74–84, 103, 108–18; ministry and, 31–32
inclusive ecclesiology, 96; synodality and, 101–5
Indiana (IN), Indianapolis, 3–8
Indianapolis, IN, employment disputes in, 3–8
infallibility, 84–85
injustice, 55, 79, 106, 125, 143–44, 146–47; apathy and, 124
International Theological Commission (ITC), 101–2, 119n24, 120n27
intrinsic probabilism, 71; magisterial doctrine and, 74–82
isolation, from communities, 54–57
ITC. *See* International Theological Commission

Jesuit order, 68–69, 122n55; Brebeuf Preparatory school of, 6–8, 10, 25n23
John Paul II (pope): *Laborem Excercens*, 137; *Theology of the Body*, 75
John XXIII (pope), *Pacem in Terris*, 127–28, 136–37, 154n49
Jones, Cleve, 120n42
Jonsen, Albert R., 68, 72–73
justice, 39–40, 51–52, 57, 108, 124, 151n5; dignity and, 127, 152n12; faith and, 45–46; sex and, 80–81; in synodal schools, 149–50. *See also* social justice

Keenan, James, 68
Kingdom of God, 42–43, 106, 151, 159; social teaching and, 124–25, 148–50
knowledge, 107–8; social sciences and, 70

labor, 3–5; dignity and, 20, 137–38; social teaching and, 126–27, 136–38, 152n10; vocation and, 138, 148
Laborem Excercens (Pope John Paul II), 137
laity: Catholic leaders and, 71, 85–86, 96–97; discernment and, 101; vocation and, 11, 98. *See also sensus fidelium*
Latinx communities, 57n1
Latinx identity, 121n45
Lawler, Michael G., 80
laxism, morality and, 69, 72
legal action, ministerial employees and, 8–9, 25n29
legal strategies, for dismissal, 2–3, 8–13
Leo XIII (pope), *Rerum Novarum*, 20, 126, 136–37, 145, 151n7, 154n50
Levada, William (cardinal), 16
LGBTQ+ Catholics, 48, 147, 150–51; synodality and, 104–7
LGBTQ+ educators: discernment and, 86–87; evangelization and, 47–48; gifts of, 33, 44–45, 86, 117, 160; human rights and, 128–29, 144; justice and, 52; as ministerial employees, 43–44; Paschal Mystery and, 53–56; as role models, 22, 32, 37, 45–53, 55–57, 114; suffering and, 53–54; synodal schools and, 114–17
LGBTQ+ employees, 12, 26n39, 134–36, 143; vocation and, 20–21
LGBTQ+ inclusion, xviii–xix, 103; probabilism and, 74–84; synodal model for, 108–18

LGBTQ+ people, 20, 31, 57n1, 58nn2–3; preferential option for the vulnerable and, 21, 35, 125, 136, 142–43, 146, 150; representation and, 22, 46–47, 70–71
LGBTQ+ students, 46; belonging and, 21–22, 28n65; mentorship and, xv–xvi; struggle and, 31–33, 36–37, 160
LGBTQ+ youth: families and, 35, 59n14; risks to, 21–22, 32, 35
liberation, 44–45; oppression and, 50–52
local communities: global Church and, 96, 117; hierarchy and, 95–103, 145
Lumen Gentium, 98

magisterial authority, *sensus fidelium* and, 99
magisterial doctrine, 69; dissent from, 2, 26n36, 65–67, 82; extrinsic probabilism and, 82–83; intrinsic probabilism and, 74–82; LGBTQ+ students and, 46; morality and, 4–5, 15, 27n48, 34–35; social sciences and, 77; theology and, 82–83, 93n72
Maher, Michael, 36
Marianism, 65, 122n55
Martin, James, 26n39, 144
mass, in schools, 6–7, 24n19
Medina, Bartolomeo, 68, 71–72
mentorship, 143; belonging and, 49–50; LGBTQ+ students and, xv–xvi
ministerial employees, 5–6; archbishops and, 3–4; consistency and, 11–13, 26n39; doctrine and, 17; legal action and, 8–9, 25n29; LGBTQ+ educators as, 43–44; morality clauses and, 8–13
ministerial exception, 8–11, 26n35; religious liberty and, 12, 20, 129–30, 133, 136, 147
ministry, 3–5, 10–11, 104; disagreement and, 48; inclusion and, 31–32; sexual morality and, 66

mission, 55–56; of Catholic education, 38–41, 60n26; spirituality and, 47
Mominee, Mick, 36
moral doubt, 66–67, 73
morality, 148–49; Catholic leaders and, 125; communities and, 19–20; confession and, 68–69; faith and, 98–99; homosexuality and, 80; laxism and, 69, 72; magisterial doctrine and, 4–5, 15, 27n48, 34–35; religious liberty and, 130; rigorism and, 69, 72, 135–36
morality clauses, 3–5, 8, 11–14, 139; dialogue and, 17; personal life and, 9–10
moral theology, xvii, 19, 71–74
Morey, Melanie, 13–14, 38, 108
Moss, Candida, 15n48
Murray, John Courtney, 130–33

natural law: homosexuality and, 74–75, 77, 79; identity and, 106; queer, 81–82; rights and, 154n50
needs: of communities, 22, 145; spiritual, xvi, 21, 45–46; of students, xviii–xix, 18, 31, 33–37, 49
non-Catholic educators, 11, 47
non-Catholic students, 11–12, 26n41
Noonan, John T., 86, 153n26

O'Malley, John W., 100
O'Neill, William, 128
openly queer role models, 32, 116, 159
opposite scandal, dismissal and, 18–20, 138, 140
oppression, 63n79; liberation and, 50–52; personal life and, 142; queerness and, 105–6; social teaching and, 123; spiritual harm and, xviii–xix; vocation and, 115
Orsy, Ladislas, 134
Osheim, Amanda C., 102
O'Sullivan, Gus, 22

Pacem in Terris, Pope John XXIII, 127–28, 136–37, 154n49
Palmer, Parker, xv
paradigm shift, probabilism and, 84–85
Park, Peter, 61n48
parochialism, 40, 109
participation, in Catholic Church, 12, 42, 97–100, 138, 145–46, 150, 152n12
participatory action research, 44, 61n48
Paschal Mystery, LGBTQ+ educators and, 53–56
pastoral care: discrimination and, 36; homosexuality and, 77–78; the vulnerable and, 21–22, 35, 37, 49–50
pathologized identity, 77–78, 81, 104
Paul VI (pope), 119n20; *Humanae Vitae*, 77, 93n72
Payne-Elliot, Joshua and Layton, 6–7, 10, 28n65
pedagogies, synodality and, 112–13
Peddicord, Richard, 62n74
People of God, Catholic Church as, 87–88, 98, 101–2, 160
personal lives, 1; doctrine and, xvi–xvii; morality clauses and, 9–10; oppression and, 142; secrecy and, 138–39; witness and, 15–16
personhood, 39–41, 132
Piderit, John, 13–14, 38, 108
Pius IX (pope), 127
Pius X (pope), 100; *Vehementer Nos*, 98
pluralism, xvii, 13, 17; sexual morality and, 84; theology and, 73; Vatican II and, 69–70, 84–85
pneumatology, 102, 120n31. *See also* Holy Spirit
popes: Benedict XVI, 137; John Paul II, 75, 137; John XXIII, 127–28, 136–37, 154n49; Leo XIII, 20, 126, 136–37, 145, 151n7, 154n50; Paul VI, 77, 93n72, 119n20; Pius IX, 127; Pius X, 98, 100. *See also* Francis
Porter, Billy, 32

preferential option for the vulnerable, 21, 35, 125, 136, 142–43, 146, 150
preparation, of students, 40–41
privacy, 146–47; dismissal and, 141, 156n68; sex and, 139–40, 156n67; social teaching and, 138–42
probabilism, xvii, 70; casuistry and, 68–69; Catholic tradition and, 61n36, 74, 79, 82–83, 85; communal discernment and, 86–87; disagreement and, 110; dismissal and, 83–84; diversity and, 87–88; extrinsic, 71–72, 82–83; freedom and, 69; intrinsic, 71, 74–82; LGBTQ+ inclusion and, 74–84; moral doubt and, 67; moral theology and, 71–74; paradigm shift and, 84–85; religious liberty and, 134–36; synodality and, 85–86, 96–97
prohibitions, on sexual activities, 4, 66, 74–75
protests, 5, 7, 14, 21–22

queer educators, liberation and, 44–45
Queer Educators in Religious Schools (Qu.E.I.R.S.), xvi
queer epistemology, 32–33, 106–7, 115–17, 149
queer natural law, 81–82
queerness: dignity and, 149–50; oppression and, 105–6
queer theology, 105–7, 120nn43–44, 121n45
Qu.E.I.R.S. *See* Queer Educators in Religious Schools

religious liberty, 2, 11; affirmative defense and, 8–9, 25n28, 26n35; Catholic identity and, 13; communities and, 128; corporate, 132–34, 146–48; discrimination and, 8–9, 125; dissent and, 133–34; human rights and, 20–21, 23, 133–34, 146–48; ministerial exception and, 12, 20, 129–30, 133, 136, 147;

morality and, 130; probabilism and, 134–36; US and, 130, 153n26; Vatican II and, 130–31
representation, LGBTQ+ people and, 22, 46–47, 70–71
Rerum Novarum, Pope Leo XIII, 20, 126, 136–37, 145, 151n7, 154n50
research, participatory action, 44, 61n48
respect, 17–18, 23, 54–55, 128, 148; disagreement and, 42, 97; for students, 39, 41
responsibility, synodality and, 101, 120n27
revelation, 84–85, 96, 98–99, 111–12, 117; cultural context and, 17, 88n11
rights: natural law and, 154n50; transgender people and, 139–40; to vocation, 148–49; of workers, 20, 136–38, 146–47. *See also* human rights
rigorism, moral, 69, 72, 135–36
risk: of dismissal, xvi–xvii, 45–46, 53–54, 159; to LGBTQ+ youth, 21–22, 32, 35; safe spaces and, 31, 113
role models, 143, 160; communities and, 49–50; diversity and, 11–12; in doctrine, 45–48; LGBTQ+ educators as, 22, 32, 37, 45–53, 55–57, 114; openly queer, 32, 116, 159; service and, 50–53; vocation and, 46, 56–57
Rush, Ormond, 98, 103

sacraments, 6–7, 39–41, 47
safe spaces, xv–xvi, 49; educators and, 32; evangelization and, 32; hostility and, 50; for LGBTQ+ Catholics, 104; risk and, 31, 113
Salzman, Todd A., 80
same-sex marriage, xvi–xvii, 128–29, 140; dismissal and, xixn4, 5–10, 28n65; doctrine and, 156n67
same-sex unions, 71, 78, 83–84, 86; sexual activities and, 140–41

San Francisco, CA, 14–15; employment dispute in, 3–5, 22
scandal, 18, 20, 111, 140–41; doctrine and, 15–16, 27n49; fear of, 19, 138
schools, 97, 112, 118; bishops and, 25n30, 76, 110, 145; Brebeuf Jesuit Preparatory, 6–8, 10, 25n23; Catholic identity of, 10, 13–14, 16–18, 53–55, 83, 108–10; governance and, 4, 7, 10, 25n23; GSAs and, 36, 49; mass in, 6–7, 24n19; *sensus fidelium* and, 111, 113–14, 117. *See also* synodal schools
Second Vatican Council (Vatican II), xviii, 13, 17, 38, 77, 127, 145–46; *Dei Verbum*, 98–99; *Gaudium et Spes*, 69, 98; *Lumen Gentium*, 98; pluralism and, 69–70, 84–85; religious liberty and, 130–31; synodality and, 88, 97–100
secrecy, xv, xvii, 51, 119n14; authenticity and, 1–2, 53; personal lives and, 138–39. *See also* privacy
sectarianism, 40, 109
secular culture, 17–18, 28n58, 38–39, 111; belonging and, 58n5; evangelization and, 40–41
secularism, 127; freedom and, 126, 152n8
sensus fidelium, 71, 84–85, 96–98, 100–101, 104–6, 160; dialogue and, 102–3; magisterial authority and, 99; schools and, 111, 113–14, 117
service, 42–44; role models and, 50–53
sex, 105; gender and, 75–77; justice and, 80–81; privacy and, 139–40, 156n67
sexual activities, 16, 77–81, 139, 142, 156n67; prohibitions on, 4, 66, 74–75; same-sex unions and, 140–41
sexual morality, 23; magisterial doctrine and, 15, 27n48, 34–35; ministry and, 66; pluralism and, 84; social justice and, 62n74
Shue, Henry, 148

sin, 19–20, 31, 135, 139–41; homosexuality and, 77–79
Smith, Christian, 33–34, 59n6
social justice, 20–21, 111; sexual morality and, 62n74; social teaching and, 124–26, 142
social sciences, 70, 80; magisterial doctrine and, 77; students and, 110; theology and, 74
social teaching, xviii, 12, 19, 74, 123, 143–45; evangelization and, 150–51; human rights and, 127–29; labor and, 126–27, 136–38, 152n10; privacy and, 138–42; social justice and, 124–26, 142; synodal schools and, 146–50
social transitions, transgender people and, 66, 88n1
spiritual crisis, identity and, 31, 56–57
spiritual harm, 95–96; exclusion and, 31–32; oppression and, xviii–xix
spirituality, 31, 47, 58n2
spiritual needs, of students, xvi, 21, 45–46
Starkey, Lynn, 6, 8–9
Stockbridge, Kevin, xvi, 44–47, 49–56, 63n79
struggle, 1, 22, 52–53; hope and, 56; LGBTQ+ students and, 31–33, 36–37, 160
Strzelczyk, Grzegorz, 102–3
students, 1–2, 39, 143; apathy and, 32, 87; belonging and, 19; discernment and, 109–12; educators and, 15–16; empathy for, 49–50, 116; needs of, xviii–xix, 18, 31, 33–37, 49; non-Catholic, 11–12, 26n41; preparation of, 40–41; social sciences and, 110; social teaching and, 124; spiritual needs of, xvi, 21, 45–46; synodality and, 108
studies, of educators, 44–56
subsidiarity, dismissals and, 145–46
suffering, LGBTQ+ educators and, 53–54

suicide, 21–22, 32, 37, 81; Catholic leaders and, 35
Supreme Court, US, 8–9
synodality, xvii–xviii, 108, 114, 160; belonging and, 106–7; diversity and, 110–11; epiphany and, 135–36; inclusive ecclesiology and, 101–5; LGBTQ+ Catholics and, 104–7; local communities and, 96; pedagogies and, 112–13; Pope Francis and, 23, 71, 100–101, 103; probabilism and, 85–86, 96–97; responsibility and, 101, 120n27; Vatican II and, 88, 97–100
synodal model, for LGBTQ+ inclusion, 108–18
synodal schools, 97, 108–12, 118; bishops and, 113–14; justice in, 149–50; LGBTQ+ educators and, 114–17; social teaching and, 146–50
Synod of Bishops, 74, 100–101, 119n20

teaching, xv; of doctrine, 42; freedom and, 109–10; Holy Spirit and, 102–3, 107; through witness, xvi, 10
theological consistency, 22
theology, xvii–xix, 2, 91n43, 97, 159–60; discrimination and, 26n35; diversity and, 23, 65–66, 69; on gender, 75–77; homosexuality and, 79–82; magisterial doctrine and, 82–83, 93n72; of ministry, 10; pluralism and, 73; queer, 105–7, 120nn43–44, 121n45; social sciences and, 74
Theology of the Body (Pope John Paul II), 75
Thompson, Charles C. (archbishop), 6–8, 16
Thorpe, Brooklyn, 28n65
threats: to Catholic Church, 134–35, 147; to Catholic identity, 2–4, 7–8, 15–16, 27n48, 83; gender ideology as, 75–77
Toulmin, Stephen, 68, 72–73

transgender identity, 75–77
transgender people, 35, 77, 81, 91n41; rights and, 139–40; social transitions and, 66, 88n1
transgression, 105–7, 121n45; communities and, 115–16
transition, gender, xvi–xvii, 66, 76, 88n1, 141
transmission, of faith, 15–16, 21, 42, 108–10
truth, 67; freedom and, 131–32; privacy and, 139
Truth, 84, 93n74
Tutino, Stefania, 72

United States (US): religious liberty and, 130, 153n26; Supreme Court of, 8–9
United States Conference of Catholic Bishops (USCCB), 10–11, 33, 42–44, 54, 138
US. *See* United States

USCCB. *See* United States Conference of Catholic Bishops

Vatican II. *See* Second Vatican Council
Vehementer Nos (Pope Pius X), 98
virtues, 108–9, 121n52
vocation, xvi, 160; dismissals and, 2, 149–50; identity and, xv; labor and, 138, 148; laity and, 11, 98; LGBTQ+ employees and, 20–21; oppression and, 115; right to, 148–49; role models and, 46, 56–57; witness and, 52
Vogt, Christopher, 18–19
the vulnerable, 43; pastoral care and, 21–22, 35, 37, 49–50; preferential option for, 21, 35, 125, 136, 142–43, 146, 150

witness, 151, 159; diversity and, 41–42; personal lives and, 15–16; teaching through, xvi, 10; vocation and, 52
workers, rights of, 20, 136–38, 146–47

About the Author

Dr. Ish Ruiz is assistant professor of Latinx and queer decolonial theology at the Pacific School of Religion in Berkeley. He holds a PhD in ethics and theology from the Graduate Theological Union, and his research interests intersect Catholic theology, sexual morality, LGBTQ+ identity, queer theology, Latinx identity, human rights, social justice, and education. Ruiz has published several scholarly articles and presented his research at numerous academic conferences. Prior to his current academic appointment, he served as the provost's postdoctoral fellow of Catholic Studies at Candler School of Theology of Emory University, an adjunct professor at the University of Dayton, and a Catholic high school religious studies teacher for eleven years in Ohio, Hawaii, and California. Throughout his career and ministry, he has mentored many LGBTQ+ educators and youth throughout the United States. These experiences, combined with his LGBTQ+ ministry at parishes for over ten years, equipped Ruiz to facilitate numerous public lectures, workshops, and discussion groups that promote LGBTQ+ ministry and inclusion in Catholic institutions. Through his vocation, he hopes to see a Catholic global community where LGBTQ+ people are cherished for the indispensable gifts they offer and are fully welcomed into the Church.